Critical Digital Pedagogy

CRITICAL DIGITAL PEDAGOGY

A Collection

JESSE STOMMEL, CHRIS FRIEND, AND SEAN MICHAEL MORRIS

Hybrid Pedagogy Inc.

Washington, D.C.

CONTENTS

FOREWORD

RUHA BENJAMIN

In reflecting on this historic moment in the life of the planet, one of my favorite writers and thinkers, Arundhati Roy, in "The Pandemic is a Portal," wrote: "Historically, pandemics have forced humans to break with the past and imagine their world anew. This one is no different. It is a portal, a gateway between one world and the next. We can choose to walk through it, dragging the carcasses of our prejudice and hatred, our avarice, our data banks and dead ideas, our dead rivers and smoky skies behind us. Or we can walk through lightly, with little luggage, ready to imagine another world. And ready to fight for it."

The image of "dragging the carcasses of our prejudice and hatred... our data banks and dead ideas," has been nagging me...in a good way. At exactly the moment we need to be imagining and crafting a world that is more livable, more just, and joyful for all of earth's inhabitants, will we hang on desperately to the familiar, pining for a return to normality?

I am convinced that without a deep engagement with critical digital pedagogy, as individuals and institutions, we will almost certainly drag outmoded ways of thinking and doing things with us. If we do not reckon honestly with what all we have been carrying, many dead ideas are sure to be repackaged as new and innovative "tech solutions" for the converging public health, social, political, and economic crises we face.

In Amer and Noujaim's 2019 documentary, *The Great Hack*, there is a moment when the narrator is explaining the goal of those who used fake news and digital propaganda to manipulate the electorate on both sides of the Atlantic, during the 2016 U.S. presidential election and the Brexit referendum. The aim of disinformation architects is to "break society." In the words of one of the chief architects, "It is only when you break it, that you can remodel the pieces into your vision of a new society."

Their "new" vision is nothing new, of course, just more white supremacy, more class oppression, more patriarchy, more ableism, more imperialism. And to get more, they need to break (or, continue to break) the social contract, by deepening divisions and amplifying hierarchies using what Vaidhyanathan terms "anti-social media." In short, there are powerful people and organizations working overtime to undermine the very premise of this thing we call "society."

So, what are the responsibilities of educators and educational institutions in a context where this is a deliberate campaign to break society, erode mutuality, grind down our ability to care for one another, eat away at any notion of a collective good, and destroy the institutions upon which our society depends? In this context, I think educators are called on to be champions of the social contract and to model and cultivate caring forms of sociality that are everywhere under siege.

What could be more important? That those of us who have a radically different vision — one that insists on everyone having, according to Erik Wright, broadly equal "access to the social and material means for a flourishing life," use every tool at our disposal to ensure that no one be sacrificed at the altar of progress. This brilliant collection of essays offers a set of political, pedagogical, and practical tools that are essential as we move through this portal.

When the late-great writer and builder of speculative worlds, Octavia E. Butler, was asked, *what is there to do about the state of the world*, she responded, "I mean there's no single answer that will solve all of our future problems. There's no magic bullet. Instead there are thousands of answers — at least. You can be one of them if you choose to be."

Without a doubt, *Critical Digital Pedagogy* energizes all of us to be an answer, if we choose to be!

INTRODUCTION: THE URGENCY OF CRITICAL DIGITAL PEDAGOGY

JESSE STOMMEL, CHRIS FRIEND, AND SEAN MICHAEL MORRIS

"The world is not a *cul-de-sac*."
~ Paulo Freire, *Education for Critical Consciousness*

There is no hope for the future without education.

For the past ten years, *Hybrid Pedagogy* has worked to help craft a theory of teaching and learning in and around digital spaces, not by imagining what that work might look like, but by doing, asking after, changing, and doing again. Since 2011, *Hybrid Pedagogy* has published over 400 articles from more than 200 authors focused in and around the emerging field of critical digital pedagogy. This book gathers together a selection of those articles. Much of the writing on *Hybrid Pedagogy* feels just as timely now as it did when it was written (and even more prescient). The journal has spent the last decade working to support voices which are "emotionally resonant and intellectually vital" and their vision of an equitable, resilient, critical pedagogy, and a hopeful future toward which education might arc. That work has become more vital and must continue.

Critical digital pedagogy is activism as much as it is a field, practice as much as it is theory, derived from experience and then reflection upon that experience. In his definition, Jesse asserts that when "we're looking for solutions, what we most need to change is our thinking and not our tools." He further argues that critical digital pedagogy is more defined by its questions, by the problems it poses, than it is by answers, and that it "will not, cannot, be defined by a single voice but must gather together a cacophony of voices" ("Critical Digital Pedagogy: a Definition"). It's not a stack of content or a bibliography; critical digital pedagogy is a way we treat one another.

We have long held that "every voice is needed within academe, within education. The more we leave out, the less we have to offer" (Morris, "Call for Editors"). *Hybrid Pedagogy*'s collaborative peer review process is decidedly not "blind" and typically includes open discussion about the overall direction of a piece and its author's voice as much as the specifics of its rhetorical strategy. We work to build personal relationships between and among authors and editors. Writing requires trust. Editing requires trust. Building communities of trust is at the center of our work.

Hybrid Pedagogy authors have written about and around some of the most vital issues in pedagogy and digital learning. The writing done on the pages of the journal are a critical, in-depth resource for teachers, administrators, instructional designers, and others as they begin to navigate digital, remote, and hybrid learning.

As *Hybrid Pedagogy*'s work continues, we recognize that education is, in many ways, at a vital moment. The response to the COVID-19 pandemic has abruptly shifted more than one million students to fully online or remote instruction. And what has become immediately clear is that students face much more than technological hurdles. As Jesse writes in an article for AAUP's *Academe*: "When so many higher education teachers have almost no training at all, it's hard to imagine how faculty could be adequately prepared for working with students who are increasingly nontraditional and often lack access to basic needs such as food and housing." The work of students and teachers is increasingly precarious.

Critical Digital Pedagogy: A Collection is the first peer-reviewed book centered on the theory and practice of critical digital pedagogy. The collection represents a wide cross-section of both academic and non-academic culture and features articles by women, Black people, indigenous people, Chicanx and Latinx writers, people with disabilities, queer people, and other underrepresented populations. The goal of this collection is to provide evidence for the extraordinary work being done by university and college faculty, librarians, instructional designers, graduate students, technologists, and more — work which advances the study and the praxis of critical digital pedagogy.

WHAT IS CRITICAL DIGITAL PEDAGOGY?

There are three words in "critical digital pedagogy," and it is not a neat and tidy triptych. The pieces of this collection circle around, and through, these three words. Too often, folks privilege "digital" at the expense of "critical" and "pedagogy." This reduces the practice of critical digital pedagogy to tools and technologies, mistaking it for best practices inside a learning management system, or sequestering it strangely within other fields, like digital humanities or open education.

Similarly, focusing too much on "critical" instrumentalizes the work of teaching, relegating the work of thinking about teaching to the humanities, and isolating criticality from STEM fields. This not only diminishes the potential of critical work, it underestimates the much broader swath of teaching and learning which must (and does) benefit not just from *criticality* and *critical* thinking, but from a mission that is *critical*, a practice that asks questions in order to dismantle (*criticize*) institutional or societal impediments to learning.

Perhaps the most confounding and contentious of the three words, "pedagogy" too often refers to work done in classrooms with children. When conversation turns to andragogy and heutagogy, and crude distinctions between adults and "kids," learning and teaching become age-specific, institution-specific, environment-specific instead of human endeavors, *practices of freedom*. The word "pedagogy," as we use it, defines the work of education at the intersection of theory and practice — the act of teaching that derives from reflection and which inspires reflection again. Pedagogy is both where "critical" and "digital" terminate, and also the whole terrain of teaching.

All three of these words, "critical," "digital," and "pedagogy," do real work in the world — each individually, and also in combination. In *Teaching to Transgress*, bell hooks asserts that when "there is a split between theory and practice" we perpetuate "conditions that reinforce our collective exploitation and repression." When, however, we let words do work, when "no gap exists between theory and practice," we allow teaching to be more than instrumental, and digital learning to be more than edtech. We reclaim the critical aims of education, its questioning and reflection, its imperative toward justice and equity, and its persistent need to read the world within which it takes place, whether that's a classroom, a living room, a playground, or a digital device.

There are no easy answers in critical digital pedagogy. It can't tell us how to shift face-to-face teaching online. It can't tell us how the learning management system can be refashioned for 6-year-olds fumbling through remote karate lessons. Critical digital pedagogy can't, of its own volition, keep at bay the absurd siren song of Turnitin or ProctorU. It can't solve the problem of recreating online a 3-year-old's Montessori language-immersion preschool.

ABOUT THE COLLECTION

Articles in this collection have been organized into five sections, with each section standing alone but also building on what precedes it. In other words, though the chapters of this collection have been arranged in a specific order, they need not be read in that order.

The book acknowledges the humanity behind critical digital pedagogy and its influence on the people with whom we work. In **Politicizing Critical Digital Pedagogy**, we critique the connection between education and efforts to use power to dominate or control others — and the urgency of resistance. This section establishes the need for critical digital pedagogy and its foundation of liberation and care. Through these chapters, we see the practice of teaching as embodied compassion, a theme we revisit throughout the book. We see that practice as essential in today's world, for as Chris writes in *Hybrid Pedagogy*'s "Politicizing Critical Digital Pedagogy" CFP, "we can no longer afford to push politics to the side because it affects us all, at every turn." This opening section works best for readers who want to engage with the effects of pedagogy on educators and learners alike.

In **Practicing Critical Digital Pedagogy**, the articles take a hands-on turn, focusing on what can be done, today, to implement the fundamental principles of critical digital pedagogy into any classroom — whether online or on-ground, humanities or STEM, taught or designed. This section connects with our past ("Building in the Humanities Isn't New"), engages our present ("Best Practices: Thoughts on a Flash Mob Mentality"), and looks to our future ("Why Start With Pedagogy?"). Each chapter examines the potentials of critical digital pedagogy within a specific context, showing the tangible benefits of this approach to education. Readers already familiar with the tenets of critical digital pedagogy but considering implementation will find wisdom and clarity within this section.

Contingency and Academic Labor steps away from explicit discussions of pedagogy to consider working conditions in the academy from the perspective of the oft-marginalized. Here, adjuncts, librarians, mothers, and others share their experiences as professionals in problematic or precarious positions. Educators in similar situations may find shared experiences expressed by authors in this section. But these chapters are also a call for those in positions of authority and secure employment — administrators and tenured faculty — many unaware of the gulf separating their working conditions from those of their more marginalized and precarious colleagues.

Pedagogical Alterity questions assumptions about the broad applicability of our pedagogies. These chapters ask us to face difference and consider its effects on students, instructors, institutions, and learning environments. Through the narratives in this section, authors remind us that we cannot shape a pedagogy without acknowledging the backgrounds, social location, bodies, and intersectionality of teachers and students alike.

In **The Scholarly and the Digital**, authors consider the nature not just of teaching but of scholarship in the digital age. From matters of publication and peer review, to issues of access and recognition, this section encourages us to look closely at our use of digital technologies and the human connections they engender. This section ends by asserting that institutions, processes, and pedagogies must remain focused on the people we serve and the compassion they deserve.

A compassionate pedagogy is more necessary now than ever before: to see the student beyond the screen, to recognize the limits and affordances of body, space, and technology, to identify issues of privacy in an increasingly surveilled digital world, and to be conscious of the basic needs of students which must be met to make learning possible.

THE PRESENT MOMENT

This introduction is written in a peculiar present.

As we write this, the coronavirus pandemic has thrust human and educational experiences into online spaces without preparation. Presently, there will be no graduations or ballet recitals. There will be no last days of senior year. And online learning and digital pedagogy are failing as a salve or a lifeline in a moment of uncertainty and panic. Tools like Zoom were not built to meet the moral challenge of a present moment like this one. Nothing in edtech was built for humans. Thus far, our edtech machines were taught only to speak to other machines. If we imagine we can just "pivot" out of classrooms and into online class portals, the *what* of education, the *how-to* of technology, and the *why* of our humanity will continue to break down. At a moment like this, a pause with one eyebrow raised is the most necessary work that critical digital pedagogy can bring.

What we can only hope to be left with after this month, and next month, and next year is a certainty that we do not yet know how to learn online. We do not yet know what education can be in the wake of such political, social, ideological, technological unrest. What we can only hope to end up with is the understanding that we didn't ever know. Students are burdened by massive amounts of debt, face increasing basic needs insecurity, and the work of teaching has become increasingly precarious. Critical digital pedagogy must be an utterance of the hopeful and haunting question, *what now?*

We have known (and written) all along that the stuff of teaching in a classroom does not port, or shift, or "pivot" into digital spaces. The culture of a classroom is unique, and the architecture of the Web is unique as well. The physical environment of a bricks-and-mortar classroom is not equivalent to the 1s and 0s of a learning management system. In fact, these digital spaces (and the ways they traffic in educational data) are sometimes, or often, anathema to the relationships at the center of the work of teaching and learning.

Ultimately, digital pedagogy is about human relationships, the complexity of humans working together with other humans — the challenge (as Sean has said elsewhere) of finding ways to teach *through* a screen, not *to* a screen. The work of critical digital pedagogy is to inspect our tools, understanding them — *reading them* — as part of the world of education. But before we can turn to tools, we must reflect on who we are as teachers, where our pedagogies come from — the *wherefore* of our teaching. "The answer does not lie in the rejection of the machine," Freire tells us in *Education for Critical Consciousness*, "but rather in the humanization of man." These words are all the more apt when we are faced with such uncertainty.

In *Teaching Community: A Pedagogy of Hope*, bell hooks writes, "At its best, teaching is a caring profession." It's a simple statement. It is also, in the way hooks so often does, aimed at correcting a misperception. Namely, that *caring* and *teaching* are not part and parcel of the same profession. But hooks' critical pedagogy insists, as much as that education is a practice of freedom, that caring and teaching are intimately bound.

We must come to grips with the fact that, right now, the work of teachers is not just to teach. We are also responsible for the basic needs of students. Helping students eat and live, and also helping them find the tools they need to reflect on the present moment. This is in keeping with Freire's insistence that critical pedagogy be focused on helping students *read their world*; but more and more, we must together *reckon* with that world. Teaching must be an act of imagination, hope, and possibility. Education must be a practice done with hearts as much as heads, with hands as much as books. Care has to be at the center of this work.

PART I.

_____

POLITICIZING CRITICAL
DIGITAL PEDAGOGY

_____

"In this world we now occupy, everything is political. Everything, we so often think, except our schools. We somehow believe learning in schools can be isolated from the surrounding society, even when that society creates, funds, and staffs our schools. We can no longer pretend our classrooms are separate from current political conditions and discourse."

~ Chris Friend, "CFP: Politicizing Critical Digital Pedagogy"

CHAPTER 1.

OCCUPY THE DIGITAL: CRITICAL PEDAGOGY AND NEW MEDIA

PETE RORABAUGH

Teaching is a moral act. Our choice of course content is a moral decision, but so is the relationship we cultivate with students. Both physical and digital learning spaces require us to practice a politics of teaching, whether we're conscious of it or not. However, traditional relationships between students and teachers come freighted with a model of interaction that often impedes learning. They are hierarchical. Progressive teaching, informed by a critical attention to pedagogy, resets the variables and insists on the classroom as a site of moral agency.

Jesse Stommel and I have outlined the ways that the "critical" in critical pedagogy functions in several registers:

- Critical, as in mission-critical, essential;

- Critical, as in literary criticism and critique, providing definitions and interpretation;

- Critical, as in a reflective and nuanced approach to a thing;

- Critical, as in criticizing institutional or corporate

impediments to learning;

- Critical Pedagogy, as a disciplinary approach, which inflects (and is inflected by) each of these other meanings.

The Brazilian educator Paulo Freire began his experiments in progressive education by teaching peasant farmers to read in 1962. By 1969 he had published his landmark work *Pedagogy of the Oppressed*, had been exiled from Brazil, and was teaching as a visiting professor at Harvard University. Freire's work remained focused on raising the consciousness of institutionally marginalized populations by rethinking education. Critical pedagogy, the academic discipline that emerged from his work, remains committed to an openly leftist critique of educational institutions that silence or displace dissent.

A critical approach to pedagogy is consistent with the goals of a digitally-infused curriculum. Critical and digital pedagogical collaboration is lately proliferating, in widening ripples and across disciplines. At the end of a recent blog post / interview titled "The Rise of MOOCs" about the development of the MOOC model, Stephen Downes asserts that academic discourse is too rigid and abstract. He writes: "[Our objective] is about actually empowering people to develop and create their own learning, their own education . . . We (those of us working in MOOCs) have also been clear about the influences of people like Ivan Illich and Paulo Freire."

Several scholars in critical pedagogy recognize the potential power of networked technology, once viewed as the zone of corporate colonization. In "Critical Pedagogy in the Twenty-First Century" in *Critical Pedagogy: Where Are We Now?* (2007), Joe L. Kincheloe suggests, "If critical pedagogy is to matter as we move toward the second decade of the twenty-first century . . . then it must meet several contemporary challenges . . . In an era when open-access publishing on the Internet is a compelling issue in the politics of education, I contend that open-access writing and speaking about critical pedagogy are also profoundly important.

Such a populist form of criticality does not in any manner undermine our intellectual rigor and theoretical sophistication; instead it challenges our pedagogical ability to express complex ideas in a language that is understandable and germane to wide audiences." Kincheloe echoes Downes's assertions 1) that academic work must be useful beyond its tower and 2) that digital culture offers new opportunities to achieve that goal.

The same thread exists in the work of Anya Kamenetz, whose *DIY U* (2010) documents the shift of education away from burdensome, hierarchical institutions. Kamenetz summarizes why students have been increasingly "priced out" of a college education in the last three decades. In a Chelsea Green Publishing video — "Anya Kamenetz on Alternative Education" — associated with the release of *DIY U*, Kamenetz says: "We don't have to be locked into this situation of constantly spiraling [higher ed] costs because there are ways to use technology to bring down the cost of higher education. [That includes] everything from a free lecture that's available through video-on-demand or an open-source textbook . . . or peer-group learning that happens in social networks . . . and hybrid models of technology with experiential education". Kamenetz's research on the shifting nature of learning represents a new strand of critical analysis from outside the academy that recognizes the potential of critically re-imagined digital learning communities.

Critical pedagogy, no matter how we define it, has a central place in the discussion of how learning is changing in the 21st century because critical pedagogy is primarily concerned with an equitable distribution of power. If students live in a culture that digitizes and educates them through a screen, they require an education that empowers them in that sphere, teaches them that language, and offers new opportunities of human connectivity. Digital tools offer the opportunity to refocus how power works in the classroom. In its evolution from passive consumption to critical production — from the cult of the expert to a culture of collaboration — the critical and digital classroom emerges as a site of intellectual and moral agency.

In *The Moral University*, Maurice and Claire Berube examine recent debates over morality in higher education. They cite Derek Bok, Stanley Fish, and John J. Mearsheimer as outspoken critics against the indoctrination of students in moral principles. They also quote Fish's 2008 *Save the World On Your Own Time*: "Teachers cannot . . . fashion moral character . . . My contention is that academization is the only thing that should happen in the classroom . . . This position [is] sometimes called derisively the Ivory Tower position." Faculty in support of a moral teaching imperative — among them Henry Giroux, Michael Berube, and Bruce Wilshire — argue that a moral curriculum does not mandate a specific moral position.

As educators, it behooves us always to consider the situations of our students — their actual material circumstances. To assume the primacy of the educational institution over the student is regressive. Institutions, by their nature, seek their own perpetuation; pedagogues pursue the increasing agency of their students. This is not to say that these goals are never compatible, but they are sometimes at odds.

As scholars, we come through the professional birthing canal and inherit the theoretical DNA of our disciplines — theories of postmodern fragmentation, of colonial evil, of textual deconstruction, of material embodiment. What many of us do not receive from our early development as academics, but hopefully accumulate on our own, is a theory of student empowerment.

In the same way that we can buzz, electrified, in the presence of a powerfully delivered lecture or vigorous classroom discussion, we can also achieve a certain glow from the move to a digital educational landscape, where the interaction of co-learners can explode virtually across the media frames of the Internet. Electrified teaching can happen in the physical classroom, and genuine academic engagement can happen between keyboards, cameras, and smartphones in a committed learning community.

But this does not happen by accident. It is the product of a critical pedagogue who understands and selects tools and activities, blending them with the interactive community that meets her in the learning landscape.

The formal discipline of critical pedagogy is political. It unearths and disrupts the nest of political powers that orbit educational structures. It unapologetically ascribes to particular political principles that are liberal in nature. It would be overly simplistic to describe critical pedagogy as holding values that are anti-racist, anti-patriarchal, anti-capitalist, anti-fundamentalist, but these values are the nucleus of critical pedagogical work.

Most of us do our work within the boundaries of institutions. However, the principles of critical pedagogy are extra-institutional. Questions of power, access, and technology are moral; they have been critical for progressive educators for decades. The commitment to learners, to their exploration, their community, their authentic engagement, and their ultimate agency and empowerment, governs our work. Sometimes these principles find themselves in conflict with the material or political goals of the institution. At such a point, the critical pedagogue must negotiate mandates while adhering to principles.

This is the stuff of progressive pedagogy: a principled commitment to the engagement of the learner and the democratic discovery of their own empowerment.

CHAPTER 2.

TECHNOLOGY 101: WHAT DO WE NEED TO KNOW ABOUT THE FUTURE WE'RE CREATING?

HOWARD RHEINGOLD

"...A crucial turning point comes when one is able to acknowledge that modern technics, much more than politics as conventionally understood, now legislates the conditions of human existence. New technologies are institutionalized structures within an existing constitution that gives shape to a new polity, the technopolis in which we do increasingly live. For the most part, this constitution still evolves with little public scrutiny or debate. Shielded by the conviction that technology is neutral and tool-like, a whole new order is built — piecemeal, step by step, with the parts and pieces linked together in novel ways, without the slightest public awareness or opportunity to dispute the character of the changes underway. It is somnambulism (rather than determinism) that characterizes technological politics — on the left, right, and center equally."
                               ~ Langdon Winner, *Autonomous Technology*

Are we awake to the world we're building, or are we, as an old Sufi saying goes, merely asleep in life's waiting room?

The petroleum economy, nuclear power, biotechnology, artificial intelligence, lasers, organ transplants, telephone and television and personal computer networks — today's technologies have put staggering amounts of power into the hands of billions of people. More power is on its way in the next several decades, as present scientific knowledge drives future technological capability. Do we know what to do with the powers over matter, mind, and life that tomorrow's technologies will grant us?

If we don't already know the answers to these questions, what do we need to know to design, deploy, control, and live humanely with the tools we are creating?

Like millions of other baby-boomers, the evolution of technology isn't just something I study, it's the backdrop of my life. The importance of technology in the daily life of most human beings has multiplied more within my lifetime than in any previous era in history. Interstate highways and the transformation of American life by the automobile were just getting into high gear when I was born in 1947. When I was an infant, television and nuclear power were also in their infancy. I can remember using propeller-driven aircraft and vinyl record albums. I can remember black and white TV. Like most Americans, the foundation of my beliefs about the future was a strong faith in "progress" — the assurance that tomorrow will be different and better than today because of new technologies.

I'm still immersed in technologies. I'm fascinated by them. I make a good living using computers and networks to write about computers and networks. In the process, I've became quasi-famous, and learned more than I ever imagined I would know about the mass media's love-hate affair with technology. Somewhere along the way, I started spending hours of my day in front of a computer screen. But I've been paying more attention to the cracks in my worldview lately, especially the place where progress and somnambulism meet.

I am compelled to begin with a confession of not just my complicity in the creation of today's digital culture, but my outright seduction by high-tech tools. I must describe my love for mind-extending technologies before I can describe how I started to think more critically about tools, minds, and civilizations.

I speak now directly to others like myself who are admitted, even enthusiastic, technophiles. For that reason, I don't want anyone to mistake this for an orthodox neoLuddite rant. I lack the certainty of the true believers — both the orthodox technophiles and the convinced technophobes. I confess up front that I know of no theology or ideology that will answer the questions I can no longer avoid asking.

Where are we going? Do we want to go there? Is there anything we can do about it? I have written this because I hope we can think together about where these questions lead. Perhaps there are solutions that can only be found by many of us, working together.

Thinking critically about the technosphere we inhabit, which defines who we are and dictates how we live and die, is scary — like thinking about performing surgery on yourself. Your internal denial alarms are going off already, I know. But I urge you to repress the urge to rise to the defense of penicillin and civilization, and consider how I came to rethink my attitudes.

You're reading this on the web, after all. I do all the HTML myself. I upload it to the server. I do a little PhotoShop, a little Unix. I'm not an archgeek, but neither am I totally unaware of how this new stuff works. It is possible to think critically about technology without running off to the woods — although, I must warn you, it is possible that you will never be quite so comfortable again about the moral dimensions of progress and the part we all play in it. I know that I'm not.

We are all partaking in, and many of us are helping to build, something that none of us understands. There are taboos against looking too critically at the real politics of technology. Marx was just as deluded as Adam Smith when it came to understanding the real invisible hand that has influenced how humans work, live, and think for the past several centuries. Although a few people understand the urgency and relevance of the history of technologies, most people aren't even aware that progress wasn't always our most important product.

One of the things that makes technology dangerous is the way people forget where tools come from, and what they were designed to do.

We have forgotten, and have been encouraged to forget, about the origins and provenance of fundamental thinking tools we all benefit from — rationality, progress, democratic self-governance, universal acceptance of the superiority of the scientific method to other ways of knowing. A specific manner of systematically examining the world, extracting knowledge, and applying that knowledge to extend power, a system that was developed only a few centuries ago, has been so extraordinarily successful that it has totally sucked our attention. Our technologized culture shapes and fascinates us to the extent we don't even see other ways of knowing and interacting with the world and each other. As Langdon Winner claims above, people in industrial, megatechnological civilization seem to sleepwalk through the world we've created, oblivious to the worlds that have been destroyed, never really thinking about the worlds technology will engender in years to come.

One crashes into a fundamental paradox when one tries to determine whether one is sleepwalking, so I ask you to stipulate only that most people in the world are unaware of the true dimensions of the revolution that has taken place since the time of Descartes and Bacon. We know we live in a world of 747s and heart transplants and perpetual change, but we don't know — aren't taught — how we got here. Knowing how we got here is particularly important now because civilization is facing a crisis about thinking about tools that was caused, in part, because we learned how to create tools for thinking.

People didn't know how to think systematically about the material world until 17th and 18th centuries, despite millennia of attempts by philosophers to understand the nature of the energy and matter. In the 16th and 17th centuries, in an unpleasant era of plagues, witch-burnings, Inquisitions, devastating religious wars and civil conflicts, a small number of European philosophers proposed that if we could discover a better method of thinking about the world — a systematic means of discovering truth — we could govern ourselves in a more equitable manner, we could relieve the suffering of disease and hunger and improve the living conditions of many, if not all.

These thinkers postulated, not too many centuries ago, that the human condition could be improved by way of a magical mental operation that had yet to be discovered. In their search for this mind-magic, the founders of modern science drew their hints from the alchemic, hermetic, cabalist magical traditions of the past. The search for meaning in the stars or in the manipulation of magical symbols turned to the search for meaning in matter and the manipulation of mathematical symbols.

Newton's astrological speculations are forgotten, but every school child learns what Newton discovered about gravity and motion. Science and technology seem to have trumped metaphysics, but it's important to know that metaphysical inquiry is what triggered the quest that led to science and technology. We take it for granted now, but the premise of this quest was a radically new view of human nature when it emerged, four hundred years ago: Humans are perfectible, are capable of discovering the means of our own perfection, and human institutions thereafter can be improved by perfected people: This was the blueprint for the modern idea of progress, in its original form.

Rooted in Platonic transcendental idealism and Christian eschatology, the notion that history has a direction prepared the way for the "new method" of recent centuries. Egyptians, Greeks, Hebrews, and Christians all contributed components to the foundations of science, but the idea of scientific progress emerged as something wholly new.

One of the reasons technology's shadow side is more or less invisible is because progress has been such a winner. The seekers found their grail, and it proved to be as potent as the alchemic philosopher's stone had promised to be. Introducing rationalism into human affairs and scientific enterprise was a noble vision, with many successes. A great deal of human misery has been relieved because those European thinkers began concocting this notion of perpetual discovery, perpetual change, perpetual improvement — and inventing tools for bringing about this transformation of the human condition.

In response to that call for what came to be known as "the Enlightenment Project," thinkers including Descartes, Bacon, Newton, and Galileo applied themselves to the task of thinking in a wholly new manner. Between their individual insights, this small number of European intellectual adventurers came up with a "new method" that was extraordinarily successful. First, doubt everything. Then, gather evidence by examining the world and performing systematic experiments. Then formulate theories, preferably with mathematical formulae, that allow you to explain the evidence and predict the outcome of further experiments. In the beginning, few foresaw the limitations of the wondrous discovery. We can see now, however, how this successful transformation of human thought caused side-effects that were not visible for centuries.

At the end of the twentieth century, it is easy to see that technological progress based on systematically gathered scientific knowledge, coupled with industrial capitalism (or socialism, for that matter), requires continuous growth, damages the environment that supports life, diminishes both biological and social diversity, and everywhere seems to move us toward societies in which humans learn how to be components in larger social machines. No matter how convenient it makes life for billions, this process of extracting resources, expanding power, and stimulating perpetual growth in energy consumption seems to be headed for ecological, political, economic catastrophe within the next few decades, at most.

Although our present crisis is so threatening precisely because it plays out on the physical plane, where our bodies and other creatures live, it is a crisis of knowledge. We lack a crucial mental skill. I contend that our position today regarding the way we make decisions about technologies is similar to the dilemma that pre-Enlightenment scientists faced in the sixteenth century. We simply don't have a good method for thinking and making decisions about how to apply (and not apply) the powerful tools of rationality, the scientific method, reductionism, the combination of logic and efficiency embodied by technology.

That we don't now know how to think and make decisions about technology doesn't mean we are incapable of discovering a "new method" for thinking about technology. If ever our species needed thinkers of the caliber of Descartes and Newton, it is now. But first we need to think about a new way to think about technology.

I don't hope to discover that method by myself. But I would like to help encourage a more widespread public discourse about the problem, in the hope that our process of thinking together can help lead to this future mindset. And I hope that the people who will be designing and distributing tomorrow's technologies can do so with a thorough knowledge of the systemic effects of their enterprise.

We must be careful that we don't destroy what we set out to save. The assumption that there is a rational solution to every problem is at the heart of Enlightenment rationalism. Relentless and successful problem-solving is what brought us from Mesopotamia to Metropolis in five thousand years. Let's begin by not mistaking "thinking together" for "rushing for a solution."

Perhaps the answer is not in the realm of "problem —> solution." Perhaps we need to think/feel outside that frame.

Without claiming I have an answer to the problems of technology, I'd like to tell other technology-lovers, technology-designers, technology users, about a few of the things I've learned.

I have to start with my own fascination with technologies, especially those that amplify intellectual functions. I know that many people have fallen in love with the virtual life, as I have, and you and I are the people — the ones who are designing tomorrow's technologies — who most actively need to know about what I've been learning. For those who are not technophiles, I want you to recognize the beauty in digital technology as a creation of the human mind, on a par with music or painting or architecture.

Our compulsion and talent for changing our world and ourselves is hardwired in our frontal lobes and opposable thumbs; our extremities evolved to walk upon and grasp the world, to roam it and use it. If the Devil is in the details, so is God, or at least the Demiurge. The seduction of digital technology in particular is not demonic, but Faustian. Faust didn't sell his soul for ordinary wealth or power, but for the transformative development of progress, his and society's. Faust's problem was not in the nature of his goal, but in the coin he paid.

All our stories these days are Faustian.

Originally published in 1998 as the start to a five-part series on his own blog, Howard's piece was republished on Hybrid Pedagogy *in 2014, because it productively considers so many of the issues explored elsewhere on the journal (and in this collection).*

CHAPTER 3.

MAGGIE'S DIGITAL CONTENT FARM

AUDREY WATTERS

Over the course of the last 6 months or so, I've felt a real shift in what it means (for me) to write — to work, to be — online. And let's be clear: this affects me offline too.

I'm hardly the first or the only person to notice that the great promises of the web — freedom! knowledge! access! egalitarianism! creativity! revolution! — are more than a little empty. I'm hardly the first or the only person to notice that the online communities in which we participate increasingly feel less friendly, less welcoming, more superficial, more controlling, more restrictive.

Online, we seem to be more and more short-tempered and sharp-tongued. It feels less and less sustainable. It's taking a toll on me, personally — the status updates, the sneers, the threats, the responsibilities, the accolades, the comments, the deadlines. All of it.

I've long been "a critic" of edtech, to be sure. That's what my work, my writing is known for.

But what I'm feeling now is new. It's different. As such, I recognize — for me, my work, my writing — with a growing sense of urgency that I need to re-evaluate my own use of digital technologies — as a writer, as a worker, as a human.

I ain't gonna work on Maggie's farm no more
No, I ain't gonna work on Maggie's farm no more
Well, I wake in the morning
Fold my hands and pray for rain
I got a head full of ideas
That are drivin' me insane
It's a shame the way she makes me scrub the floor
I ain't gonna work on Maggie's farm no more

It's hard to mark the moment in the early 1960s when Bob Dylan "changed," when — as we'd tell the story now, at least — enough was enough.

Bob Dylan recorded "Maggie's Farm" in 1965. There are lots of interpretations of the song's lyrics, and much to be said about the song's origins and its subsequent performances.

The song first appeared on *Bringing It Back Home* — an album that's often used to mark one of the many shifts in Dylan's career; but it was the performance of the song at the Newport Folk Festival that same year — loud and electric — that elicited those infamous boos from the audience and prompted that final split between Dylan and the folk music movement.

Some point out that, like a lot of Dylan's music, the song is simply an adaptation of an earlier folk song — in this case the Bentley Brother's 1929 recording of "Down on Penny's Farm," which also criticizes rural landlords who systematically exploit day-laborers.

Some say "Maggie's Farm" is a pun on the surname of Silas McGee, on whose farm in Greensboro, Mississippi Dylan performed "Only a Pawn in Their Game" during a voter registration rally, as featured in the D. A. Pennebaker documentary *Don't Look Back*.

Some argue that "Maggie's Farm" is a protest song against protest music, condemning those in "the scene" who are quick to profit off of the creativity and the fury of others, all the while pretending that they do so as part of some larger progressive political project.

> *I ain't gonna work for Maggie's brother no more*
> *No, I ain't gonna work for Maggie's brother no more*
> *Well, he hands you a nickel*
> *He hands you a dime*
> *He asks you with a grin*
> *If you're havin' a good time*
> *Then he fines you every time you slam the door*
> *I ain't gonna work for Maggie's brother no more*

New Media, we were told, would displace Old Media. The Internet would change things. Radically.

Old institutions — those which controlled who could be published, those who would be deemed experts, and as such who could be heard — would crumble. New voices would be recognized; new voices would be heard.

A radical democracy of "the folk," if you will.

The readable, writable web would encourage a flourishing of cultural production, distributed and supported through more equitable frameworks. Creatives, no matter who or where, would be able make a living being creative.

As a freelance writer on the web, I write. I speak. My writing is read and shared widely. Despite that, as a freelance writer on the web, I still struggle to be heard. I struggle to make ends meet. I have to hustle for gigs, and I have to hassle folks for payment. I always have to hassle folks for payment.

> *I ain't gonna work for Maggie's pa no more*
> *No, I ain't gonna work for Maggie's pa no more*
> *Well, he puts his cigar*
> *Out in your face just for kicks*
> *His bedroom window*
> *It is made out of bricks*
> *The National Guard stands around his door*
> *Ah, I ain't gonna work for Maggie's pa no more*

I've long been an advocate for writers — well, all of us really — to own our own domains. A domain of one's own, much like a room of one's own as Virginia Woolf insisted, is an important and necessary space to think and to work.

In this so-called Information Age, having a domain of one's own isn't simply a means to *produce* writing; it's a means to distribute it as well. To publish. To manage and control one's "intellectual property." To manage and control the metadata surrounding its dissemination and consumption.

The web promised openness. Open access. Open knowledge. Collaboration. Distribution.

Instead what we have today is a mass of information silos and content farms.

What we have today, if we're honest with ourselves, are old hierarchies hard coded onto new ones.

New media, new websites often demand we sign over our intellectual property. If they don't ask outright for copyright, they demand a license to such — "you grant us a non-exclusive, transferable, sub-licensable, royalty-free, worldwide license to use any IP content that you post on or in connection with [whatever]."

[Whatever] sells ads against that content. [Whatever] grants access to data to their partners.

[Whatever] [Whatever] [Whatever] — that seems to be the response from most folks in edtech. A shrug. An acquisition, one that is seemingly happy to work on someone else's farm — the LMS, the academic journal. But to work there oneself is one thing; to demand one's students work in these silos, on these farms as well… that's horrifying.

That's wrong.

I ain't gonna work for Maggie's ma no more
No, I ain't gonna work for Maggie's ma no more
Well, she talks to all the servants
About man and God and law
Everybody says
She's the brains behind pa

She's sixty-eight, but she says she's twenty-four
I ain't gonna work for Maggie's ma no more

I'm frustrated with so much of edtech. Surveillance. Control. Frustrated and exhausted by the demands that we participate in technologies that are exploitative and extractive. I'm increasingly concerned that we're asking people to participate in technologies, practices, online communities, "farms," — that are profoundly, profoundly unsafe.

How does one protest that?

Refuse to participate online?

Move one's participation elsewhere? New songs? New communities?

Dylan's protest in 1965 was to plug in. Mine, I don't know... it might be to unplug.

But if nothing else, I tell you this: I ain't gonna work on Maggie's Farm. And I think you need to think about your own work. Where you work. For whom.

And then you must consider where you demand your students work. For whom they work. Who profits. Where that content, where that data, where those dimes flow.

On whose farm are you working? On whose farm are you demanding your students work? To what end? For whose profits?

Are they safe there? Are you safe there? Are you sure?

I ain't gonna work on Maggie's farm no more
No, I ain't gonna work on Maggie's farm no more
Well, I try my best
To be just like I am
But everybody wants you
To be just like them
They say sing while you slave and I just get bored
I ain't gonna work on Maggie's farm no more

CHAPTER 4.

A GUIDE FOR RESISTING EDTECH: THE CASE AGAINST TURNITIN

SEAN MICHAEL MORRIS AND JESSE STOMMEL

"Students often find themselves uploading their content — their creative work — into the learning management system. Perhaps they retain a copy of the file on their computer; but with learning analytics and plagiarism detection software, they still often find themselves having their data scanned and monetized, often without their knowledge or consent."
~ Audrey Watters, "Education Technology's Completely Over"

A funny thing happened on the way to academic integrity. Plagiarism detection software (PDS), like Turnitin, has seized control of student intellectual property. While students who use Turnitin are discouraged from copying other work, the company itself can strip mine and sell student work for profit.

For this bait-and-switch to succeed, Turnitin relies upon the uncritical adoption of their platform by universities, colleges, community colleges, and K12 schools. All institutions that, in theory, have critical thinking as a core value in their educational missions. And yet they are complicit in the abuse of students by corporations like Turnitin.

The internet is increasingly a privately-owned public space.

On April 3, 2017, Donald Trump signed into law a bill over-turning Obama-era protections for internet users. The new law permits Internet Service Providers (ISPs) to access, without permission, data about our internet use patterns — from the sites we visit to the search terms we use. And this data isn't restricted to the work we do on computers. Thanks to the "internet of things," all our various connections can be monitored by our ISPs — from our physical location to the temperature we keep our homes to the music we ask Alexa to play for us. (In fact, Alexa processes all of our speech when it is on, even when we are not addressing it.)

Every day, we participate in a digital culture owned and operated by others — designers, engineers, technologists, CEOs — who have come to understand how easily they can harvest our intellectual property, data, and the minute details of our lives. To resist this (or even to more consciously participate in it), we need skills that allow us to "read" our world (in the Freirean sense) and to act with agency.

Critical Digital Literacies

Tim Amidon writes in "(dis)Owning Tech: Ensuring Value and Agency at the Moment of Interface",

> Educational technologies, as interfaces, offer students and educators opportunities to discover and enact agency through strategic rhetorical action. Yet, realizing this agency is complex work … [that] requires an increasingly sophisticated array of multiliteracies.

Developing these critical multiliteracies is vital if we want scholars and students — and all the digital citizenry — to retain ownership over their intellectual property, their data, their privacy, their ideas, their voices. Even tools we love — that have potential to do good work in the world — need careful scrutiny. It is, in fact, part of our care for those tools and students who use them that demands we approach educational technology critically. There is no good use in tool fidelity. For example, uncritical belief in the superiority of the Mac OS over Windows or Linux may lead us to overlook how single-platform solutions exclude those without access to them. Tools (and software) are not something we should ever be "loyal" to. Even when a company's ideology is sound, the execution of that ideology through the platform may be flawed. For this reason, it's important to understand how to look deeply at any digital tool.

This isn't, as Howard Rheingold writes in *Net Smart: How to Thrive Online,* "rocket science. It's not even algebra. Becoming acquainted with the fundamentals of Web credibility testing is easier than learning the multiplication tables. The hard part, as always, is the exercise of flabby think-for-yourself muscles." There is no special magic to digital literacies, whether we're assessing information or which word processing tool to use — and no pre-defined set of "transferrable skills" that can only be drawn upon by "experts" in the field. Rather, the work involves a shift in orientation and acknowledgement that the Web works upon its objects and people in specific and nuanced ways.

In Digital Pedagogy Lab courses we've taught, there's one exercise in particular we return to again and again. In our "crap detection" exercise (named for Rheingold's use of the term), participants use a rubric to assess one of a number of digital tools. The tools are pitted, head to head, in a sort of edtech *celebrity deathmatch.* Participants compare Blackboard and Canvas, for instance, or WordPress and Medium, Twitter and Facebook, Genius and Hypothes.is.

We start by seeing what the tools say they do and comparing that to *what they actually do.* But the work asks educators to do more than simply look at the platform's own web site, which more often than not says only the very best things (and sometimes directly misleading things) about the company and its tool. We encourage participants to do research — to find forums, articles, and blog posts written about the platform, to read the tool's terms of service, and even to tweet questions directly to the company's CEO.

This last has led to some interesting discussions on Twitter. One CEO, for example, wondered defensively what his own politics had to do with his tool. Others have been incredibly receptive to the conversations this activity has generated. We would contend that this is the exact kind of work we should do when choosing what tools to use with students. (Jesse has also done the activity with a group of digital studies students at University of Mary Washington.) Educators should be looking under the hood of edtech tools and talking more directly with technologists. Meanwhile, edtech CEOs should be encouraged (and sometimes compelled) to better understand what happens in our classrooms. Otherwise, we end up with tools — like ProctorU and Turnitin — that not only try to anticipate (or invent) the needs of teachers, but ultimately do damage by working directly at odds with our pedagogies.

Critically Evaluating Digital Tools

"To teach in a manner that respects and cares for the souls of our students is essential if we are to provide the necessary conditions where learning can most deeply and intimately begin." ~ bell hooks

"Learning to be a critical consumer of Web info is not rocket science. It's not even algebra. Becoming acquainted with the fundamentals of Web credibility testing is easier than learning the multiplication tables. The hard part, as always, is the exercise of flabby think-for-yourself muscles." ~ Howard Rheingold

1. Who owns the tool? What is the name of the company, the CEO? What are their politics? What does the tool say it does? What does it actually do?

2. What data are we required to provide in order to use the tool (login, e-mail, birthdate, etc.)? What flexibility do we have to be anonymous, or to protect our data? Where is data housed; who owns the data? What are the implications for in-class use? Will others be able to use/copy/own our work there?

3. How does this tool act or not act as a mediator for our pedagogies? Does the tool attempt to dictate our pedagogies? How is its design pedagogical? Or exactly not pedagogical? Does the tool offer a way that "learning can most deeply and intimately begin"?

Photo by flickr user JD Hancock

The goal of the exercise is not to "take down" or malign any specific digital tools or edtech companies, but rather for participants to think in ways they haven't about the tools they already use or might consider asking students to use.

Here's the rubric for the exercise:

1. Who owns the tool? What is the name of the company, the CEO? What are their politics? What does the tool say it does? What does it actually do?

2. What data are we required to provide in order to use the tool (login, e-mail, birthdate, etc.)? What flexibility do we have to be anonymous, or to protect our data? Where is data housed; who owns the data? What are the implications for in-class use? Will others be able to use/copy/own our work there?

3. How does this tool act or not act as a mediator for our pedagogies? Does the tool attempt to dictate our pedagogies? How is its design pedagogical? Or exactly not pedagogical? Does the tool offer a way that "learning can most deeply and intimately begin"?

Over time, the exercise has evolved as the educators we've worked with have developed further questions through their research. Accessibility, for example, has always been an implicit component of the activity, which we've now brought more distinctly to the fore, adding these questions: How accessible is the tool? For a blind student? For a hearing-impaired student? For a student with a learning disability? For introverts? For extroverts? Etc. What statements does the company make about accessibility?

Ultimately, this is a critical thinking exercise aimed at asking critical questions, empowering critical relationships, encouraging new digital literacies.

Sean sees these kinds of literacies as a vital component of teaching and learning in digital spaces:

What lies at the heart of these literacies also forms the primary concern of critical digital pedagogy: that is, agency. The agency to know, understand, and thereby be able to act upon, create, or resist one's reality. For the student, this can mean anything from knowing how and why to read terms of service for a digital product or platform; recognizing the availability of networks and community in digital spaces, even in the LMS; understanding the multitude of ways that digital identity can be built, compromised, and protected; discovering methods for establishing presence and voice, and the wherewithal to reach out to others who are trying to discover the same. ("Critical Pedagogy and Design")

This is ethical, activist work. While not exactly the Luddism of the 19th Century, we must ask ourselves when we're choosing edtech tools who profits and from what? Audrey Watters reminds us that, for the Luddites, "It was never about the loom per se. It's always about who owns the machines; it's about who benefits from one's labor, from one's craft" ("Education Technology's Completely Over"). Because so much of educational technology runs on the labor of students and teachers, profiting off the work they do in the course of a day, quarter, or semester, it's imperative that we understand deeply our relationship to that technology — and more importantly the relationship, or "arranged marriage," we are brokering for students.

Because what's especially problematic in all of this is that instructors compel students to comply with the terms of these software and tools. And administrators or institutions compel faculty to compel students to comply. Meanwhile, everyone involved is being sold a "product," some of which, like Turnitin, are designed to eat our intellectual property and spit out control and hierarchy on the other end. When adopting new platforms, we shouldn't invest in or cede control to for-profit companies more interested in profit than education. And, when our institutions (or teachers) make unethical choices, we must (if we are able) find ways to say "no."

In "Bartleby, the Scrivener," Herman Melville writes, "Nothing so aggravates an earnest person as a passive resistance." We must become conscious of, as Jesse has elsewhere observed,

the ways we respond (both actively and passively) in the face of institutional demands we find unethical or pedagogically harmful

... And if we object to the increasing standardization of education, how and where do we build sites of resistance? What strategies can we employ to protect ourselves and students? What work-arounds can we employ as we build courage and community for revolt? What systems of privilege must we first dismantle? ("MMDU: 'I would prefer not to'")

Critical analysis is resistance. Questions are our sabots.

Turnitin: Academic Integrity at $2 per Student

Some platforms are not agnostic. Not all tools can be hacked to good use. Critical digital pedagogy demands we approach our tools and technologies always with one eyebrow raised. Some tools have good intentions squandered at the level of interface. Some tools have no good intentions at all. And when tools like these are adopted across an institution, the risks in mounting a resistance can be incredibly high, especially for contingent staff, students, and untenured faculty.

Turnitin isn't selling teachers and administrators a product. The marketing on their website frames the Turnitin brand less as software and more as a pedagogical lifestyle brand. In fact, the word "plagiarism" is used only twice on their home page, in spite of the fact that the tool is first and foremost a plagiarism detection service. The rest of the copy and images are smoke and mirrors. They are "your partner in education with integrity." They are "trusted by 15,000 institutions and 30 million students." (We feel certain they didn't ask those 30 million students whether they "trust" Turnitin.) The "products" most prominently featured are their "revision assistant" and "feedback studio." For the teachers and administrators using Turnitin as a plagiarism detector, these features function like carbon offsetting. When asked whether their institution uses Turnitin, they can point to all the other things Turnitin can be used for — all the other things that Turnitin is not really used for. The site even attempts to hide its core functionality behind a smokescreen; in the description for the "feedback studio," plagiarism detection is called "similarity checking."

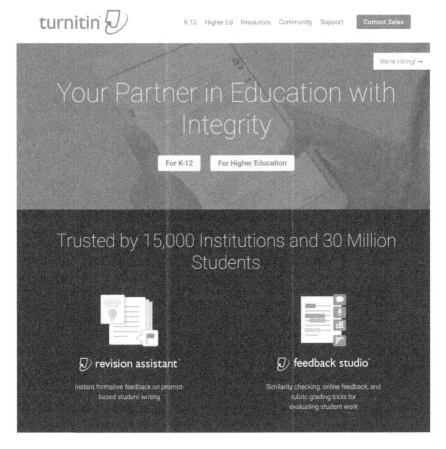

Turnitin.com Home Page

As we wrote above, thinking critically about digital tools means *weighing what the tools say they do against what they actually do*. In the case of Turnitin there are some marked discrepancies. For example, at the top of Turnitin's Privacy page (which they grossly call their "Privacy Center"), a note from the CEO declares, "Integrity is at the heart of all we do; it defines us." Then later, Turnitin declares that it "does not ever assert or claim copyright ownership of any works submitted to or through our service. Your property is YOUR property. We do not, and will not, use your intellectual property for any purpose other than to deliver, support, and develop our services, which are designed to protect and strengthen your copyright." Even if it is true that Turnitin doesn't assert *ownership* over the intellectual property it collects, their statement is misleading. They are basically saying *our brand is your brand* — that by helping them build their business we all simultaneously protect our own intellectual property. This is absurd.

Robin Wharton encourages educators, at the end of her 2006 piece "Re-Thinking Plagiarism as Unfair Competition," "to take a long hard look at how their own practices may foster an environment in which students are disenfranchised and relegated to the status of mere consumers in the education process."

In a recent conversation where he tried to explain why Turnitin's violation of student intellectual property was a problem, Sean's argument was countered with a question about whether that intellectual property was worth protecting. After all, most student work "isn't worth publishing." Ignoring for a moment this flagrant disregard for the value of student work, the point to make here is that Turnitin actively profits (to the tune of $752 million) from the work of students.

Let's look closer at Turnitin's terms of service, keeping in mind that complying with these terms is not optional for students required to submit their work to Turnitin.

> **Any communications or material of any kind** that you e-mail, post, or transmit through the Site (excluding personally identifiable information of students and any papers submitted to the Site), including, questions, comments, suggestions, and other data and information (your "Communications") **will be treated as non-confidential and nonproprietary. You grant Turnitin a non-exclusive, royalty-free, perpetual, world-wide, irrevocable license to reproduce, transmit, display, disclose, and otherwise use your Communications on the Site or elsewhere for our business purposes.** We are free to use any ideas, concepts, techniques, know-how in your Communications for any purpose, including, but not limited to, the development and use of products and services based on the Communications. [emphasis added]

As Jesse wrote in a piece for the *Chronicle of Higher Education*: "What we see there is a blur of words and phrases separated by commas, of which 'royalty-free, perpetual, world-wide, irrevocable' are but a scary few. The rat-a-tat-tat of nouns, verbs, and adjectives is so bewildering that almost anyone would quickly click 'agree' just to avoid the deluge of legalese. But these words are serious and their ramifications pedagogical" ("Who Controls Your Dissertation?"). Note also that this rather crucial paragraph is currently buried in the middle of Turnitin's TOS, over 5000 words in.

For papers submitted to the site specifically, the Turnitin TOS states "You hereby grant to Turnitin, its affiliates, vendors, service providers, and licensors a non-exclusive, royalty-free, perpetual, worldwide, irrevocable license to use such papers, as well as feedback and results, for the limited purposes of a) providing the Services, and b) for improving the quality of the Services generally." The gist: when you upload work to Turnitin, your property is, in no reasonable sense, YOUR property. Every essay students submit — representing hours, days, or even years of work — becomes part of the Turnitin database, which is then sold to universities. According to the company's website, as of this writing, Turnitin has a "non-exclusive, royalty-free, perpetual, worldwide, irrevocable license" to more than 734 million student papers.

734 million student papers.

Turnitin doesn't reveal its pricing on its website, going instead for a "get a quote" model, but as Ian Wylie reported in the article "Schools have the final word on plagiarism" for *Financial Times*, the cost per student was around $2 per year. So, that means an institution of 10,000 students will pay Turnitin $20,000 per year so the company can build its business. But Turnitin does not do a large chunk of the labor it sells. Students do. And even if students don't actively object to donating that labor, educators should never be in the business of removing student agency.

The abuse of student labor and intellectual property is only the beginning of the problem with Turnitin. If the company's financial and legal model isn't troubling enough, consider then how the application of its services affects the pedagogical relationship between students and teachers.

Tim Amidon observes:

> iParadigms' Turnitin employs a rhetoric of fear to turn educators away from, as Rebecca Moore Howard puts it, "pedagogy that joins teachers and students in the educational enterprise [by choosing] … a machine that will separate them," but also leaches the intellectual property students create within educational systems only to sell it back to schools.

Turnitin supplants teaching. Whereas intellectual property is a multivalent issue in the academy (especially in a digital age when authorship and ownership are mutable and contested), Turnitin's solution is writ in black and white. "Students uploading their work to Turnitin are turned from learners into potential plagiarizers," Jesse writes, "and the teaching moment (about attribution, citation, and scholarly generosity) is given away to an algorithm." To an issue of academic integrity that has been the project of teaching for decades, educational technology answers with efficiency. Plug it in. Add it up. Point a finger.

Behind this surrender to efficiency over complication, Turnitin takes advantage of the perennial mistrust of students by teachers. Turnitin relies on suspicion of plagiarism as an assumed quantity in the teacher-student relationship, and it feeds that polemic through its marketing. In their "Plagiarism Spectrum" infographic, for example, student writing is reduced to quaint icons and graphics. Plagiarism comes in flavors — from CTRL-C to Hybrid, from Remix and Recycle to 404 Error — which assign students to 10 discrete types. Easily managed, simple to define, less than human.

Rebecca Moore Howard writes that:

> Many of our colleagues are entrenched in an agonistic stance toward students in the aggregate: students are lazy, illiterate, anti-intellectual cheaters who must prove their worth to the instructor.

Turnitin and its automated assessment of student writing is a tool for that proof... ("Arguing against Turnitin")

There's something terribly parasitic about a service that plays on our insecurity about students and our fears of cheating. And it's not just leaching student intellectual property, and reinforcing teachers' mistrust of students, it's actually preventing teachers from exercising pedagogical agency. Carl Straumsheim reported in 2015 that:

> The Council of Writing Program Administrators has noted that "teachers often find themselves playing an adversarial role as 'plagiarism police' instead of a coaching role as educators." As a result, the "suspicion of student plagiarism has begun to affect teachers at all levels, at times diverting them from the work of developing students' writing, reading and critical thinking abilities," the organization wrote in a statement on best practices from 2003. ("What Is Detected?")

So, if you're not worried about paying Turnitin to traffic your students' intellectual property, and you're not worried about how the company has glossed a complicated pedagogical issue to offer a simple solution, you might worry about how Turnitin reinforces the divide between teachers and students, short-circuiting the human tools we have to cross that divide.

These arguments and others led the CCCC Intellectual Property Caucus to issue a statement about Turnitin and other plagiarism detection services. In short, the statement cites five irreconcilable problems with Turnitin (none of which even begin to mine its problematic business model):

Plagiarism detection services

1. "undermine students' authority" over their own work;

2. place students in a role of needing to be "policed";

3. "create a hostile environment";

4. supplant good teaching with the use of inferior technology;

5. violate student privacy.

Resisting Turnitin

How does a student push back against the flood of a tool like Turnitin, especially when that tool has been adopted across an institution? Resistance has to be on multiple fronts, offering individual students ways to respond when they are asked to compromise their intellectual property, while also addressing the systemic issues that lead to the institutional adoption of Turnitin in the first place. Many students instinctually understand the problems with a tool like Turnitin. Many have told us both how it feels to hit submit, turning over their work to an algorithm, and how helpless they feel to challenge a system that has distrust at its core. As educators, we can advocate and work to educate others about the problems of tools like Turnitin, but we find ourselves wanting better solutions, in the moment, for students who find themselves staring down the requirement of submitting to Turnitin.

Toward that end, we've put together a draft letter that students can send to faculty, that faculty can send to administrators, to help them better understand the problems with Turnitin. The tone of the letter is intentionally non-combative, and it includes a list of further resources. **We encourage anyone to fork, remix, re-imagine this letter at will. Help us by offering suggestions on how we can continue to revise. And, if you send some version of it, let us know.**

—————

Dear [Name]:

In 2014, the Conference on College Composition and Communication, a branch of the National Council of Teachers of English, concluded that plagiarism detection services, like Turnitin by iParadigm, "create a hostile environment" in classrooms, "undermine students' authority" over their own work, and violate student privacy. Despite this fact, I am asked to submit my work frequently through Turnitin in the name of academic integrity. Unfortunately, the use of student intellectual property and labor for profit by a third party is neither academic in practice or spirit, nor does it model integrity.

Plagiarism detection services rely upon the labor of students as their business model. Although Turnitin markets itself as a "partner in education," "trusted by 15,000 institutions and 30 million students," in fact the service does what no collaborator should do—forces me to license to them my intellectual property and makes it impossible for me to reclaim my full rights to that work. Turnitin's terms of service state very clearly:

> **If You submit a paper or other content in connection with the Services, You hereby grant to Turnitin, its affiliates, vendors, service providers, and licensors a non-exclusive, royalty-free, perpetual, worldwide, irrevocable license to use such papers**, as well as feedback and results, for the limited purposes of a) providing the Services, and b) for improving the quality of the Services generally.

This means that, not only do I surrender the license to use my work in perpetuity to this plagiarism detection service, but Turnitin *sells my work* back to you.

Please stop using Turnitin at our institution. Choose instead to keep academic integrity a human problem with human solutions. Or, at the very least, allow me to individually opt out. Should I ever unintentionally plagiarize, I would rather have the opportunity to speak with my instructor about my mistake than receive a machine-generated report. Please put teaching back in the hands of teachers, where it belongs.

There is no reason to surrender this institution's tradition of teaching and academic integrity to a third-party technology solution. Thank you for your support.

Sincerely,

[Name]

CHAPTER 5.

DISRUPTIVE PEDAGOGY AND THE PRACTICE OF FREEDOM

JULIE FELLMAYER

"The purpose of education, finally, is to create in a person the ability to look at the world for himself, to make his own decisions... What societies really, ideally, want is a citizenry which will simply obey the rules of society. If a society succeeds in this, that society is about to perish. **The obligation of anyone who thinks of himself as responsible is to examine society and try to change and fight it — at no matter what risk.** This is the only hope that society has. This is the only way societies change."
~ James Baldwin, "A Talk to Teachers"

Despite the edgy tone that accompanies ubiquitous calls for "disruption," I have yet to hear any edtech expert or 21st century education guru refer to disruption in the transgressive sense that Baldwin was evoking 54 years ago. The difference, of course, is that Baldwin was not worried about preparing students for "the jobs of the future." Too many modern educational calls for disruption tout themselves as progressive and revolutionary, and yet ultimately do not see students so much as they see future employees. Baldwin, on the other hand, was demanding the disruption of this "ideal citizenry" through transgressive education.

This was well before any app, coding system, or pedagogical trend had come along and claimed to carve out a pathway to societal utopia.

Ultimately, what is missing from these modern calls for disruption in education is an acknowledgement of the humanity of students and the societal perils many of them have to negotiate. Dissimilarly, in *Teaching to Transgress,* bell hooks urges teachers to contemplate "education as the practice of freedom" as their point of departure for praxis. A phrase originating from the work of Paulo Freire, hooks writes that "education as the practice of freedom" will come easiest "to those of us ... who believe that our work is not merely to share information, but to share in the intellectual and spiritual growth of our students. To teach in a manner that respects and cares for the souls of our students is essential if we are to provide the necessary conditions where learning can most deeply and intimately begin." Transgressive education and disruptive thinking therefore begin with the soul, and not the prospective career opportunities, of students.

What does it mean, therefore, to care for a student's soul in a disruptive sense? When I first read the hooks passage, I didn't even stop to consider and contemplate the meaning behind it. I blindly believed I understood it — that educators should endeavour to practice freedom for all and if we care about students as individuals we can help them to be intellectually and spiritually free. I care about my students, I care about, understand, and respect them as individuals. I differentiate for their needs; surely I am engaging in education as the practice of freedom? Surely my inclusive and individualized practice is disruptive of traditional educational constraints?

One nagging caveat of my reading of hooks was the realisation that, for the past eight years, I have been playing it pretty safe in my career. If I as a teacher, an individual with more power than any student, have not been challenging myself to be intellectually and spiritually free in my practice, how much freedom can my students possibly experience?

In referencing Buddhist philosopher Thich Nhat Hanh, hooks states, "teachers must be actively committed to a process of self-actualization that promotes their own well-being if they are to teach in a manner that empowers students." One might ask, is this self-actualization only about self-care, mindfulness and full mental and physical health? Or does self-actualization demand something much deeper and more difficult to acknowledge?

I am a straight, white, cisgender, mostly able-bodied, "appropriately" secular, middle-age, middle class, highly-educated, married woman. For just about every element of societal interaction or social participation, I am the "default" or even the "preferred" option. One might think that, from the perspective of Maslow's Hierarchy of Human Needs, I am actually pretty close to self-actualization.

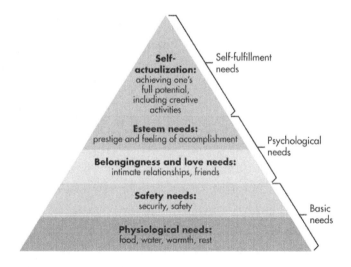

Maslow's Hierarchy of Human Needs

Much of my privilege provides me with considerable safety, of life, limb and personal property. Societal norms support and reinforce my accomplishments, choices and physical appearance, providing me with ample self-esteem. It appears that my "well-being," as hooks puts it, is being met. It is important to acknowledge, therefore, that I can reach Maslow's heights of

self-actualization not only because I have a number of my fundamental needs met, but more importantly because I benefit from
white supremacy, and from cis-het supremacy, and from the class
system.

There isn't much that stands in my way in life. I will never
have to worry that my students or their parents might find out I
am gay. I will never feel the anxiety of being the only person of
colour in my school. I worry more about the number of steps I
can accumulate in a day than I am concerned about negotiating
physically inaccessible buildings. I walk into my gender assigned
washroom confidently and without fear. I speak my mother-
tongue in cities around the world with the assurance that *someone*
will be able to communicate with me. I always know where my
next meal will come from.

I believe that to correctly understand bell hook's conception
of self-actualization one has to be willing to acknowledge their
privilege. If I reap the rewards of an unequal society, I cannot, as
hooks requests, "be actively committed to a process of self-actualization that promotes [my] own well-being." Without acknowledging my privilege, I can never be truly self-actualized. Without
using my privilege to actively disrupt the status quo, I can never
be self-actualized.

Therefore, I must admit to myself that my initial response to
engaging in true disruption through "education as the practice of
freedom" can be summed up as, "Well, that's just too hard." Ultimately, I am aware that to appropriately incorporate freedom in
praxis is to be willing to take on some risk.

In my case risk relates to the potential sacrifice of privilege. By
demanding that education be the practice of freedom I risk rocking what is, for the most part, an extremely comfortable boat.
The truth is, I don't ever have to do anything to combat oppression, and my life will be just fine. However, for anyone marginalised by systemic oppression, incurring risk is an unfortunate
but necessary element of speaking truth to power. On the daily.

For those of us on the frontline of K-12 teaching, "education as the practice of freedom" requires forthright discussion and action regarding subjects that are *messy* (at least in terms of their challenge to the agreed narrative and the cultural status quo) and this messiness can potentially make people *uncomfortable, confused, upset, angry,* and even potentially *confrontational* or worse, *violent.* Administrators and teachers and colleagues generally do not want to embrace the concept of education as the practice of freedom if it means rocking the boat too much.

Furthermore, it requires most of us to stop talking and to listen and promote the voices of people often marginalized in education. With the majority of teachers still being white women — and those in educational positions of power being mostly white men — the majority of us need to thoroughly educate ourselves in order to self-actualize. A small, but essential, first step is to immerse yourself in the work of as many POC, feminist, activist, and academic writers, bloggers, podcasters and tweeters as possible. I personally have been inspired by the work of educator and blogger Sherri Spelic, educator and author Rusul Alrubail, authors and journalists Ijeoma Oluo and Nikole Hannah Jones, podcaster and academic Dr. Hannah McGregor, and the authors and academics Dr. Roxane Gay, Dr. Adrienne Keene, Dr. Tressie McMillan Cottom and Dr. Robin Diangelo. Ideally, this self-education would also follow the lead of Dr. Erin Stutelberg — a professor of education who teaches about racism using the pyramid of white-supremacy — by making anti-white supremacy a core part of my teaching practice. This is the level of risk-taking in teaching that I'm talking about.

So be honest. It is much more comfortable to couch our true feelings in generalities that insinuate progressive ideals than to speak truth to power. We might believe we can incrementally move the conversation towards a brighter and more inclusive realm by incorporating some kind of "universal humanistic" approach to education. Unfortunately, in such a paradigm, it's more important that people avoid feeling uncomfortable and avoid challenging the status quo until a moment arises that presents us with a real shot at "success." One day we can truly practice freedom, but for now that freedom is still merely an aspiration.

Perhaps you think me cynical — even if *I* need to work on checking my privilege, I am ignoring the many well-intentioned, thoughtful, engaged educators out there that want to make the world a better place. Many teachers make equity issues a core element of their teaching. Many schools consider equity to be their reason for being. I applaud their efforts and encourage them to push themselves to do even more. As Jesse Stommel stated in his keynote address, "Queering Open Pedagogy," at the Vancouver Digital Pedagogy Lab, "There's a shit-load more work to do... The point that you think you've made it an inclusive event is the point that you've just dead failed at making an inclusive event." The same is true of schools and classrooms — to refer to oneself as inclusive without consistently challenging that assumption is to avoid hearing voices that may disrupt our belief that our inclusive values and good intentions are enough.

Freire writes in *Pedagogy of the Oppressed*, "There is no true word that is not at the same time a praxis. Thus, to speak a true word is to transform the world." If, as educators, our aim is to disrupt pedagogy and present our students with an authentic educational experience, then we have to be willing to name and attack patriarchy, white supremacy, and neoliberalism. In an interview with Robin Young from 2017, the incredible writer, poet and educator Clint Smith said,

> I think I fell victim to the fear of wanting to create an apolitical space in the classroom and revisiting "A Talk to Teachers" served as a really important reminder that the very decision to not discuss certain things in your classroom, is in and of itself, a political decision. Because my students' lives are impacted by political decisions every single day, and I think it's important for teachers to think about ways to try to facilitate and create a space where they can engage in those conversations in a meaningful way. ("Why James Baldwin's 'A Talk to Teachers' Remains Relevant 54 Years Later")

I have fallen victim to the same fear. As a teacher in an international school, my privilege, and the privilege of my students, has made the discussion of social and political concerns seem to lack urgency. It's not as though we don't tackle serious world issues such as child poverty, slave labour, access to clean water and the Sustainable Development Goals. From the perspective of a good, liberal, international curriculum, a focus on such topics is unequivocally important. It is easy, however, to present such topics from the perspective of a saviour and never consider our roles as perpetrators of inequality. What a difference it would make if we talked to our students frankly about the globally damaging effects of patriarchy and white supremacy. What if we critiqued political or international action (such as the SDGs) through an examination of neoliberal policy? Imagine if it was common practice to teach K-12 history through the lens of post-colonialism. The typical response to such perspectives is to label them "too political" or "too agenda driven" — as though a universal humanistic approach provides a bias-less, agenda-free educational platform. If we are honest with ourselves, as Clint Smith is, to avoid openly speaking and acting against oppressive forces (patriarchy, white supremacy, neoliberalism) is not to be apolitical but rather to shore up such forces.

To interpret bell hook's definition of "freedom" is to acknowledge that education in its current form advantages or disadvantages people to different degrees. Consider Kimberlé Crenshaw's definition of intersectionality as a weight or influence originating from systems of power that affect individuals with varying degrees of pressure. From the perspective of intersectionality, schools, curriculum and pedagogy are bound to the same systemic forces that perpetuate systemic inequality. hooks and Friere's understanding of freedom is an unparalleled level of disruption; it demands a de-centering of the standard narrative within society and education. Despite the best intentions of schools and individual praxis, without an acknowledged and proactive deconstruction of power structures, education cannot deflate the pressure of an oppressive system. "Education as the practice of freedom" demands that self-actualized educators open and centre the conversation and the cannon around marginalised voices and their narratives.

For those of us knowledgeable of bell hooks, Paulo Freire, Kimberlé Crenshaw, Clint Smith and James Baldwin, and who *get* the problematic strains within "the business of education," the ideas I am unpacking are nothing new. To embrace "education as the practice of freedom" is to understand that there is no legitimate conversation about disruption in education that doesn't include a focus on fighting oppression. Ultimately, what all teachers want is to provide a profound educational experience for students. In order to genuinely pursue such a profound educational experience, those of us with considerable privilege need to heed Baldwin's words and begin deliberately incurring risk.

CHAPTER 6.

OUR BODIES ENCODED: ALGORITHMIC TEST PROCTORING IN HIGHER EDUCATION

SHEA SWAUGER

Cheating is on the rise, we can't trust students, and the best strategy to protect academic integrity is to invest in massive surveillance systems. At least, that's the narrative that edtech companies catering to higher education are selling based on their products and marketing campaigns. One of the products that's currently being adopted by colleges and universities is algorithmic test proctoring — essentially software designed to automatically detect cheating in online tests — but we haven't had enough critical conversation about what values are embedded in these systems and the potential harm they can cause students. If I take a test using an algorithmic test proctor, it encodes my body as either normal or suspicious and my behaviors as safe or threatening. As a cisgender, able-bodied, neurotypical, white man, these technologies generally categorize my body as normal and safe, and because of this, they would not endanger my education, well-being, employment, or academic standing. The majority of the students on my campus don't share my identities and could have a very different experience being read by test proctoring algorithms. We need to understand the potential ways that algorithmic test proctoring can discriminate against students based on their bodies and behaviors, why higher education is willing to endanger students in the first place, and what we can do about it.

What It Is and Why It's Here

Over the last fifteen years, higher education has been increasing the number of online courses and programs it offers. While the methods for cheating in online classes are often the same as those used in-person, the institutional fear of increased cheating from online students has encouraged a new and lucrative market for ed-tech companies. Common online cheating methods include using unauthorized information aids while taking a test and/or having someone besides the student enrolled in the class take the test on their behalf, practices that predate both the internet and online tests. While in-person test proctoring has been used to combat test-based cheating, this can be difficult to translate to online courses. Ed-tech companies have sought to address this concern by offering to watch students take online tests, in real time, through their webcams. If the outsourced test proctor sees any evidence of cheating, as defined by the company or the institution, they can flag the behavior to be reviewed later by the course owner. After tests are completed, a course owner will be made aware of any flagged behavior. It is ultimately up to the course owner, not the test proctor, to determine if flagged behavior is a violation of academic misconduct and, if so, how to address it. Some of the more prominent companies offering these services include Proctorio, Respondus, ProctorU, Honor-Lock, Kryterion Global Testing Solutions, and Examity.

Several companies including Proctorio, Respondus, ProctorU, and others have adapted the outsourced human-proctoring model to include algorithmic proctoring, sometimes called "automated proctoring." Instead of a third party employee watching students take tests individually, tests are recorded, including audio and video of students, and run through internally-developed machine learning algorithms that "watch" each video and flag suspicious behavior in real time. Flagged sections of the test are sent to the course owner who, as before, determines if cheating was present or not. In order to do this, these algorithms require a large dataset to establish a baseline of "normal" bodies and behavior from which to make decisions. In this case, the data are recordings of people taking tests, exhibiting both cheating and non-cheating behavior, and the algorithm is taught by developers which bodies and behaviors are suspicious and which are "normal". At some point, with enough data and modifications, these companies deem their algorithms to be able to accurately identify cheating. While it's unclear exactly how many institutions are implementing algorithmic test proctoring, on the low end we can say there are at least tens of thousands of online tests every month proctored by third parties. From my conversations with representatives from Proctorio and ProctorU, in 2018 they administered about four million algorithmically proctored tests combined.

Potential Harms

Algorithmic test proctoring's settings have discriminatory consequences across multiple identities and serious privacy implications. For example, certain test settings flag loud noises or leaving the view of the camera as suspicious. These settings will disproportionately impact women who typically take on the majority of childcare, breast feeding, lactation, and caretaking roles for their family. Students who are parents may not be able to afford childcare, be able to leave the house, or set aside quiet, uninterrupted blocks of time to take a test. Even though Title IX includes protections for pregnancy and parental status, default test settings like these classify the day-to-day logistics of caring for children and dependents as a threat to academic integrity.

Students with certain medical conditions such as neuromuscular disorders or spinal injuries that prohibit them from sitting for long periods of time, those who need to use the restroom frequently, or anyone who needs to administer medication during a test will be flagged. In order for a student to identify themselves at the beginning of a test, they have to hold their ID stationary in front of their computer's camera and reverse-orient it to a frame on the screen, a task that requires fine motor skills that able-bodied students sometimes struggle with, and which students with certain disabilities may not be able to do. When eye-tracking is used, students with visual impairments such as blindness or nystagmus or students who identify as autistic or neuro-atypical may be flagged. Even common test-taking behaviors such as reading the question out loud, listening to music, or behaviors such as hyperactivity associated with ADHD can be flagged. While there can sometimes be accommodations for things like bathroom breaks, the fact is that most proctoring software's default settings label any bodies or behaviors that don't conform to the able-bodied, neurotypical ideal as a threat to academic integrity.

While racist technology calibrated for white skin isn't new — everything from photography to soap dispensers do this — we see it deployed through face detection and facial recognition used by algorithmic proctoring systems. Students with black or brown skin have been asked to shine more light on themselves when verifying their identities for a test, a combination of both embedded computer video cameras and facial recognition being designed by and for white people. A Black student at my university reported being unable to use Proctorio because the system had trouble detecting their face, but could detect the faces of their white peers. While some test proctoring companies develop their own facial recognition software, most purchase software developed by other companies, but these technologies generally function similarly and have shown a consistent inability to identify people with darker skin or even tell the difference between Chinese people. Facial recognition literally encodes the invisibility of Black people and the racist stereotype that all Asian people look the same.

At the beginning of a test, these products ask students to verify their identity by matching their appearance with a photo ID. As Os Keyes has demonstrated, facial recognition has a terrible history with gender. This means that a software asking students to verify their identity is compromising for students who identify as trans, non-binary, or express their gender in ways counter to cis/heteronormativity. If a student's gender expression or name on their ID are different from their current gender expression or name, the algorithm may flag them as suspicious. When this happens, they may have to undergo another level of scrutiny to authenticate their identity, an already common and traumatic experience for trans and gender non-conforming students. If these students are not alerted of this possibility before the test begins, it may force them to either discontinue the test and risk their grade, or out themselves to their course owner when they may not want to, risking more trauma and discrimination including being denied financial aid, being forced to leave their institution, or have their lives put in physical danger.

Course owners who use these products are given access to recorded video and audio of their students when they take tests, which can include the inside of students' homes and bedrooms. A common feature of proctoring systems is to allow course owners to download the recordings of their students to keep on a local device, and course owners can view the recordings of their students as many times as they want, when and wherever they want. These features and settings create a system of asymmetric surveillance and lack of accountability, things which have always created a risk for abuse and sexual harassment. Technologies like these have a long history of being abused, largely by heterosexual men at the expense of women's bodies, privacy, and dignity. For example, university professors have used texting and social media to stalk their students, TSA employees targeted women to scan their bodies and share the images, police helicopters recorded people naked and having sex, National Security Agency employees shared sexually explicit photos they intercepted and used wiretapping technology to spy on current or former lovers, civic employees used CCTV to watch women undress in their homes, and domestic abusers used IoT devices to gaslight wives and partners. These are just a few examples, but they represent how toxic masculinity has used technology to abuse women.

Additionally, proctoring systems often record the approximate location of where a student is when taking the test, which if not on campus is often in their homes. Having a course owner know where their students live can be dangerous for students, as is enabling course owners to have unaccountable access to video recordings of their students' bodies and homes.

Why Are We Encoding Bodies?

Given that these products create so much potential harm to students, it raises the question of why universities license them. Even if the risks to students were acknowledged by higher education institutions — and at present, they aren't — these companies are offering a product that resonates with several implicit values and practices of higher education that ultimately outweigh the risk to student safety: discriminatory exclusion, the pedagogy of punishment, technological solutionism, and the Eugenic Gaze.

Discriminatory Exclusion

Anytime people from a non-dominant group seek to participate in education, predictable counter arguments emerge that rest on the belief that their inclusion would harm current students, academic standards, productivity, etc. Algorithmic proctoring companies capitalize on colleges' and universities' preexisting discriminatory fears by first stoking those fears and then selling products to alleviate them. Below is an excerpt from a Proctorio promotional video [Editor's note: this video was removed just after the publication of this article.]

> Online education is moving the world's students into the future at an alarming rate. With the ability to take learning outside the brick walls of our institutions, a vast number of people now have access to

education. But this presents a problem of how to maintain academic integrity in a globally competitive job market. Instructors and students alike want to make sure they're on a level playing field when it comes to academic achievements. Proctorio defends your accomplishments by holding dishonest people accountable, all the while protecting your privacy...

This promotional video plays upon the fear that if we include people not normally inside the "brick walls of our institutions" they will somehow threaten academic integrity. In short, we on the inside are honest, those on the outside are dishonest, and the rate at which "they" are joining "us" is cause for alarm. Proctorio is not an outlier in this; their messaging is representative of how most test proctoring companies market themselves to higher education.

Colleges and universities have a long history of this kind of exclusion. In 1956, a group called the Educational Fund of the Citizen's Council began distributing pro-segregation propaganda claiming that if we allow Black students to attend white schools, Black students will lie, cheat, and generally cause disciplinary problems and the best response to them is increased disciplinary and policing tactics. In "The Case Against Coeducation: An Historical Perspective," Carol K. Coburn outlines some of the biological inferiority arguments given to exclude women from men's only institutions. Rosie Bradbury tells us that, when Cambridge University held a vote to determine if women should be granted equivalent degrees to men, male students protested by "burning effigies of female scholars and throwing fireworks into the windows of women's colleges." Higher education in the United States has feared including marginalized people from the beginning and test proctoring companies market directly to that fear. Their promotional messaging functions similarly to dog whistle politics which is commonly used in anti-immigration rhetoric. It's also not a coincidence that these technologies are being used to exclude people not wanted by an institution. As Os Keyes explains in *Vice*, biometrics and facial recognition have been connected to anti-immigration policies, supported by both Republican and Democratic administrations, going back to the 1990s.

Without having to say so directly, test proctoring companies are communicating *firstly*, that non-traditional students, students of color, international students, and students typically excluded from higher education are threats because they are more likely to cheat and need to be held accountable, and *secondly*, that additional surveillance technology (which they will sell you) would protect your institution from them.

The Pedagogy of Punishment

Algorithmic proctoring companies are the logical fulfillment of higher education's proclivity for disciplinary practices applied to academic integrity in an online environment. Borrowing from Henry A. Giroux, Kevin Seeber describes the pedagogy of punishment and some of its consequences in regards to higher education's approach to plagiarism. The pedagogy of punishment ignores that what constitutes cheating, plagiarism, and citation are culturally constructed, seemingly arbitrary on first approach, and a source of anxiety for incoming students, especially those not acculturated to higher education. When introducing new students to academic conduct policies, we create an environment based on threats and fear, communicate to them that they aren't trustworthy, and that if they break the rules, they will incur severe discipline. We've built up increasingly sophisticated surveillance methods for detecting when students cheat but fail to communicate to them the contextual, political, and historical forces that created our academic practices for citation, evaluation, and testing.

Sean Michael Morris and Jesse Stommel's ongoing critique of Turnitin, a plagiarism detection software, outlines exactly how this logic operates in edtech and higher education: 1) don't trust students, 2) surveil them, 3) ignore the complexity of writing and citation, and 4) monetize the data. That last point applies to test proctoring companies as well, but instead of stealing the intellectual property of students, these companies are monetizing data about students' bodies to increase the value of their own intellectual property: their algorithms and software. As a business model, this is an ideal scenario for the private sector. Colleges and universities require students to let companies record their bodies and collect biometric data, which these companies then use to refine their product and sell it back to universities. In some cases, institutions pass the cost of using the technology to the students who then pay proctoring companies directly, averaging about $25 per test. There isn't a clearer example of surveillance capitalism in education.

Technological Solutionism

Cheating is not a technological problem, but a social and pedagogical problem. Technology is often blamed for creating the conditions in which cheating proliferates and is then offered as the solution to the problem it created; both claims are false. Cheating predates the internet and will not be solved by a tool, a product, or an algorithm, even when that cheating happens online. Our habit of believing that technology will solve pedagogical problems is endemic to narratives produced by the ed-tech community and is tied to the Silicon Valley culture that often funds it. Scholars have been dismantling the narrative of technological solutionism and neutrality for some time now. In her book *Algorithms of Oppression*, Safiya Umoja Noble demonstrates how the algorithms that are responsible for Google Search amplify and "reinforce oppressive social relationships and enact new modes of racial profiling." Her body of work includes authoritative critiques of algorithmic bias, technological redlining, and how racism and sexism pervade technology and online culture. Another scholar at the forefront of this conversation is Anna Lauren Hoffmann, who coined the term "data violence" to describe the impact harmful technological systems have on people and how these systems retain the appearance of objectivity despite the disproportionate harm they inflict on marginalized communities. Algorithmic discrimination and data violence can sometimes be more difficult to call out than traditional forms of discrimination and violence, not just because the data and code are kept in a black box of intellectual property, but because people are less likely to believe that data and code are even capable of discrimination and violence in the first place. Lastly, Ruha Benjamin has been developing an abolitionist toolkit using race critical code studies to not only cut through technological solutionist propaganda, but deconstruct the white supremacy that underpins what she coins the "New Jim Code."

The Eugenic Gaze

Algorithmic test proctoring encodes ideal student bodies and behaviors and penalizes deviations from that ideal by marking them as suspicious, which threatens students with academic misconduct investigations and exclusion from the educational community. This system of measuring bodies and behaviors, associating certain bodies and behaviors with desirability and others with inferiority, engages in what Lennard J. Davis calls the Eugenic Gaze. To understand this, let's break down the terms "Eugenic" and "Gaze." Eugenics is an ideology with the goal of improving the genetic quality of humans through the erasure of undesirable traits. While most eugenics programs focus on race, they often expand their list of undesirable traits which have included, "...(1) the feeble-minded; (2) paupers; (3) alcoholics; (4) criminals...; (5) epileptics; (6) the insane; (7) the constitutionally weak; (8) those with specific diseases; (9) the deformed; and (10) the deaf, blind, and mute..." Eugenics programs attempt to remove people who have "undesirable" traits through anti-immigration policies, selective breeding programs, marriage restrictions, forced sterilization, murder, and genocide.

Higher education is deeply complicit in the eugenics movement. Nazism borrowed many of its ideas about racial purity from the American school of eugenics, and universities were instrumental in supporting eugenics research by publishing copious literature on it, establishing endowed professorships, institutes, and scholarly societies that spearheaded eugenic research and propaganda. Those researchers (and often university presidents) went on to promote federal policies that supported eugenics goals in areas as far reaching as immigration, economics, housing, law, and medicine. Roughly 70,000 Americans were forcibly sterilized as a direct result of these policies.

A Gaze, like the Male Gaze or the White Gaze, is a culturally dominant perspective that seeks to create a power difference between a dominant and nondominant group of people by defining the terms through which they are seen, valued, and discussed. Gazes usually share similar features such as unequal power dynamics, surveillance, control, and conformity. The Eugenic Gaze seeks to measure people's bodies and behaviors, compare them to an idealized norm, and either reform people who don't fit that norm through punishment or exclude them from the community altogether. Algorithmic test proctoring uses the Eugenic Gaze by measuring student's bodies and behavior (machine learning and facial recognition software), defining what bodies and behaviors are associated with the ideal student (cisgender, white, able-bodied, neurotypical, male, non-parent, non-caretaker, etc.), attempts to reform students who deviate from the ideal student (flagging them as suspicious), or exclude them from the community (academic misconduct investigations which can lead to expulsion). The Eugenic Gaze is a combination of white supremacy, sexism, ableism, cis/heteronormativity, and xenophobia. When we apply the Eugenic Gaze using technology, the way we do with algorithmic test proctoring, we're able to codify and reinforce all of those oppressive systems while avoiding equity-based critiques because of our belief in the neutrality of data and technology.

What Do We Do Now?

Don't use algorithmic test proctoring. Instead, focus on pedagogical techniques that you can use to design assessments, online or in person, that draw from personal experience or require students to apply concepts in unique contexts. If you have to use algorithmic test proctoring, make sure students know about the test settings and ID requirement well before they take a test, and assure them that you will not take any behavior flagged as "suspicious" into consideration that isn't described explicitly in the syllabus. Talk with students about academic integrity, not just about the rules and consequences, but the culture that constructed it and how surveillance capitalism and privacy play a role. If students are uncomfortable with algorithmic test proctoring, support and empower them to communicate this to the administration and, where possible, give them the ability to opt-out. Advocate on behalf of students; start a conversation at your institution about what this technology communicates to students who are forced to use it, what values it represents, and how those may be different from the stated values of the institution. Lastly, read Safiya Umoja Noble, Anna Lauren Hoffmann, Ruha Benjamin, Audrey Watters, and Os Keyes. Each of these scholars offers important analyses and critiques of technology, but also a vision for how it can be used towards justice and care; they've helped me understand and continue to give me hope.

Conclusion

Algorithmic test proctoring is a collection of machine learning algorithms that reinforce oppressive social relationships and inflict a form of data violence upon students. It encodes a "normal" body as cisgender, white, able-bodied, neurotypical, and male. It surveils students and disciplines anyone who doesn't conform to "normal" through a series of protocols and policies that participate in a pedagogy of punishment, ultimately risking students' academic career and psychological, emotional, and physical safety. Companies that build these technologies are able to exploit higher education's proclivity for discrimination because academia is still afraid of letting the wrong people in.

Technology isn't neutral or objective, it didn't cause cheating, and it won't ultimately stop it. It is, however, able to encode and amplify discriminatory beliefs and cast them into invisible and powerful systems that can harmfully impact our choices and our bodies.

Cathy O'Neil writes:

> Big Data processes codify the past. They do not invent the future. Doing that requires moral imagination, and that's something only humans can provide. We have to explicitly embed better values into our algorithms, creating Big Data models that can follow our ethical lead. Sometimes that will mean putting fairness ahead of profit.

Collectively, higher education has failed to embed ethical values into educational technology. Algorithmic test proctoring, and many technologies like it, sacrifice student agency in favor of discriminatory exclusion, the pedagogy of punishment, surveillance capitalism, technological solutionism, and the Eugenic Gaze. Educators have an obligation to object, resist, and subvert these systems, to push towards a practice that embodies justice, liberation, and love, and to remain vigilant for the next technological "solution" that promises to "fix" students or education.

PART II.

PRACTICING CRITICAL DIGITAL PEDAGOGY

"Hybrid Pedagogy is not ideologically neutral. The threads of our discussions and the underlying philosophy of the journal are grounded in critical pedagogy — an approach to teaching and learning predicated on fostering agency and empowering learners (implicitly and explicitly critiquing oppressive power structures)."
~ Jesse Stommel, "CFP: Critical Digital Pedagogy"

CHAPTER 7.

CRITICAL PEDAGOGY: INTENTIONS AND REALITIES

MAHA BALI

It is one thing to read about critical pedagogy in the abstract, but I believe there is much more to learn from contextual understandings of how the philosophy of critical pedagogy works in practice. When I first started reading about critical pedagogy I found the scholarship interesting but too abstract. I understood that it was intentionally non-prescriptive, but it also seemed impractical to me. Elizabeth Ellsworth's article was enlightening in her criticism of critical pedagogues for "consistently strip[ping] discussions of classroom practices of historical context and political position" (300), a view also held by Catherine Cornbleth, who suggests that a better approach to a critical curriculum would be to include both the macro issues (traditionally tackled by critical pedagogy scholars) and the micro-contextual issues of the lived experience of teachers.

I teach at the American University in Cairo (AUC) as a part-time teacher educator with no K-12 teaching experience (I am a full-time faculty developer, i.e. my day job is to support AUC faculty, and I'd had experience as a TA for undergraduates, and as a teacher of adults before). I teach educational technology to in-service school teachers who are either close to my age or much older. This means my students often have much more teaching experience than I do! Most of the experiences described below are from teaching a course on ethical, legal, social and human issues in educational technology. Teaching this course before Egypt's January 2011 revolution, some students had been more cautious about critiquing the Egyptian public school system; they have since felt more comfortable doing so. But their willingness to critique me does not come naturally to them, given the strong culture of respecting authority in Egypt.

In our first class meeting, I explain my teaching philosophy, though not in the elaborate and elegant detail Kris Shaffer has done in "An Open Letter to My Students." I do not make everything *explicit* on the first day because I am aware much of it will sound foreign to my students. I do, however, clarify the importance of learning from each other, that my syllabus is flexible and negotiable, that I want us all to learn from each other, and that I hope they can apply everything we learn in the course in their own context. I emphasize the importance of dialogue and talk about respectful disagreement and the importance of class participation. I mention the concept of "digital agnosticism" to encourage them to avoid the technopositivist attitude many of them come to the class with. None of these things directly describe the social justice orientation behind my teaching approach, but most of what I do say is completely new pedagogy for my students, and it usually takes them awhile to absorb it as they live through it in the class.

Critical pedagogy, for me, is not about knowing how to do everything right, or getting it right the first time, or every time. It is about putting faith in our learners to take control of their learning, and teach us, each other, and themselves in the process. Very often, we become better pedagogues by learning from our mistakes (see Clarissa Bezerra's heart-wrenching piece), accepting and even embracing the uncertainties, unpredictability, the messiness of learning. Understanding the contextual experiences of other pedagogues helps us reflect on our own practice.

Departing from the more prevalent sharing of good practice, I am sharing some of the unexpected consequences of my own attempts to implement critical pedagogy in my classes over five years of teaching in-service teachers about edtech.

Intention A: treat students as peers in a learning community. Ellsworth critiques critical pedagogues for discussing this in a paternalistic manner, where "treating" students as peers is a means to "empower" them so they can reach the level of knowledge of the teacher. But I truly believe each of them has valuable experience from their own context to bring to the classroom (that the rest of us have little knowledge of) and I hope my class is a place for them to learn from each other, for me to learn from them, and for them to reflect on their own experiences in ways they can take with them beyond the class so they can keep developing long after I am gone from their lives, continuing to "explore the dungeon" as Jeff Everhart recently wrote. In my first day of class, I quote Jesse Stommel's "Online Learning: A Manifesto," "Content-expertise does not equal good teaching... Once a course begins, the growing expertise of the students, and not the teacher, should be the primary focus." Making students *believe* this is a different matter.

Reality #1: Some students think I am "withholding" knowledge from them and not sharing it, when I try to decenter my own knowledge while foregrounding theirs. They usually do not realize that information, content, knowledge, are not the point. It is the process of creating that knowledge that matters, because that's what they will take with them for the rest of their lives. They don't realize that the knowledge I have isn't inherently more valuable than the knowledge they have. Part of my point is for them to understand that they can build from their own situated knowledge and not have to rely on theories that some other person (unaware of their context) has developed previously. Last semester, I introduced my students to MOOCs, then assigned them to read two different posts I had written about them. The key was to let them see how I, the same "authority" figure, could write about the same topic (MOOCs) very positively, and yet also very critically, all in the space of one week!

Reality #2: A student once commented that they thought I was *using the class environment to learn FROM the students rather than to help THEM learn.* Like I was doing some sort of covert research or something. It stems partially, I think, from an underlying skepticism towards anything affiliated with America. I had never thought of myself as affiliated with America just because I worked at an American institution. Ummm. Thankfully, that student later changed her mind about this. In hindsight, I am glad she brought it up so that we could discuss it, so I could explain myself, and so we could discuss her critique in more detail and unpack it.

Reality #3: I discovered the limitations of my collegiality with my students *when one of them plagiarized,* and when I felt that student was lying when confronted. I immediately went into power/authority/paternalistic mode. I spoke with sharpness and derision and started exerting my power in ugly ways. Ellsworth was right about the institutional authority of teachers always remaining in the background of any attempts at equitable classroom relations. In this case, it came to the fore. Even when I recognized this, there was no way to "take back" my initial reaction, it had already happened. I have apologized to my students in the past for some of my spontaneous reactions (and they usually consider it a valuable learning experience when I do). However, in this case, an apology would have been transparently disingenuous, and I just gave the student a second chance. But it made me think that I might need to rethink my entire attitude towards plagiarism (which I have done a little on inadvertent plagiarism and on the role of empathy and social justice in what we perceive as cheating).

Reality #4: On an upbeat note, at the end of one of my classes, several students commented on how they appreciated what they termed as my "modesty" in treating them as peers. This was slightly funny for me because I do not do it out of any sense of (false) modesty. I really do respect my students' experience and knowledge that they bring to class and I truly do think they can learn from each other (and I from them) much more than they can learn from me alone. I don't just believe it, I have seen it time and time again.

Intention B: use the class to promote social justice, and a stance towards social justice and challenging the status quo. The subjects of some of my classes help with this as I can cover topics like gender and access issues in educational technology.

Reality #1: I discovered that in being an authentic *non-neutral teacher on the topic of gender*, I can end up responding pretty strongly to chauvinistic male opinions on gender issues. One semester, male students asserted their views as fathers, that it was justifiable to limit girls' internet access lest they come across x-rated websites, but that there was no need to exert such control or censorship over their sons. My response to this was emotional, vehement, and I will admit, not a thought-out devil's advocate strategy. Thankfully, female students were also able to respond. I can never be sure why my strong reaction did not silence the male students: maybe they trusted me enough not to harm their grades? Maybe it is simply because they are the male (and therefore dominant) members of society as a whole, and felt no such threat. In any case, I thought that in the future, I would make my stance clear to students (no way could I hide my upper-middle class slightly Westernized feminism) BUT try not to get too involved in their arguments and see what came out naturally... Which led to...

Reality #2: I ended up getting a few responses that fell into *two dangerous camps*. The first was that educated folks nowadays no longer discriminate against girls with regards to technology (which is problematic in that it misses subtle forms of discrimination) and the second was male opinion that men are inherently better/more interested in certain computer things and it's FINE that girls don't want to. So I showed them some research. Then I went one step further and asked THEM to do research and find out in their own contexts whether there were gender differences. I let them choose whether to survey/interview other teachers, students or parents. I got interesting results from diverse research projects. Mainly, that most of their research confirmed what they already believed. Ahem. Well, this could mean one of two things: One, as novice researchers, their own bias got in the way of objective data collection, interpretation and analysis. Or two: Their environments truly are how they told me they were, and I am the one who is "biased" in trying to find gender issues in places they don't exist! I am still undecided. I am reminded, though, of Ellsworth's point about our individual inability to truly understand the suffering of others not in our place, and that it would take a lot of time and exposure (not merely a few weeks in my course) for men to start to understand how women feel in our society. And as bell hooks points out in *The Will to Change*, males are almost encouraged to *not* empathize with females in issues of patriarchy (though she speaks of American society, the case is similar here). hooks also talks about how some women adhere to patriarchal discourse themselves and reproduce it. But it is also possible that coming from my own upper middle class (slightly Westernized) privilege blinds me to other contexts, has me looking at things from a different lens than my students.

Intention C: equal participation for students, which includes students calling me by my first name, and calling each other by their first names; it also includes everyone feeling they have a voice in class, that their contribution is equally valued and equally valuable. But even though Freire suggests in *Pedagogy of the Oppressed* that "dialogue cannot exist without humility," Ellsworth is more realistic about the illusions of equality in dialogue. I experienced this firsthand.

   Reality #1: pre-existing hierarchies. Some of my students are each others' superiors at work or in other contexts outside of class. This means there are all sorts of sensitivities I am unaware of and considerations during classroom discussions where some feel uncomfortable disagreeing with others in public; and issues during group projects where someone would "delegate" work to another.

Reality #2: ageism. In a society where respecting one's elders is drilled into us from childhood, some students come in with the view that the older more experienced teachers in the class should be given more weight for their opinions (one student once told *me*, on the side, that "it is OK, you are just not a very experienced teacher"; another young colleague has similar experiences). Others come in with the view that the younger members are better with technology by default. Some students felt, as older members of the class, that they had the right to speak to me individually on behalf of the rest of the class and I had to explain to them why they should stop giving themselves that right.

Reality #3: (and this one should not be surprising) *equality does not work with a magic wand*. As Mary Stewart recently wrote,"collaborative communities construct their own power dynamics that necessarily privilege particular individuals or groups over others." Some students who are more eloquent, louder, more aggressive, more confident, willing to take more risks than others often get "heard" while others do not. When I was doing my masters, we were once asked at the beginning of a module if we wanted to work with particular people. I said outright who I wanted to work with. Another person was offended that I had spoken my mind (even though we were invited to do so) because she tried to be polite by not doing what I did! It occurs to me that whenever I try to invite students to participate and have an equal say, only some of them will participate fully while others' voices get lost. There are personality issues, but also complex underlying power dynamics within and beyond the class itself.

Having said all this, I am not claiming that the critical pedagogy approach does not work, nor that I have tried every aspect of what critical pedagogy entails. Every group of students is different, and what works for one group might not necessarily work for another. I have had much more success trying out Gloria Ladson-Billings's *Culturally Relevant Pedagogy* in my classes (documented in an upcoming publication), for example. I have had multiple students get "aha" moments midway through a semester and acknowledge that most of the learning in this class is from the process and not just the content. I have had students who say they have gone and tried what we do with their own students and had great responses. I have had final projects from students that showed growth in gender sensitivity from our initial discussions. I have had students call me months after our last classroom meeting to reflect on their learning from that class, often telling me stories about things they have done that demonstrate the long-term impact of the course on them. So sometimes I am fortunate that things work out better than I had imagined. Teaching is a humbling experience; what sounds good in theory may not work in practice. But we keep trying, and we keep reflecting. I do not claim that a few weeks will necessarily transform every single student, the practice of critical pedagogy is a journey that we start together, empowering one another to learn and grow.

CHAPTER 8.

WHY START WITH PEDAGOGY? 4 GOOD REASONS, 4 GOOD SOLUTIONS

CATHY N. DAVIDSON

I'm often asked why I start with pedagogy, given the larger institutional reforms and social ambitions that HASTAC and the new
Futures Initiative program advocate. If your goal is equality in a
world where inequality is structural and violent and pervasive,
you can at least start with your classroom as a place in which
to model a better way. Rather than feeling overwhelmed and
oppressed by the unfairness of the world, be an activist in the
realm where you have control. *You can change to a pedagogy of liberation today.* These four ways are all simple to implement. And if
you make sure to add "meta-cognition" — you discuss with your
students what it means to change power relations when you have
the opportunity — you also instill learning and life lessons that
persist far beyond your classroom.

Remember: your students have had at least twelve years of
practice/indoctrination in mastering the formal education methods where hierarchy and control displace all the complex, experi-
ence-based, interactive learning methods (i.e. the kind we all use
in our lives *outside* of formal education when we really want to
learn how to do something). Because they have been rewarded

for credential-centered and teacher-centered learning in school, some will think you are trying to get out of work or pulling a fast one by having them do the thinking and taking responsibility for their own learning. So I typically note that these are extensively researched theories, practices, and methods designed to help students learn not for the test or the grade but for the best possible retention and application of complex ideas that they will use in this class, in other classes, and in their lives beyond school.

All of this is true and it is useful to state it up front. If you are untenured, it is even useful to put this into a syllabus and to cite some great sources. HASTAC and *Hybrid Pedagogy* are two online communities and peer-reviewed open publications with lots of research and methodology in this area, but the theory goes back at least as far as Dewey, and the research is extensive.

NB: These methods work.

Why start with pedagogy? Here are four reasons, followed by four easy methods:

1. It is in your control. There are so many huge and pressing and overwhelming issues facing higher education and our society, most of which require enormous changes in funding, policy, priority, reward systems, and accreditation structures — not to mention huge social realignments of race, gender, sexuality, income, citizenship, and on and on. No one can accomplish all that needs to be accomplished. We all need to be working (and are working) to change structural inequalities at every level. While we do, we're not off the hook in our individual lives and in our professional practice.

The classroom is one of the least egalitarian spaces on the planet. There is abundant research on who gets into college, who gets out, what kind of college you go to, and how all relates to income inequality, racism, and gender issues. There is also plenty of research on how little it takes (roughly 20% participation) for a teacher to believe there is "full participation" and that "everyone is discussing" in a seminar. There is also plenty about the disproportionate time spent by race and gender talking in class, getting attention, grades, recommendations, responses to queries, all of it. And, without building in a structure of equality, the typical "unstructured" classroom replicates social inequalities (again lots of research on this) and, indeed, becomes a site for modeling inequality. Who gets to talk? Where is the teacher? Who has the knowledge? Even in seminars with "discussion," who hogs the floor, who is the boss, who is too ashamed to speak?

Learning inside formal education is different than successful learning almost anywhere else — and it is almost universally effective at learning social protocols for who has knowledge, who has power, but not so much for deeply transformative learning for every student. The student who is not likely to specialize in the field and go on to be a professor is typically the most marginalized by our traditional educational practices. Of course there are stunning educational successes in every classroom, but the structured inequality of the classroom is an obstacle great teachers, great students, and great learning must fight against. That does not happen by chance or by willing it so, but by thinking through how your own classroom is structured, overtly and covertly, and thinking about how it can be restructured according to the principles you say you espouse as a professor. And it's easy (see "how" part of this discussion below): You can restructure your classroom tomorrow. You may not solve the adjunct crisis tonight but you can rethink pedagogy and enact change in how your students learn — and change lives tomorrow. Pedagogy is your responsibility, and you can change how you teach and learn immediately, in ways large and small, in virtually any institutional setting.

2. It is free. You don't need any technology to transform your classroom from a credential-centered or professor-centered environment (information and ideas emanating from you to your students) to a student-centered, interactive, engaged, research-based, goal driven, egalitarian classroom. You can use as much or as little technology as you want. (I start with index cards, Google

Docs, and an interactive website that allows students to publish their work and comment on one another's work publicly. That can be building a WordPress site, creating a Group on HASTAC, or using available collaborative sites such as Hypothes.is).

3. It works. I don't know anyone who has tried simple student-centered techniques who hasn't had success — either spectacular success or just better luck than they have been having with a given class. I find any of the four solutions below, used at any point in a class, changes the whole temperature of the room. I've also done this in a group of five coworkers, in a class of 20 students, and in the Philadelphia 76'ers stadium with 6000 high school teachers. Also, the more you think about how giving power to others enriches everyone's learning, lightens your own load, and makes everyone less alienated, the more you see why democracy is preferable to oligarchy. You are not just modeling a classroom practice but a social ideal. That gives meaning and affect to all the other conditions of social inequality you may want to address. But even if you have no interest in social equality, as the work of physicist Eric Mazur at Harvard shows, just putting student inquiry at the center of a classroom helps everyone learn better, deeper, and more. It is just a better method for learning, in the short run, and a better goal for education, in the long run.

4. It is gratifying and gives you energy and inspiration for the bigger institutional battles. Social activism and institutional change are difficult. Victories should be celebrated because we need to keep our spirit up to fight against legislators cutting funding and programs and tenure; the horrific adjunct crisis that *must* be reversed immediately; the soaring cost of tuition and the immoral tuition debt with which we saddle the next generation; the irrelevant curriculum designed for the Taylorist era of the assembly line not for the world we live in now; the standardized metrics that test only how well prepared you are to take standardized tests (in itself largely income based); the soaring educational inequality that exacerbates income inequality.

Etc. There is so much work to do. So why not see your students thrive, see them enjoying their learning, see them becoming engaged in ways they were not before, see them learning and designing learning that is far more ambitious and thoughtful and deep than you had thought possible. All that is gratifying and inspiring. It is joyful. We need joy and positive energy to fight all the battles ahead.

Here are four easy methods for turning any classroom, of any size, in any field, into a student-centered, engaged classroom.

1. Think-Pair-Share. *Approximately 5 minutes of class time; can be done at any point in a class.* At some point in every class and every lecture, I use this technique I learned from a second grade teacher but have also seen in medical schools (it's analogue is See One. Do One. Teach One. And then I add: Share one.) In Think-Pair-Share, you hand out index cards and pencils (this is not necessary but it somehow sets the mood fast and fast is important in TPS). You set a timer for 90 seconds (really, 90). And you pose a question. For example, if this were a class on "Why Start With Pedagogy?", I would ask everyone to take 90 seconds to jot down three things (there are no right or wrong answers) they do in their classrooms to engage students. When the timer sounds, I then have students work in pairs for another 90 seconds in a very specific, ritualized way. Their objective in this 90 seconds is to, together, come up with one thing to share with the whole group — it can be a synthesis of various comments on both cards, but one agreed upon thing to share.

But before that each person has to hear the other. One member of the pair reads their three things while the other is silent; then the second person reads to a silent listener. *Hearing your own voice in a classroom — and witnessing being heard — is the beginning of taking responsibility for your own learning.* It's not only about meeting someone else's criteria but setting the bar for yourself. There is also something about the ritual of writing down, then reading to someone else, that allows the introvert to speak up in a way that avoids the panic of being called on and having to speak extemp before a group. It is extremely egalitarian — it structures equality. The final 90 seconds involves going rapidly around the room and having one person in each pair read their contribution. After this, you can go anywhere, do anything. But involvement is already 100%. A triumph. In a very large lecture class, I often have a Google Doc ready and "share" is everyone writing their one thing on the Doc. I like to make this a public contribution so we do it as an open Google Doc or we post it to the website. For more details, look at my article, "Single Best Way to Transform Classrooms of Any Size!"

2. Everyone Raise Your Hand. *No extra time needed.* The great science fiction writer Samuel Delany was shocked when he began teaching at Tufts University to find that he'd ask a question and some students would simply look ashamed and cringe. In an interview with me, he says:

> Don't you realize that every time you don't answer a question, you're learning something? You're learning how to make do with what you got, and you're learning how not to ask for a raise … you're learning how to take it. That's not good! That's not good! So, from now on, whenever I ask a question, everybody's got to put their hand up. I don't care whether you know the answer or not. You have to put your hand up … I'm going to call on you and if you don't know the answer, I want you to say nice and clear: I don't know the answer to that, Professor Delany, but I would like to hear what that person has to say. And we'll pass it on. And so this is what we started doing. And I said, whenever I ask a question, everybody put their hand up. I don't care whether you know or not … You need to teach people they are important enough to say what they have to say. ("The Single Best Method For Class (Or Any Kind of) Participation (Thx SciFi Genius Samuel Delany)")

So now I do that, I ask everyone to raise their hand. It works. It's funny, it's embarrassing, but it is a training, a practice, in participation. It also means people prepare better because they know they cannot hide behind their own shame or indifference. By the way, I learned this technique last semester from a student in our student-designed "Mapping the Futures of Higher Education" class.

3. Question Stacking. *No extra time needed.* I learned this from a student too, and they learned it from the Occupy movement. It's an alternate way of structuring equality in the classroom to the Delany method above — and it works great in department meetings too. To ensure no one hogs the discussion, when someone has a comment to make you write their name down on a sheet. You go through the sheet and ask for comments. No one asks a second question or makes a second comment until everyone else on the sheet has gone first. Also, set a time limit of one minute per question and have a timer set. People will adjust to the time quickly. It makes a difference, sets a practice of consideration, respect, and egalitarianism in a structured way.

4. The Exit Ticket. *Three minutes of class time.* I learned this from a student last semester too. End every class three minutes early — set a timer if you need to. It's an important practice in itself. On those index cards, have every student write the one question that is still on their minds at the end of the class. Ask that it be full sentences and signed. Have them also add the question, signed (if your university permits) to a public, open Google Doc that you can share with the other students in the class and the world (if you wish). Everyone leaves with a thought written out carefully which makes for deeper reading. Everyone sees the questions that remain and that causes a different kind of post-class introspection. You as a professor can read all their questions and use that to help shape the next class period — perhaps tomorrow's Think-Pair-Share. If you have 200-seat classes, this substitutes for a pop quiz and for attendance. It is efficient, engaged, useful, on many levels.

These are just four of hundreds of ways to restructure your classroom for student success, for learning, for equality, for engagement, and, if you are inclined, for activism. The main thing is that, rather than despair about the things too big to change, start changing the ones within your control and that can make a difference in the lives of your students — and in your own life too. **Let's get started!**

CHAPTER 9.

BEST PRACTICES: THOUGHTS ON A FLASH MOB MENTALITY

JANINE DEBAISE

I have colleagues who invoke "Best Practices" the way that evangelical Christians quote the Bible: God has spoken. During these conversations, I am tempted to say in a serious voice, "Best Practices dictate that teaching writing should include loud music in a public place and synchronized dancing. In short, a flash mob." I mean, if Best Practices are really going to be the end-all of pedagogy, I want them to be cool.

I had a revelation about Best Practices during a discussion with my students about a similar concept: universal design solutions. We were reading Braungart & McDonough's *Cradle to Cradle*, a book which challenges industry to become more sustainable through ecologically smart design and which raises questions about what architects call universal design solutions. Braungart and McDonough weren't talking about students. They were talking about household products like detergent. Here's how a universal design solution works: in order to market the same detergent across the country, the industry designs it to work effectively anywhere, regardless of water quality, no matter what is being washed. That means if I'm washing out my tea mug at a sink with soft water, I use the same detergent as someone 500 miles away washing a greasy pan in hard water. The ecologically devastating result is that I dump harsh chemicals, which were never necessary in the first place, into the waste stream and eventually the water supply, harming aquatic life for no good reason.

Braungart and McDonough summed it up this way: "To achieve their universal design solutions, manufacturers design for the worst-case scenario: they design a product for the worst possible circumstance, so that it will always operate with the same efficacy" (30). One of my students summed it up this way: "If you care about ecology, universal design solutions suck."

Manufacturers who want to mass-produce consumer goods depend on universal design solutions. I worry that universities, faced with pressure to churn out students who will all achieve the same "measurable learning outcomes," have also come to embrace universal design solutions, packaged as "Best Practices." For instance, when I was a grad student teaching composition at a large university, the curriculum stipulated that we were to ask each student to write a five-paragraph essay (no more, no less), with a thesis at the end of the introduction, three supporting paragraphs, and the thesis re-stated in the first line of the conclusion. We were to use that formula on every single student and every single paper, regardless of context. This teaching practice was based on the assumption that first year students couldn't possibly come up with smart ways to organize their ideas. Composition teachers have, for the most part, abandoned that particular formula, but higher education hasn't lost the quest for the Best Practices that can magically transform all students. Too often, faculty design pedagogy around the worst-case scenario and then apply that pedagogy to every student.

If you care about students, this approach sucks.

As a teacher, I prefer to assume the best-case scenario: that my students are brilliant and amazing. There is no such thing as a stupid student: they just have a different base of knowledge than I do. In fact, the different backgrounds and experiences that my students bring to the class add depth to our learning. Every student has something valuable to teach the rest of us. I've made that assumption for over thirty years now, and so far, I've never been proven wrong.

I don't know the best way to teach students how to read, write, and think. It's different for every single student. That's why I try to put students in charge of their own learning. I ask them to analyze their own learning styles and move out of their comfort zones. My responsibility is to create a space (in the classroom and, increasingly, on the Internet) where they feel safe experimenting, playing, and trying out new things. I try to create an atmosphere in which it is okay to be vulnerable.

For example, sometimes introverted students won't speak up because they "hate people looking at me." So we work around that. One time, a student turned out the lights in our basement classroom and we had class by flashlight, which prompted quiet students to speak up. Another student led a class where we used interpretive dance and communicated without words. Sometimes students bring art supplies to my literature class and add to our discussion with amazing drawings, while the rest of us doodle in solidarity. Each student brings a one-page informal piece of writing to every class: we pass these short papers around and read them, write and draw on them, and coax each other to speak up. "Once you've read each other's papers, you can nudge each other," I tell them. Students are more likely to respond to peer encouragement than to anything a teacher says.

Then there are the extroverted students, quick to blurt out opinions and jump into discussions. I'm one of them myself. We have to learn to listen carefully, to think before we talk, and to make room for everyone in the discussion. Last week in class, one student volunteered this experiment: "Okay, we're going to talk about this reading. Each person has to contribute exactly three times, no more and no less." During the next thirty minutes, I had to just take deep breaths every time there was a lull in the conversation, since I used up my three sentences pretty early in the discussion. It turns out that those lulls gave the introverts time to gather their thoughts and speak up. We extroverts have discovered, too, that there's virtually no way to dominate a Twitter chat: the 140-character limit means that we have to edit ourselves.

The Internet has given learners a bunch more options. Some introverts like Twitter chats, where they can participate in a quiet room with a laptop. Other students think the Twitter chats are too fast-paced; they like collaborative writing inside a Google Doc, which gives them time to process their thoughts. Sometimes shy students prefer to use twitter to introduce themselves. Some students are more likely to participate in online exercises where they can speak up under the cloak of anonymity, just as Harry Potter feels empowered when he puts on the invisibility cloak. Others prefer activities where they are required to sign in with their real names, because getting credit and being visible are motivating factors.

The list of activities we can try has evolved over the last thirty years. When I first began teaching, I was using a typewriter — and a ditto machine that produced purple-and-white copies that smelled wonderfully of ink. Many students later, I teach hybrid classes. For their Public Writing/Research Projects, for example, small groups of my students do primary research together, putting their field notes, photos, and videos into a shared Google Doc, and then they divide up the secondary research, each writing an individual research document, which they share with each other. They are required to make their ideas public, and they get to choose how they do this. They've come up with trailers to promote their projects, held twitter chats, created hashtags to raise awareness of environmental issues, asked the public to collaborate in writing assignments, made videos, defined terms, created brochures, offered crossword puzzles, wrote narratives, did interviews, wrote songs, created blogs, created art, and built websites. We are still exploring all the possibilities that the Internet offers us.

My teaching methods have changed over the years, but my philosophy has not. I always assume that every student has something to say. Find what that student is passionate about — whether it's dance or hunting or climate change — and that student will put in all kinds of effort to contribute to the larger discussion about that topic. Teaching is still about playing around with options, figuring out what you need to do to light that spark that will get students excited. Somedays, I am rearranging chairs in the classroom. Somedays, I'm opening up a Google Doc so that we can collaborate. Somedays, I'm jumping into a Twitter chat to learn more about a topic that my students care about.

Empowered to contribute options, my students come up with ways we can spread our ideas to the rest of the world. They held a nature photo contest on Twitter to see if we could get people to use their smartphones to become more aware of the nature around them. We've used Twitter to get folks to write lines of poetry which students then pulled into collaborative poems. We've used our bodies to show the world our hashtag. Every semester, we collaborate with students in other parts of the world. For example, we worked with Pete Rorabaugh's students in Georgia to host round two of Twitter vs Zombies. My students here in upstate New York also interact through Twitter with Bernardo Trejo's students in Taiwan. Since his students study sustainable tourism, my students try to lure them in by adding the topic of tourism to whatever environmental issue we're discussing and offering opportunities to interact. Students on both sides of the globe especially love to share photos. When my students use the Internet to begin discussions about environmental issues, we never know who is going to jump in: alumni, parents, friends, and often complete strangers. The Internet has opened up possibilities that I never dreamed of when I first began teaching.

In this evolving and exciting world of hybrid pedagogy, I'm cautious about identifying Best Practices. Figuring out what will work with any particular group of students — well, that's the work we do together. I bring to the course some expertise in writing and literature and pedagogy, but I always need to wait and see what my newest batch of students will bring to our circle of slanted desks and precariously balanced laptops.

I'm not dismissing Best Practices entirely. I like the idea of having some guidelines that teachers can learn from, ideas I can share with my students. But we should be a little more honest about what they are. Let's not pretend that universal design solutions aren't without problems. Let's call them "Practices Worth Considering" or "Things You Could Try" or "Stuff That Just Might Work." Let's not assume that our students are all moving in the same direction, listening to the same music, and singing the same song. That's not even a desirable outcome. Unless, of course, we're doing a flash mob.

CHAPTER 10.

BUT YOU CAN'T DO THAT IN A STEM COURSE!

KAREN CANGIALOSI

"I spent a whole year learning about all the different kinds of clouds. I still refer to them as 'puffy clouds', 'rain clouds', 'snow clouds', 'hazy clouds'. If I was some master of knowledge or learning like the school system tells me I am, wouldn't I remember these things?"
~ Miranda Dean, undergraduate student, "What an Open Pedagogy Course Taught Me About Myself"

In "A Call for Critical Instructional Design", Sean Michael Morris explains why he doesn't use traditional rubrics or learning objectives when he teaches. He argues that "participation is an individual choice"; "learner contributions are meaningful content in the course"; and "there are no 'right' answers to the questions I'm bound to ask." Many who teach in the 'hard' or 'natural' sciences might say: "That is just great for those of you who teach in the humanities, but you can't do that in a STEM class!" While I consider the work that I've been doing with my biology courses a pilot study on a pathway towards more deeply engaged experiments, my experiences using open pedagogy strategies suggests that yes, yes you can.

When I was a biology undergraduate years ago, nearly all of my science classes were in large lecture halls. Content was delivered by lecturers, and students spit back answers on multiple choice exams primarily graded by Scantron. We've come a long way since then, with many science teachers incorporating more active learning in their courses, developing powerful case studies (check out the National Center for Case Study Teaching in Science), and using jigsaw strategy, discussion groups, peer review, open-ended research projects, co-ops, service-learning, and more.

But these active learning strategies, while adding a great deal to the teaching of science, can often still fall short of what I consider to be the most salient and powerful features of open pedagogy. Inspired by the ideas of Robin DeRosa (see "Open Pedagogy at the Program Level: The #PlymouthIDS case study" and *Open Pedagogy Notebook*), for me, this includes 1) student agency, and 2) a commons-oriented approach to education — both of which encapsulate the ideals of equity, access, connection, and sharing. When we blend the best of what we have learned from those who have labored to transform education with ideas integral to feminist pedagogy, engaged pedagogy, constructivist pedagogy, and critical digital pedagogy, and then embed them in a larger commons paradigm, open pedagogy emerges.

Student agency is ultimately about how we share power in our classrooms and work collaboratively with students. It has historical feminist roots from Adrienne Rich's plea for women students to claim their own education to bell hooks questioning the power and authority in the teacher/student relationship where she asserts that the classroom should be "a place that is life-sustaining and mind-expanding, a place of liberating mutuality where teacher and student together work in partnership" (*Teaching Community: A Pedagogy of Hope*). And viewing pedagogy through the lens of the commons (the cultural and natural resources accessible to all members of a society) situates student agency in the praxis of equitable and inclusive access to learning, learning structure design, knowledge, sharing knowledge, creating knowledge and community participation (see diagram). The open license and the 5R permissions provide a tangible way for the knowledge commons to be manifested and for us to participate in its ongoing construction.

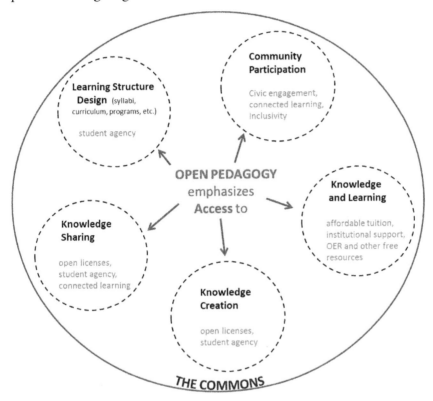

Diagram by Karen Cangialosi, licensed under CC BY 4.0

But what does this all mean on the ground? Can giving more power and control over to students really be effective for teaching in the natural sciences? Can students create scientific knowledge? How does sharing do anything for student learning?

Agency and Course Content

I often hear a version of the following objection to giving content control to students: *"But... there <u>are</u> right answers, many of them —these are called facts. And many scientific facts simply need to be memorized."* Of course there are many known facts, and especially in this brave new world where the phrase "alternative facts" is used regularly and dangerously, it is important to acknowledge that. And some questions do have right answers (although Sean probably isn't bound to ask simple scientific questions). But many scientific questions don't have right answers, or at least don't have them yet. So while facts are very important, the ways that we have come to know them as facts are even more important for students to learn, which is why we emphasize the steps of the 'scientific method' and teach that scientific knowledge is produced through observation, analysis, and experimentation. We also end up committing many facts to memory. But which facts need to be memorized? And which processes of memorization should we use? The premise that there are important facts to learn, does not automatically imply that one should rely on a stack of flash cards (whether paper or digital). In my experiences teaching biology, stimulating student interest and motivation have been far more effective than rote memorization. I think this gets to the heart of student agency in the ethos of open pedagogy. Thanks to Bryan Alexander's interview of Gardner Campbell, the primary learning outcome I have for my students is to increase their depth and breadth of interest.

Now ask me about the one connecting factor between murder, violence, and loneliness. It's dopamine. Come back in ten years and ask me again and I'll still know the answer. Why? because it's not information that was dumped on me. It's not information that I was forced to regurgitate. It's information that I voluntarily sought out and connect with my personal interests.
~ Miranda Dean, undergraduate student, In 'What an Open Pedagogy Course Taught Me About Myself'

"But... students in STEM courses can't just choose what they want to learn, there is important content to cover that can't be missed." So much has already been written that challenges the idea of 'content as king' in teaching and learning. For example, in "Through the Open Door: Open Courses as Research, Learning, and Engagement," David Cormier and George Siemens argue that "the true

benefit of the academy is the interaction, the access to the debate, to the negotiation of knowledge — not to the stale cataloging of content." But it's not usually instructors of STEM courses that challenge the importance of content. The position for content as king in STEM often comes down to the argument that there is an appropriate order in which material must be learned. The way that concepts incrementally build on one another is the reason why instructors must control the order in which they are presented, usually in a step-by-step method that builds from simple to complex ideas. You can't understand a complex molecule if you don't even know what an atom is, the argument goes.

So it's really *'foundational* content as king'. *"But... there are basic foundational ideas and terms that need to be understood first, without those basics and scaffolding the concepts, students will be lost."* This objection brings to mind a non-scientist friend of mine who had spent months and months researching information about her illness and said to me, "Have you heard of these things called oxidation-reduction reactions? Fascinating how they work!" My friend's enthusiasm and passion intrigued me. Anyone who teaches basic chemistry and has experience with saying something like, "OK class, today we are going to cover oxidation-reduction reactions" can say that, in most cases, glazed over eyes are more likely than fascination as your equations and electrons begin filling the board.

Is it really true that memorizing all the basics must come before tackling more complex questions, such as "What is the nature of a cancerous cell?" Does one need to learn all of the details of atomic structure, bonding, molecules, chemical properties, macromolecules like DNA, RNA, protein structure and function, cell structure and function, DNA replication, transcription, translation, cell cycle, etc., in (or close to) that order? Ask someone who has been diagnosed with cancer (or is close to someone who has) what they know of these foundational topics. The answer might surprise you. You can research quite a bit, starting at the end and working your way back down, or in the middle and jumping around. What is that? How does that work? Yeah, but what does that mean? Yeah, but what does THAT mean? It is all driven by interest, motivation, a passion to learn or even a burning necessity to learn. Our primary role as teacher can be simply to create the best culture chambers for students to flourish. They will find the content. Examples from my tropical-marine biology course are students who chose to learn about the Effects of Plastic on Marine Life and Ocean Acidification. These led to a need to understand ocean gyres, the corioliseffect, amplification of chemicals via food chains, the chemistry of ocean carbonic acid formation from atmospheric carbon dioxide, and more. My instruction: explore some environmental threats to coral reefs.

Agency and Course Design

"But... science students can't design courses; they need to be provided with a clear syllabus, assignments and a grading structure from experts who know best." Recently, when reading my students' final self-assessments, I was struck by the different ways in which each student approached the course. The more nebulous I was about my expectations, the more they had to work to find their own way. They had to figure out how much time to put into the labs, which labs to work on more deeply, how many blog posts to write, whether to cover a broad range of groups or focus on a few, how to structure their websites, and so on. Essentially, what they were grappling with was determining the pieces that were motivating enough for them to spend their precious time.

A student taking a journey into discovery, who is encouraged to pursue their own interests and take any pathway using any tools, assignments, practices, and policies that they want, may end up stumped or confused — but also intrigued. The desire to know more is the genesis of learning. And a wonderful synergy happens as a student figures out both *what* they are trying to learn and *how* they learn best. As instructor, knowing just when to strategically intervene is challenging, but letting go of control can have powerful effects on student learning. Students will only be frustrated by "not knowing what you want" as long as you take the fear of grades away and communicate as clearly as you can that what you most want as a teacher is for them to find their own way to uncover their passions. When we stop judging students they stop judging and censoring themselves. They begin to actually learn. Even in a STEM class.

As open pedagogy instructors in science classes, we can ignite the spark for the search that leads to foundations, and facilitate (not direct) the process along the way. Then students make their own connections and find the social contexts in which science *needs* to be understood. When my tropical-marine biology class arrived to our field trip destination, they stated: "We are not drinking water from disposable plastic bottles." The whole class felt united in this, not just the one student who wrote the post about ocean plastic, because they were reading, sharing and talking about their openly licensed work. This is where writing in the open, sharing ideas, connecting to others (including professionals in social media spaces like Twitter), and deciding what you want to pursue next results in real and significant learning, and continues beyond the course itself. At the time of this writing, one year after the course ended, these students are still tweeting about marine biology and issues in ocean conservation.

Open Licenses, Sharing, Connection and Open Science

"But... students can't create scientific content, they aren't yet capable." Scientific practice and undergraduate pedagogy would suggest otherwise. For science educators have led the way in facilitating student contribution to academic content via the incorporation of undergraduates into faculty research programs. Even including first and second year students in the PI research lab has been the norm for decades. While for some this has meant more peripheral participation such as data collection only, others have had their students participate in all stages of research — from hypothesis formation, experimental design, data analysis and sci-

entific writing. Outside of the PI lab, many students complete self-designed research projects. Such projects don't usually result in original data or publishable findings; but the remixing and recombining of materials in posts or articles that summarize, synthesize, and shape information so that the work is more accessible and relevant to other students is its own kind of originality. And sometimes, just the fact that another student wrote it makes it more enticing or interesting to them and sparks ideas and confidence for new investigations. As students share their experimental designs, data and analyses with an open license, they contribute to the open science commons and can benefit from constructive criticism and feedback from a much broader audience than their instructor and peers.

Undergraduate scientific research conferences and journals have been around for decades, and students have been contributing valuable content. But only a few privileged students are able to attend conferences or get their work published in conventional journals. We can increase the value and reach of student work by teaching students how to engage in the global learning networks of scientists who are using open platforms and social media in academic and effective ways. If we model ways for students to be transparent about all of the stages of the research process — encouraging them to publicly post and openly license their methodology and data long before it is polished into a final paper, they can receive broad and sometimes expert feedback on their work. Our role should be to indoctrinate students into those processes that emphasize collaboration and communication, and how to work as an authentic scientific community.

The growing Open Science movement, and what I am calling the Pedagogy of Open Science, has the potential to revolutionize both the teaching of science and scientific practice itself. The open science and open data communities envision a future where, according to the Center for Open Science, "the process, content, and outcomes of research are openly accessible by default." When every step of the scientific process is transparent, all students can have greater capacity to distinguish "alternative facts" or "fake news" from actual scientific knowledge. As science undergraduate educators, we need to teach and model these values and practices to our students now — before they are in graduate school, before they have lab or corporate jobs, before they are publishing their work, before they are writing grants, before they are worrying about promotion and tenure guidelines and before they are shaping those guidelines for the future.

Agency, curiosity, questioning, creativity, design, experimentation, collaboration, contribution, connection, communication and discovery: These activities are embedded in the processes of both scientific investigation and open pedagogy. Not only can you "do that" in science courses, but the assertion that one 'learns science by doing science' (an idea widely championed in the science educator community) is manifested by adopting open pedagogical practices in STEM.

Acknowledgements

I am greatly indebted to Mark Long, Jenny Darrow, and Robin DeRosa for their comments and suggestions on several earlier drafts of this article.

CHAPTER 11.

TRAVELLING IN TROY WITH AN INSTRUCTIONAL DESIGNER

JONAN PHILLIP DONALDSON

Paulo Blikstein's *Travels in Troy with Freire* demonstrated how digital technologies can be used as agents of emancipation when grounded in the principles of constructionist learning. Technologies can be used to perpetuate entrenched authoritarian and didactic approaches to teaching, or they can be used as Trojan Horses to liberate learners as they transform themselves into agentic, autonomous, self-directed learners. In my work in instructional design and technology support in many institutions of higher education I have worked on at least five hundred online courses. With the rapid expansion of online learning over the last decade I have witnessed a tendency to translate classes into online modalities with designs closely resembling those of the face-to-face classes. Textbooks become eBooks, lectures become narrated presentations, and paper exams become online exams. Even when multimedia and interactive technologies are used, they are designed to "teach" rather than to facilitate learning. By this I mean that the overwhelming majority of online courses I have seen are designed to deliver content — to transfer knowledge into the minds of students.

The job of the instructional designer is often reduced to that of a technologist and project manager in charge of building online courses which mirror the face-to-face lecture/textbook/exam versions. However, when the design of learning is structured around constructionist principles and authentic problem-based learning, instructional designers become energized and empowered as they unleash the transformative power of digital technologies as Trojan Horses. My journey as an instructional designer (ID) led me to a learning experience design philosophy of building online and digitally-mediated courses in which technologies are used as Trojan Horses for emancipation through constructionist problem-based learning with an emphasis on learner agency, situating learners as designers, and focused tinkering.

Grounding the Designer

Conceptualizations of the nature of learning determine our practices as learners and educators. The two most common conceptualizations can be described according to the metaphors in which they are grounded. The dominant metaphor sees learning as the *acquisition* of information by learners, or conversely as the *transfer* of information from external sources into the minds of learners. This conceptualization of learning has been characterized by Freire in *Pedagogy of the Oppressed* as a *banking* approach to teaching and learning, and by Papert in *The Children's Machine* as the *instructionist* approach. Another metaphor is common in the learning sciences and some lines of educational research, a metaphor which sees learning as the individual, collaborative, and collective *construction* of meaning. This *construction* metaphor as applied to learning can be traced back to the works of Piaget, Vygotsky, and Bruner. The *transfer/acquisition* metaphor leads to practices involving textbooks, lectures, exams and prescribed learning objectives. The *construction* metaphor leads to practices involving collaborative learning, situated learning, authentic problem-based learning, self-directed learning, and creative problem-solving. Critical pedagogy is grounded in the *construction* conceptualization of learning, and educational practices that facilitate critical consciousness and emancipation are, as Kincheloe argued, "incompatible with a view of teaching as a technical act of information delivery" (*Teachers as Researchers: Qualitative Inquiry as a Path to Empowerment*). So incommensurate are the *construction* and *transfer/acquisition* conceptualizations of learning that Freire stated: "Those truly committed to liberation must reject the banking concept in its entirety."

Both conceptualizations of learning described above can be found among IDs, but perhaps due to the prominence of backward design and instructional design models such as ADDIE there is a tendency toward the *transfer/acquisition* metaphor. Most instructional design projects begin with the creation of clear and measurable learning objectives, followed by articulation of the means by which learner mastery of those objectives will be assessed. Only then are learning activities and materials considered. This approach encourages the design of learning around only things which can be "objectively" assessed.

My work as an ID and critical theorist is guided by my conceptualization of learning which is grounded in the *construction* metaphor. Therefore, my starting place with any instructional design project is a consideration of what sort of learning environment would be optimal in facilitating individual, collaborative and collective construction of meaning. In other words, my design decisions regarding the environment and activities come before decisions regarding learning objectives, assessment and materials. Although extremely difficult in the majority of instructional design projects due to the nature of the academic environment and conceptualizations of learning held by subject matter experts, my approach is not "instructional design," but "learning environment design." In the spirit of a learning scientist, I continually experiment with new ways of designing online learning environments which place upon learners the responsibility and authority over decisions regarding learning objectives and assessments.

My involvement in the community of IDs over the years has led me to believe that the majority of IDs have strong grounding in instructional design models, standards and professional community norms. However, the field generally lacks grounding in a conceptual or theoretical framework regarding the nature of learning. One of the most promising frameworks is constructionism which conceptualizes learning as the construction of meaning and development of learners as agents of change.

Design Principles for Constructionist Learning

Instructional design projects usually begin with a meeting between the instructional designer and the subject matter expert — usually a professor or instructor in the contexts in which I have been involved. During this meeting the scope and sequence of the project are discussed, and then the conversation moves to discussion of the nature and structure of previous versions of the course when it was taught in face-to-face contexts. It is at this point that I often say: "Imagine no textbooks, no lectures, no exams. Now what can we do?" Reactions have ranged from horrified disbelief, to mild interest, to enthusiastic embrace.

That question stems from my groundedness in constructionism. Principles of constructionist learning as articulated by Papert flow from a conceptualization of learning defined largely in contrast with "instructionism." Learning is context-dependent. It is the result of interactions between people and between learners and features of their environments such as tools, resources, language, social structures, and so on. Therefore, the focus of constructionism is on the design of learning environments, not of instructional materials — because learning is not the result of acquisition of knowledge, but the construction of meaning. Assessment is not about mastery of learning objectives, but a reflective practice. Technologies are put in the hands of the learners for the purpose of constructing artifacts for real-world audiences, rather than in the hands of the instructors for the purpose of delivering information. Constructionism provides a set of principles for the design of learning: placing making at the heart of all learning activity, facilitating learner agency, situating learners as designers, engaging learners in designing for authentic audiences, and engaging learners in focused tinkering.

Making

Constructionist learning starts with the proposition that learning is most powerful when learners make things of their own design. The constructed artifacts mirror the construction of meaning occurring in the minds of the learners. The artifacts also serve as tangible "objects-to-think-with" (*The Children's Machine*) — tools of embodied cognition.

Learner Agency

In order for the construction of artifacts to facilitate optimal learning, the artifacts must be personally meaningful. The meaningfulness depends on several preconditions. The first of these is the agency of the learner. When learners have autonomy and authority over the goals, processes, roles, and nature of the artifacts, those artifacts take on personal significance. This leads not only to student ownership of learning, but ownership of the artifacts of learning. Artifacts are embodiments of the meanings the learners have constructed, and the act of constructing meaning involves constructing one's own mind. Therefore, learner agency in constructionist learning leads to ownership and authorship of self.

Situating Learners as Designers

Learners are situated as designers in constructionist learning environments. As designers on design teams, they engage in negotiation of goals, roles, procedures, tools, and meanings. They collaboratively design, prototype, iterate, and deploy their artifacts in the real world.

Authentic Audience

Another precondition to meaningfulness of artifacts is the authenticity of the intended use of the artifact. If learners create artifacts which they know will only be seen by their fellow learners and teachers, construction of artifacts is akin to drill-and-practice activities. Learners need to know that the artifacts they are creating will have real-world impact. They need authentic audiences.

Focused Tinkering

Resnick and Rosenbaum define tinkering as "a playful, experimental, iterative style of engagement, in which makers are continually reassessing their goals, exploring new paths, and imagining new possibilities." Situating learners as designers fosters a more focused form of tinkering (the book *Invent To Learn: Making, Tinkering, and Engineering in the Classroom* by Martinez and Stager is an excellent deep dive into this concept) which facilitates development of skills characterized by Donald Schön as framing and reflection-in-action.

Focused tinkering provides a means of balancing the product-driven activity of artifact construction with the joy and freedom of exploration: what Seymour Papert (2002) calls the "hard fun" of learning which is painfully absent in courses designed using instructional design models which are obsessed with learning objectives.

Making, learner agency, authentic audience, situating learners as designers, and focused tinkering are the core principles in designing for constructionist learning. But how can we translate these powerful principles into course design work? It is through these principles that a more powerful conceptualization of learning can be applied in the practical work of designing for learning.

Designing Learning Environments

The use of instructional design models leads many instructional designers to focus on the design of learning activities and content. Instructional designers are trained to start all design projects by creating learning objectives, often in the form "after successful completion of this course, you will be able to..." followed by phrases describing observable and measurable competencies. The next task is to figure out how we will assess the degree to which the students demonstrate these competencies, and then the activities that will help students develop the ability to meet the objectives. Finally the instructional designer (usually working with faculty members or subject-matter experts) develops or curates a set of materials like textbook readings, videos, or multimedia content. This process reinforces the tendency to think of learning as acquisition of knowledge or skills.

It is very difficult to swim against the current when the culture of instructional design is dominated by concepts such as alignment. Popular rubrics and standards for assessing the quality of online course designs demand that there be clear alignment between learning objectives, assessments, learning activities, and content. Instructional designers ask "What do we want students to learn? How will we assess how well they learned it? What activities will they do to learn it? What readings, videos, and other resources will they need first before engaging in the activities?" This focus on alignment leads to designs of learning which dictate what students will learn, when they will learn it, and how they will learn it — and limiting student agency to whether or not they will comply. The resulting designs for learning do not allow students to engage in the hard work required for true learning to occur. By predetermining what material is relevant and beneficial, the students deprived of the need for processes crucial to learning including exploration, evaluation, framing, and problematization.

Designing according to the principles of constructionist learning requires abandoning the standards and norms of the instructional design community and shifting the focus from alignment and "instructional" design toward the design of learning environments. Such a learning environment is not a free-for-all cacophony of unstructured explorations. There is structure. The purpose of the structure in constructionist design for learning is different than in traditional instructional design, and therefore the structuring principles are different.

A constructionist learning environment design is structured around students creating authentic artifacts for authentic audiences. What the learners create, how they go about creating, and for whom they create are matters for the learners to determine, often through structured negotiation and collaborative articulation of goals, roles, and processes. Therefore, the instructional designer must provide the tools for collaboration and negotiation, as well as guidance — built into the structure of the course — regarding the processes and skills involved in negotiation and collaboration. Instructional designers can use a number of strategies to design effective environments for learning.

Digital Portfolios

One design strategy I have found particularly powerful is to structure courses around learner construction of digital portfolios in conjunction with group projects. In many of the courses I designed, each week the students individually created digital artifacts related to the topic of the course. They published their artifacts through their digital portfolios, which are websites open to the public. Those individual artifacts were part of a bigger picture because students were simultaneously working with their groups in collaboratively creating a larger work which was deployed (published, implemented or launched) in the final weeks of the course. These larger works have taken many forms, including magazine articles, documentary videos, assisting a library in designing a makerspace and organizing a local conference. The form is always dictated by real-world needs the students identify. The group projects provide the structure for collaborative learning, and the weekly addition of artifacts to the digital portfolios provides the structure for individual meaning-making in relation to the collaborative meaning-making. Throughout these processes, learners are frequently prompted to engage in focused tinkering, reflecting upon their role as a designer, and reflecting upon the relationship between the artifact they are constructing and the meaning they are constructing.

Authorship Learning

Digital technologies have created affordances rarely leveraged in instructional designs. The shift in society from information consumerism to information production by the masses is not reflected in the use of technologies in most learning environments. When leveraged in constructionist learning environments, the power of digital technologies as tools for learner creation and publishing of artifacts can be transformational. For example, in one of the courses I designed the students collaboratively planned, wrote, and published a book. They used the discussion features in a learning management system for planning, Google Docs for collaborative writing, and Amazon's CreateSpace to publish and sell their book. Through this process they developed new identities as experts on the topic and as published authors.

Learning Environments

Due to the nature of the current structure of academia, the syllabus for a course must include learning outcomes. However, they do not have to be the focus of the course design process. If they are content-knowledge outcomes, they become topics around which learners gather for collaborative construction of knowledge. For instance, in the courses described above there were readings and videos every week, but they were not presented as "content" to learn, but rather as "setting the stage" material. They provided a background, a starting point, and an atmosphere. If the learning outcomes describe skills, the guidelines for the individual and collaborative construction of artifacts emphasized those skills, which also are embedded in prompts for reflective and metacognitive activities.

Designing learning environments — as opposed to designing instruction — requires a particular kind of skill informed by the literature in collaborative learning, engagement, motivation, and metacognitive strategies. The instructional designer must also develop the ability to see all technologies from a unique perspective: not what the instructional designer can do with the technology, but what affordances of the technologies can be leveraged by putting them in the hands of the students for the construction of artifacts with real-world impact.

Interpretation

The journey I have described has not been easy. Cognitive dissonance is a constant companion. I have worked as an instructional designer who rejects the concept of instruction. There have been times when I felt deeply troubled using the term *instructional designer* as my job title. I am a designer of spaces where communities of learners engage in purposeful construction of meaning and authorship of self and society through collaborative construction of meaningful artifacts with real-world impact.

There is also cognitive dissonance in designing courses where agency is situated in learners who have authority, autonomy, and responsibility — and yet these courses are in academic environments where final grades must be assigned and students have been enculturated into a community where the purpose of everything they do is to earn grades and eventually a diploma.

I have often noticed a disconnect between my conceptualization of learning (based on the *construction* metaphor) and the conceptualization of learning held by the majority of my colleagues and students — based on the *transfer/acquisition* metaphor. I find myself forgetting to exercise empathy and consider how the learning environments I design may look from their perspectives. I have to remind myself that people whose conceptualization of learning is based on the *transfer/acquisition* metaphor may question the effectiveness of course designs which implement collaborative problem-based student-directed learning, just as I question the effectiveness of course designs based on lectures, textbooks, and exams.

Despite the struggles inevitable in my journey as an ID, travelling in Troy has been an immense pleasure. With guidance and inspiration from the experiences of those who have traveled in Troy before such as Papert, Freire, Resnick, Kafai, Blikstein, and many others in the community of learning scientists, I have discovered that a simple set of design principles can guide the work of instructional designers as they design far more than instruction:

- First, focus on the design of the learning environment, not on instruction. Build up the courage to resist the immense pressure of the dominance of instructional design models and keep the learners at the forefront in all your design moves.

- Second, design environments in which learners construct meaning through focused tinkering in the construction of artifacts. Think of technologies as tools in the hands of learners rather than tools for delivering content.

- Third, design environments which shift the authority, autonomy, and responsibility of learning to the learners. This shift will be uncomfortable for some learners, so we must design for gradual scaffolding of learners' abilities in assuming authority and responsibility.

- Fourth, situate learners as designers by insisting that the artifacts learners create be intended for authentic audiences and meet real-world needs. Avoid designing assignments which will be seen and assessed only by an instructor, as this undermines the learners' emerging identities as designers. Instead, design projects which carefully scaffold the design process such as a design thinking model and designerly ways of knowing, and also engage learners in frequent reflection on their processes and identities as designers.

- And finally, design the learning environment to shift learners' conceptualizations of learning from the passive and oppressive *transfer/acquisition* metaphor toward the active, agentic, transformative, and empowering *construction* or *authorship* metaphor of learning.

With these strategies in our tool belts, instructional designers can build learning environments that facilitate powerful learning and transform learners into reflective, critical, and empowered agents of change.

CHAPTER 12.

BUILDING IN THE HUMANITIES ISN'T NEW

ROBIN WHARTON

"For children can accomplish the renewal of existence in a hundred unfailing ways."
~ Walter Benjamin, "Unpacking My Library"

"Turn your data into a story, into a game, into art."
~ Mark Sample, "The Poetics of Non-Consumptive Reading"

I initially encountered Walter Benjamin's essay, "Unpacking My Library," during my first semester of graduate school. Ten years later, as my oldest daughter started kindergarten, and I prepared to teach my first upper-division seminar on Chaucer, I found myself returning again and again to Benjamin's discussion of children and collecting. Charting a course from theory to praxis as both a parent and a teacher over the past several months has, for me, demanded the decomposition of many received binaries: personal/professional, K-12/"higher" education, consumptive/productive reading, student/scholar, pedagogy/scholarship.

Within the post-secondary academy, we often talk about building, curation, and creative production as if they are new methods for approaching the study of literature, history, philosophy, language. Learning alongside my daughter as she has built, collected, and created her way through kindergarten in a Waldorf school, however, I've begun to wonder if our turn to these methods in college and university classrooms is actually in fact a *return* — to pedagogical strategies already familiar to many of our students from their primary school days. I've also become concerned pedagogies of building, collecting, and creative play with texts and information in primary and secondary settings are endangered by a one-way "conversation" in which post-secondary educators are making increasingly strident demands that K-12 educators "prepare" our young people for college and the workplace.

Benjamin and Serious Play

One of the most striking things I noticed when I first visited the school my daughter now attends was the variety of activity in the classroom. At all levels, the curriculum involves engaging the body and senses as well as the mind. In kindergarten and the younger grades, instruction might require children to combine physical gestures with recitation of their multiplication tables, or a poem about how plants grow from seeds. In the older grades, material demonstration of scientific and mathematical principles plays an important role. Art, handwork, music, woodworking, and even recess are core parts of the curriculum. And, perhaps most relevant to my purpose in this piece, literature is a means of conveying information about self and the world, as well as the material of creative production. Children learn by listening and reading to, and also by reinterpreting, retelling, performing, and remediating stories drawn from a variety of cultural and historical sources.

Walter Benjamin says,

> For children can accomplish the renewal of existence in a hundred unfailing ways. Among children, collecting is only one process of renewal; other processes are the painting of objects, the cutting out

of figures, the application of decals–the whole range of childlike modes of acquisition, from touching things to giving them names.

As I prepared the syllabus for my Chaucer class this past Fall, and reviewed articles in my role as production editor for Hybrid Pedagogy, I became acutely aware of how impoverished most post-secondary pedagogy might appear to a teacher or a student coming to a college or university classroom from the methodological richness of this sort of K-12 experience. I recalled Benjamin's beautiful image of children making the world new and newly available to their perception through the serious work of play. I also returned, via copyediting my own writing, to considering how digital humanities scholarship, like Bruno Latour's compositionism, sometimes productively and problematically blurs the aesthetic boundaries we usually draw between the products and the objects of literary analysis. For the most part, the study of "literature" has historically produced literary scholarship, mostly non-fiction books and essays offering "objective" analyses of novels, plays, and stories. In the work of some digital humanities scholars, however, the end result of literary scholarship is often what Mark Sample would call an "expressive object," something that is both a work of art *and* a scholarly artifact.

I wondered what might happen if I designed a syllabus whose object was to facilitate activity as well as discussion, to engage the hands as well as the mind. I tried to imagine what a "grown up" version of a Waldorf kindergarten classroom might look like. The result of all this musing was a course in which students learned about medieval literature and culture by reading, discussing, and writing about it, and also by producing their own manuscript and digital editions of Chaucer's work.

For anyone who has ever been around children for an extended period of time, and especially for early childhood specialists, the idea of "serious play" is probably nothing new. Children learn — to communicate, to use tools, to count — by playing. Curricula in many early childhood educational settings are designed around this basic principle. In using my daughter's experience in a Waldorf school as an illustrative example here, I'm not trying to advocate for the superiority of the Waldorf approach, but rather drawing upon my own admittedly limited and very personal knowledge to make a point. I see a potentially useful convergence between the long-standing and relatively well-studied use of certain pedagogical strategies in early childhood settings and the still-emergent, and relatively untested use of what appear — on the surface at least — to be similar pedagogical strategies in post-secondary education.

This convergence between early childhood and K-12 pedagogies on the one hand, and emerging post-secondary pedagogies involving building, curation, and non-consumptive reading on the other seems, as it was for me, to have resulted from serendipity for the most part. It is largely the product of "screwing around" (Ramsay) and a general alignment of interests and goals, an unexpected result that still requires a more carefully articulated understanding of influence and shared methodologies. For example, although some discussions do give a nod to the importance of play in early childhood development, I have seen few that treat seriously with the substantial literature studying how play as a pedagogical strategy is implemented in a wide variety of developmental curricula. Are we concerned linking what we're doing in college and university classes to what is going on in K-12 classrooms might dilute the prestige value of university education? Why is making K-12 classrooms look more like post-secondary classrooms (often through the implementation of technology) decidedly a good idea, but thinking about how we might make post-secondary classrooms look more like K-12 classrooms (e.g., through learning by doing, integrating play, emphasizing social values like sharing and concern for others, etc.) doesn't seem to have caught on in the same way, especially at the institutional or curricular levels?

Education and Its "Purpose"

One of the most important things we can learn from reading Freire or Thoreau — or Motessori or Steiner — is to ask the important questions: What is education doing, and what should it be doing? Should education be the means through which children and adults are indoctrinated in and made obedient to the dominant ideology? Or should it be the means through which political, social, and economic agency are more evenly distributed throughout a democratic system? Should kindergarten be the first step in preparing our children for college, and eventually, a job? Or should it be, as I think my daughter's teachers might argue, a preparation for *first grade* in the short term, and for *life* (which may or may not include college, and may include a job that doesn't exist yet) in the longer term?

In "The Poetics of Non-Consumptive Reading" Mark Sample states,

> I want to advocate for a poetics of non-consumptive reading in the digital humanities. Scholars and students of art, literature, history, and culture ought to transform more of our non-consumptive research into expressive objects. Nonexpressive use of texts is a dead-end for the humanities. A computer model surrounded by a wall of explanatory words is not enough. Make the computer model itself an expressive object. Turn your data into a story, into a game, into art.

In "Unpacking My Library," and in his other work on the figure of the collector, Walter Benjamin argues for the existence of subject-object (or maybe object-object) relations that, even though they cannot exist *outside* of the exchange economy, nevertheless resist the ontological consequences of that economy in highly productive ways. I see that potential in Sample's description of non-consumptive reading. Non-consumptive reading resists the ontological consequences of the current regulatory system, transgressing distinctions between the products and objects of literary analysis upon which its operation depends. It blurs the distinction between producer and consumer, or artist and critic — categories with substantial legal, social, and economic significance. Because non-consumptive reading causes us to re-examine foundational and often implicit discursive assumptions, it has potential value not only as a scholarly practice in the digital humanities, but also as a critical pedagogical practice in the humanities, and perhaps even other disciplines more broadly.

To put it another way, digital humanities scholarship has caused us to examine more carefully how the discursive forms — including the channels of distribution — within our discipline perpetuate both a failing academic hierarchy and an out-of-control copyright regime. We should also be asking what our pedagogy, designed to teach students how to reproduce those discursive forms, is doing. Too often in post-secondary pedagogy we ask students to iterate discursive forms without asking whether that is the best way to teach them — either the forms or the students. Yes, certainly, it's the best way to train students to become members of our own professional discourse communities, but given the precarity of the academic labor market, we should at least be questioning the wisdom of that justification.

We should be open to the possibility that developmental, K-12 pedagogies have been specifically designed to take advantage of and to foster what Benjamin identifies as "childlike" processes of "renewal." And that, consequently, such pedagogies have something to offer post-secondary scholar pedagogues as we re-examine how current forms and methods may contribute to the commodification of learning and knowledge. As Audrey Watters and others have urged, we should be suspicious of overly simplistic narratives that erase the complex history of modern K-12 and post-secondary education to paint a grim picture of a uniformly languishing, antiquated system in need of a technological savior. Let's stop simply taking for granted that the whole purpose of K-12 education is to prepare students for college and a job, and also that the social, political, and economic functions of the academy are all unquestionably good. Instead, let's have a genuine, dialogic conversation about what the purposes of life-long learning should be and how best to design our pedagogy to fulfill those purposes at every stage in a learner's experience.

Transformed and Transformative Classrooms

Since this piece is just one of the initial phases of a research project in progress, I have done more to generate questions than to answer them here. I *can* give some insight into how reconsidering my own pedagogy in this way has transformed my classroom practice, however. For a start, rather than presuming serious discussion should be the model for every seminar meeting, I've become much more mindful of how what I want to accomplish in a given period, the learning preferences of my students, and the material under consideration should determine the methods I employ. I've also become more open to the possibility of field trips, games, physical activity, show and tell, and other "childish" things need not be left behind once students enter college. Similarly, the spaces in which learning takes place may be as variable as the activities that take place within them. I am more attentive to the affective dimensions of the learning experience. Ensuring learning is pleasant, engaging, and pleasurable — as well as challenging, sometimes difficult, and transformative — *does not* necessarily reduce a pedagogue to an entertainer.

Even while I have started to refashion my own pedagogy, I have also become increasingly worried about what might result from unreflective calls for increased "rigour" and greater "accountability" in K-12 education. Standardized testing, the controversial common core standards, proposed MOOC-ification of remedial education, these "innovations" are all arguably attempts to address students' "underpreparedness" for college and the workplace. Meanwhile, art, music, physical education, and recess are disappearing from the curriculum. I fear in our zeal for "reform" we may be eradicating the very things about K-12 education that might teach us and our students about where curation, building, and non-consumptive reading fit in humanistic inquiry. Further, even where we have begun to acknowledge their value, our obsessive emphasis on end results may actually empty out their potential. For Benjamin, "childlike processes" and collecting — processes that work against or at cross-purposes with the logic of capital — are strategies of material and ontological renewal precisely *because* they are done for themselves rather than as a means to a consciously articulated and pre-determined end.

Let me be clear, essays, discussions, even quizzes — all of these still have an important place in my classroom. As a lawyer and legal scholar, I am absolutely aware of how essential the ability to interpret and reproduce the discursive forms in which power speaks to power can be. Yet, what is truly empowering is understanding such forms are constructed, contingent, open to interpretation, negotiable, and also knowing where they fail and when other forms are better suited to the task at hand. I have seen in a variety of contexts how process and methodology work to establish personal and professional identity in ways that can be liberating and also limiting. We should constantly be re-examining how our own processes and methodologies as teachers, students, scholars, and artists position us in relation to one another and the subjects/objects of study within our classrooms. Rather than simply allowing social, economic, political, legal, and disciplinary regulatory structures to dictate the shape of what we do, we should be more mindful of how what we do helps give rise to and reinforce such structures. I think questioning the continuing utility of the physical, conceptual, pedagogical, and rhetorical walls we've erected between K-12 and so-called "higher" education might be a great place to begin.

CHAPTER 13.

THREE LINES OF RESISTANCE: ETHICS, CRITICAL PEDAGOGY, AND TEACHING UNDERGROUND

KRIS SHAFFER

It is easy for those of us invested in critical pedagogy to see need for major change in education in the U.S. It is also easy for us to write highly ideological manifesti that make sweeping philosophical statements about how things should be. One question I often hear from those getting their feet wet in critical pedagogy is *where do I start?* Many agree with the ideology and the goals of critical pedagogy and other movements seeking major change, but we cannot simply drop those changes into our current institutional structures. Never mind the fact that we have colleagues and students to win over before we can implement these changes with a chance at success.

But some of the issues raised by critical pedagogy are major *ethical* issues. It's not that we can do something more efficiently or effectively, it's that we see what we're doing on the whole as being actually *wrong*. As a critical pedagogue, I can go along with something less effective much more easily than with something that goes against my newly pricked conscience. So when I disagree fundamentally with the direction something is headed, but am powerless to change it singlehandedly, what do I do? Do I forget about it and wash my hands of the situation? Do I leave in disgust? Do I bide my time until I can *really* do something? (And hope it doesn't get worse in the mean time!) Do I try to make incremental changes, appeasing my conscience with the knowledge that I am improving things, albeit slowly?

As I've thought about various issues in various contexts, I've come to believe that I should work on at least three different planes — or resisting along three different fronts. Sometimes, only one is an option; sometimes all three. But by framing my thoughts and work this way, it helps me to identify what I can and can't do, and to not feel like every class I teach needs to be a major revolution. I hope these three lines of resistance can help other people seeking to make changes where they are.

The first and highest line of resistance is pushing for major institutional change in policies and practices, like I did at Charleston Southern University with the social media policy. This is where we should push for large, sweeping changes — where our full ideology, even our manifestos, should come to the fore.

The second line of resistance is changing our own day-to-day practices. Major institutional change comes slowly, if at all. And we are unlikely to get everything we want on the highest level. But we can effect significant change on the local level. These changes are often incremental because of the lack of major institutional change, but they are no less important.

Often, I find myself working on both of these levels simultaneously. For example, I may speak against the use of letter grades or standardized tests (first line of resistance). But until there are major university-wide changes, I cannot operate entirely outside of the world of grades and SAT/ACT/GRE scores. However, I can ignore, or at least heavily de-emphasize, GPA and GRE scores in favor of writing samples and unique elements on the C.V. when considering graduate school applications to my department (second line of resistance).

Likewise, I can employ assessment practices in class that focus on formative assessment and verbal feedback over summative assessment and final grades. I can also use a standards-based, or criterion-referenced, grading system where I assign grades of P, B, A, or N (passing, borderline, attempted, not attempted) — encouraging students to think less about ABCDF grades, and to think more about the *meaning* of an assessment. (The fact that the letter grades stand for a word, and that B is better than A, both contribute to that.) Since these grades are assigned in reference to concepts or skills, rather than assignments, it also invites students to focus on the content we are exploring together and their intellectual development in light of it, rather than just a series of scores. This is by no means ideal, but it is an improvement that still fits inside university policies and draws student attention to the problems with those policies. It also allows me to demonstrate the value of other systems, and have data and student feedback to point to if and when the university actually considers changing its policies.

Not every change we would like to make can be accomplished within the policies set forth by our university, though. That's where the third line of resistance comes in: *teaching underground*. Academic instructors can influence the intellectual and social development of our students outside the boundaries of the course. We can also influence the way our colleagues think about things. Further, our role as critical pedagogues need not be limited to the professional relationships we have with students and colleagues. We have an educational role to play outside the university, as well.

For example, while what we do during class, prep, and grading time is important, what happens during office hours often has a greater impact on our students. Even better can be meetings over coffee or the throwing of a frisbee. And education need not be limited to our tuition-paying university students. As a parent and the member of a vibrant faith community, I have two very important educational charges outside my professional life, in which I seek to put my critical-pedagogy ideals to work. Social media is another locus of pedagogy, if we use it as such. Many of us teachers use social media for pedagogical development, seeking the ideas of others that we can can appropriate for our own teaching. But we can also use it as an others-oriented place to teach other educators, especially given the large population of educators seeking to learn from others on those platforms.

These are not the only ways in which we can seek change and resist harmful practices in education. But I have found it helpful to frame my educational work in these three ways. For instance, I used to try and do *everything* that I found important in *every* class. When institutional policies or student preferences got in the way, I became frustrated — either with the policies, or the students, or with my own inability to make it all work. However, recognizing the difference between the first and second lines of resistance helps me see the value in making *incremental local changes* while pursuing big change outside the immediate context of my classes. Likewise, taking opportunities to "teach underground" helps me accomplish aims outside of class that I cannot (yet) accomplish in class. (Don't underestimate the value of having coffee with education majors, for example, especially if they just read Paulo Freire in one of their education classes!)

Among the *Hybrid Pedagogy* community, we often focus on the ideology, and thus the first line of resistance. Of course, most of us live in a world where we can have our biggest influence on the second and third lines of resistance. (And communities like *Hybrid Pedagogy* are examples of that third line of resistance.) We do not live in Luther's Wittenburg or Calvin's Geneva; most of us live in Cranmer's England. Reformation, if it comes at all, will come slowly and incrementally, and we may risk our livelihood if we push too hard on the first line of resistance too soon. But we all have things we can do on the second and third lines of resistance. The more we push there, and the more people we can bring along with us, the greater chance we'll have of success when we do make that assault on the first line.

As a community that teaches each other underground, let's

keep our eyes fixed on the broad goals and help each other to make significant, incremental gains on the local level, both in class and off the books.

———————

The following is a letter to my first- and second-year music theory and aural skills students at The University of Colorado–Boulder. This is my second semester at CU, and the music students and I are still getting to know each other. For some, this will be their first semester with me; others are still getting used to my pedagogical quirks. To help frame the semester, I will have them read and discuss this open letter.

My most profound educational experience was not a lecture, or a test, and certainly not a homework assignment from a workbook. My most profound educational experience was playing second horn for a brass sectional for our conservatory orchestra. We were playing Richard Strauss's *Ein Heldenleben*, a piece full of difficult passages for the brass players. Our principal horn was away for an audition on that day, and our horn professor, Dale Clevenger (principal horn of the Chicago Symphony), played in his place. I sat right next to him, seeing and hearing what he was doing first-hand, and trying to match or complement him as I played. Even though he only talked to me for a fraction of the time, that single two-hour rehearsal was easily worth a year of lessons, or dozens of concerts. And no amount of lectures or readings could have accomplished what was accomplished by playing a hard piece alongside the greatest horn player in the world, trying to match his sound as I heard it.

Now I'm not the world's greatest music theorist. But I am an expert in the things we will be studying, and I care deeply about fostering the best opportunities I can for you to learn them for yourselves. With that in mind, I'd like to set the tone for this semester by offering a few things to keep in mind as we work together. Though these are not part of the course content, do not appear on the syllabus, and will not be assessed, they are *more* important than the course content. These things will help us lay the groundwork to be successful in our engagement with the course material, and, even more importantly, they have broad applicability to learning processes in general — in this course, in other courses, and outside the classroom. We will occasionally reflect on these in class, as they apply to specific situations in which we find ourselves.

First, *education is more than the transfer of information*. Education *involves* the transfer of information, of course. However, there are things more important, and more difficult, than simply memorizing information. In our class, those things include the assimilation of concepts and the application of those concepts in musical activities. Assimilating concepts often requires engaging multiple perspectives on the same information — multiple theories about the same musical concept, multiple ways to perform the same kind of passage, etc. It also requires attempts at applying the material, such as composing, analyzing, or performing. These things are harder than taking notes and regurgitating them on a test, and often take longer than a single class meeting or homework assignment to figure out. For those of you who are used to courses that "test early and test often," this may be uncomfortable and may feel, initially, ineffective. However, doing hard things and working to apply concepts leads to deeper, longer-lasting learning than lecture, baby-step homework, and a test you can cram for. That's a big reason that I rarely lecture and don't use workbooks: we need to do hard things and engage multiple routes through the material in order to truly understand and master it.

Education is training for life, not just a career, and certainly not just a job upon graduation. You are paying too much money and putting too much time into your education for it to be valuable for a few years of work only. Your education should help you develop skills that will last your entire career (which could be upwards of 50 years). We don't have all the information that will be required of musicians working in 2060. However, what we do in these classes can help you develop the skills of inquiry and analysis you'll need to figure out how to work in those new settings. We will also take multiple approaches to a single topic so that you can 1) see that there are always a diversity of ways to understand a single topic, and 2) have more tools at your disposal to choose from when facing something new that was not anticipated by your textbook's authors or your professors.

Ask your private studio teachers, ensemble conductors, or other seasoned professionals you respect (in any field) what their most valuable educational experience was that has prepared them for their life and career. Was it a series of lectures? Was it a textbook reading? A workbook assignment? Or a hard project — maybe even one they created themselves — for which there was no textbook or how-to guide, but which pushed them to develop new ways of thinking about their work, and led them to create something they didn't think they were capable of? You will get plenty of lectures and readings in your college education. I want you to find the tools and experiences that will help you develop the ability to do good, hard work when there are no lectures and readings.

In other words, *I want you to learn how to learn*. That means that at times you will be teaching yourself. This is an intentional choice. One of my chief goals is for you to take charge of your own education. Though I will help set a frame in which this will take place, many of you will feel uncomfortable, even overwhelmed, at this. That's normal. It's what independent learning feels like quite often. (Because it's what *teaching* feels like.) However, if at any time you feel lost, please talk to me. I have gone through the same process many times before, both as a student and as a teacher. I may not remove the discomfort immediately, or at all, but I will help you learn to manage it and harness it to a positive outcome.

Education is about far more than grades. I understand that grades feel incredibly important. The university puts stock in them, your scholarships depend on them, and many of you are only able to be here because of those scholarships. You're working hard to make sure you can stay here. Other students are, admittedly, minimizing their workload while maximizing their GPA, so they can spend time doing other things, often very good things. However, in both cases, focusing on grades leads us to miss the best things an education has to offer. Some of the most important things in a class are things that are hard to assess, so they're not part of the grade. You have the opportunity to work with world-class scholars and creative professionals here, some of whom are your fellow students. Take advantage of that! Don't think about your education as work for a boss who tells you what to do. You are making an investment. Do what you can to reap the greatest return on your investment (which is not only, or even chiefly, financial). Education is not a commodity that can be purchased; it is a process, and your tuition does not buy learning; it buys an opportunity to learn. That means figuring out what else a professor, or a book, or a piece of music, or a campus, or a city, or a group of fellow students has to offer you besides what is on the syllabus or in the course catalog. Yes, grades can be important, but they are not the goal: the goal is an intellectual, musical, professional, and social maturity that will allow you to get the most out of, and contribute the most to, your life.

A class is a negotiated space. Every class is full of students — and an instructor — whose backgrounds, goals, and attitudes differ. Even when students' goals are congruent, the "best" route for each student towards those goals is different. Thus, a class activity is always a compromise that seeks to enable as many students as possible to make as much progress as possible towards those goals. And even though this means more freedom for all of you, there will be times when I have to make decisions for the group. But they will be made with this need for compromise in mind.

Teaching is not performance. My goal is not to dazzle you with my intellect or to blow your mind with the course content. Nor is it to entertain you or to charm you with my personality (though I may). Instead, my goal is to create an environment that is conducive to your musical and intellectual growth. While I do have some tricks up my sleeve that will help you "get it" quickly, and I do have some class activities that may be entertaining or inspiring, much of our work will look like your daily work in the practice room. Mastering something new is like that, as you know from the hours you've spent composing or practicing. However, I will make sure that everything we do, whether mind-blowing or mundane, will have value.

Finally, *I am not perfect*. Nor are any of your other professors. We are experts in the fields we teach, and some of us are experts in the art of teaching. However, we make mistakes. We also have an imperfect university structure to work within (semesters, grades, class schedules, etc.), and each pass through the material brings new students with different experiences, backgrounds, skills, sensitivities, prejudices, loves, career goals, life goals, financial situations, etc. There is no one way — often not even a best way — to teach a topic to a student, let alone one best way to teach a topic to 15 or 40 (or 400) students simultaneously. So even when we do our jobs well, it won't fit everyone. And even if it did, you will have bad days, too. This is why I will provide you a variety of resources and tasks to help you learn. If you take charge of your own education, make full use of the resources most helpful to you, and make full use of the *people* around you (myself and your fellow students), you will make significant strides in your musical growth.

Most of you did not come to music school so that you can make lots of money. And I doubt any of you came here just to get good grades. In fact, I bet all of you are here because you love music. And most of you enjoy making and talking about music together with others. That's exactly what these classes are about. If you focus on making and exploring music collaboratively in this class, deep learning will happen. (And, yes, good grades will follow.) You will also grow as musicians who can continue to educate yourselves when you leave CU. So let's make the most of our time together not by seeing how much information we can get from my notebook into yours, but instead by learning how to make music, and to make insights about music, in new ways.

CHAPTER 14.

LISTENING FOR STUDENT VOICES

SEAN MICHAEL MORRIS AND CHRIS FRIEND

Teachers don't teach; instructors don't really instruct. The lecture-based course fell out of favor years ago, and we know today to bring front and center the role students play in their own learning. "Education," says Paulo Freire, "becomes the practice of freedom, the means by which men and women deal critically and creatively with reality and discover how to participate in the transformation of their world" (*Pedagogy of the Oppressed*). When critical and independent thinking are the most valuable products of learning, we must ask and make space for students to work and create on their own. It isn't enough for them to take notes and then recite; learners must invent — not just the products of their knowledge, but also their own learning.

These lofty goals require risk. If we give students the freedom to choose their own path, they might choose poorly or make mistakes on our watch. But we must be willing to allow them the challenge of this authority, the dignity of this risk, and the opportunity to err and learn from their mistakes. They learn and gain expertise through experimentation. We are given responsibility for a classroom because we are experts in our fields, which we become after years of work and experience, learning things that are very difficult to put in a textbook or instruction manual. These experiences require time, and often frustration. We have to try, and risk failure, so that we *also* can learn.

The words *experience* and *expert* both come from the Latin word *experiri* meaning "to try". If we want our students to become experts, we have an obligation to give them the opportunity to try things, without the real danger that otherwise exists outside a classroom environment. Our students must have the chance — and the compulsion — to experiment in their thinking and with their work. That's what school is for. Because one day it ends, and everyone involved in this grand experiment, both experienced and novice, must become experts in their own right.

If we decide that our classrooms are places where *trying* happens, then we transform them into laboratories; and in a laboratory, with happy people of varying skill sets working side by side, anyone can make a discovery. As lab managers, then, we do not approach our work as "I've solved this problem, let's see if you can too" but as, "here's a problem with many possible solutions." Everyone is invited to try, allowed to fail, encouraged to succeed. Our job becomes making sure that all the appropriate equipment is available for success to occur.

> @caty_posch @HybridPed Internet and general play are important to learning. We often teach ourselves out of pure interest. #digped
> ~ Valerie Robin

They don't need *us* to let them do what we hope they will do in our classes. Our students need to work through each experience on their own apprenticed terms, not on ours. In "The Novice as Expert: Writing the Freshman Year," Nancy Sommers and Laura Saltz explain, "freshmen build authority not by writing *from* a position of expertise but by writing *into* expertise." And because "being a novice allows students to be changed by what they learn," we have an obligation to our students — indeed, a mandate — to make our classrooms sites of trial and experimentation, rather than routine and repetition.

There's only one of us, but plenty of them, so is it really *our* classroom? When we view a class as "ours", the term brings with it an inherent sense of ownership and even domination. We want students to have control over their learning. But because they're in school, an institution built around hierarchy, at most they can have the *illusion* of control within the limits set by the instructor or the institution.

This is the fly in the ointment of critical pedagogy. Teachers must teach students to think for themselves, to feel empowered, and to cultivate their own learning processes. And yet, to teach that is to assert the educator's own authority. Even when we step aside from the podium, the act reminds everyone in the room under whose power the podium really is, and who has the ability to resume that position at will.

Good teachers bemoan the separation of instructor and student, and ply our trade to bring student voices into academic conversations. We may make efforts to publish student work, involve students in conferences and discussions, create student-led courses, let students set class rules or evaluation standards, and more. But too often these efforts reinforce the division they mean to overcome. A good teacher works to give students the space, the opportunity, and the motivation to learn on their own. The best teachers upend the hierarchy and strategically use their authority to make teachers unnecessary. In her recent blog post about listening to learners, the author reticulatrix states,

> Some people feel excluded from dominant discourse. Some do not want to contribute to the dominant discourse. Some of us are fed up of being consistently on the wrong end of power structures with the academy. Furthermore, many of us have already been doing just fine creating our own conversations and resource repositories ... it now seems to me even more than before, that academics are often busy talking to themselves inside their own bubbles.

Learners of all stripes are having conversations about learning, networked collaboration, and open education entirely outside the academic environment. In fact, many of these conversations eschew academics because of the myriad complexities those "authorities" bring into discussions of teaching and learning. Learners are talking about learning, and they might share with educators… if educators are willing to listen more than speak.

> @HybridPed Students literally own their education. They must be allowed to co-create and steer it in order to reach their own goals. #digped
>
> ~ Lans Pacifico

Teachers should not be gatekeepers for student voices, and once we suppose we are, we miss half the conversation. When teachers serve as gatekeepers, when we tell students explicitly what they should learn for our courses, when we establish requirements or procedures for their learning, we aren't functioning as teachers; we aren't allowing students to engage in genuine, self-directed, natural learning. We are instead being scriptwriters. The more elaborate direction, specific instruction, and constraining requirements we provide, the less our students rely on themselves to think and learn. They work to adopt *our* mindset, to decipher and satisfy *our* expectations, and to gain *our* knowledge and experience, rather than using their own curiosity and their own experimentation to risk learning something new… and we stifle learning. Instead, we need to be in the business of manufacturing opportunities.

Classrooms murmur. They hum and buzz — with experimentation, with discoveries at all scales. Underneath the lectures, slideshows, and exams, voices rustle. These are the voices of students, learners of all shapes and variety, online and on-ground, higher ed and K-12, formal and lifelong. These voices don't talk just of course materials and content. They talk about what is taught, and how, and about what and how they want to learn. They talk about the things that *matter to them*. Students have plenty to say about learning, about the failings of higher education, about their own futures and careers. If we think they're only concerned with life outside of school, we're mistaken; learners have a deeper investment in our teaching than we do.

PART III.

CONTINGENCY AND
ACADEMIC LABOR

"For many, contingency isn't just a political status, it's a personal matter; at the same time, serious discussion of the situation in higher education deserves thoughtful, scholarly dialogue. Only a balance of both approaches will get to the heart of the matter."
~ Sean Michael Morris, Robin Wharton, and Jesse Stommel,
"CFP: The Problem of Contingency in Higher Education"

CHAPTER 15.

ON, ON, ON

"Life *chez* Simpson was not normal, Helen now reflects, principally because a constant eye had to be kept on anything that might affect Simpson's performance, whether he was racing or not ... 'Social life [as a couple] was non-existent. I often used to think it would be really strange living a normal life, going out and having a meal with people.'"

~ William Fotheringham

"In the past 4 months I have kept seeing accolades to Andy's amazing productivity — the 100+ articles, the zillions of case books, etc., and I have always told people that yes, he led a normal life, yes, he got plenty of sleep and yes, he even took plenty of naps. But that's not really true. His life was not normal, at least not to me, and it certainly wasn't balanced."

~ Patty Sun

It's Tour de France time again, and I've been reading William Fotheringham's sensitive and ambivalent search for the story of British cyclist Tom Simpson, who died on Mont Ventoux in 1967. In the history of professional cycling, it's one of the landmark stories of ambition, risk and terrible loss — the grainy prequel to all the doping scandals that came later. Fotheringham spoke directly to Simpson's widow Helen, and to those who were closely involved at the time of his death, including Harry Hall, the mechanic who helped Simpson back onto his bike on the mountain, and was the last to hear him speak.

> He had seen riders pedal themselves into a state of exhaustion or hypoglycemia before, but of Simpson collapsed against the bank telling him to put him back on his bike, he can only say, 'At that moment I don't know what I thought. I just don't know.' What Hall does know is that Simpson's last words were murmured, in a rasping voice, just as he was pushing him off: 'On, on, on.' He could have been exhorting the mechanic, or telling himself to keep going; Hall seems to think it was both. (34)

500 metres further up the mountain, Tom Simpson fell again, and did not survive. He was 29, and he left Helen and two tiny daughters.

What can we possibly do with this kind of career sacrifice? When someone pushes himself to these limits, who takes responsibility? Who exploits ambition, and who profits from it? Fotheringham puts a subtle case historically against both the Tour organisers and the newspapers that followed the race, both of whom had an interest in promoting the heroic struggle of cyclist against mountain.

> At the turn of the last century, the public appeal of the Tour de France lay in the fact that the competitors were pioneers, setting off to do things no right-thinking mortal would attempt … That was the great attraction for its first organiser, Desgrange; that was why his paper's circulation went up during the Tour. (111)

Fotheringham also lays out sympathetically the personal and cultural circumstances under which any individual might calculate that the price paid for professional success can't be too high. It's such a sad read; I can't imagine how it must feel for his family to have lost someone so publicly, even to the extent that his final wavering moments on the mountain are preserved in shaky black and white footage on YouTube, remixed to funereal sound-tracks by many cycling fans. And those fans — and all of us couching it through the Tour again — are part of the problem. Isn't this exactly what we came to see?

Patty Sun is the wife of law professor Andrew Taslitz, who died earlier this year. Like Helen Simpson, her loss has been shaded by public celebration of her husband's professional work made in comments like this:

> He is one of the most amazing faculty members I have ever met. So many of us excel at one of the three major aspects of being a faculty member. Taz excelled at all three. I was always amazed at how he could write reports for committees, facilitate tenure files, attend events, write multiple law review articles a year, write a book every other year, and still manage to be one of the most effective teachers in the country … He was certainly one of a kind, and of the kind that this world could use much more.

Let's think about this for a moment. What happens when academics celebrate each other's achievements in these terms? What happens when we think this is something the world needs more of? *Which world?* All I can think of is the cyclists who make the pilgrimage to Tom Simpson's lonely memorial on Mont Ventoux and leave their water bottles there, passing on a powerful message to every young rider who comes along after them, hoping for a spot on a pro team.

When I was diagnosed with cancer, I started to think about the connection between why professional cyclists dope and why academics overwork, and got about half way there: that it's impossible to keep up with a doping peloton unless you're willing to entertain the same personal cost. Richard Hall has taken up this post a couple of times, in a way that has cleared up something for me. In his latest discussion of academic labour within the "anxiety machine" of the university, he connects the shame culture of performance management to practices of self-care, and ultimately to the ways in which both our hidden and attention-seeking gestures of overwork entangle us with the lives of others:

> Just as the high-performing athlete recalibrates the performance of those around her, and creates a productive new-normal, so the workaholic professor does the same. And the irony of my sitting here at 11.22pm writing this is not lost on me. And maybe this is because I am committed. And maybe this is a form of flight or a defence against the abstract pain of the world. Maybe it is a form of self-care, through which I am trying to make concrete how I feel about my past and my present. And maybe as Maggie Turp argues, this form of overwork and performance anxiety is a culturally acceptable self-harming activity. I am performance managed to the point where I willingly internalise the question "am I productive enough?", which aligns with "am I a good academic?", which aligns with "am I working hard enough", which risks becoming a projection onto those around me of "are you working/producing enough?"

This is such a vital step: to connect the personal pathology of overcommitment (including to the welfare of others) to the creation of profit from machines and systems that facilitate labour. And then to think about what it means to understand universities in these terms, especially as we lurch towards a more competitive and more marketised higher education system. In other words, in thinking about the hamster-wheel cultures of academic overwork, we don't need to look much further than the mechanics of the wheel itself, whose whole design and purpose is to keep on keeping on, which is precisely the problem. As Harry Hall, the mechanic who put Tom Simpson back on his bike, later reflected, cycling and rowing were the two most dangerous sports for athletes because of their mechanised nature: "The individual is pushing a machine which doesn't know when to stop. It always asks for another pull of the oars, another pedal stroke" (41).

But the anxiety machine of the academy isn't a component, like a bike or even a hamster wheel: it's the whole system. It's all of us, helping each other on, on, on. It's the formal incentives and rewards for overwork that we chase, and it's all the informal ways in which we perform, celebrate and even lament our own willingness to work to exhaustion — without ever stopping long enough to think about how we could change this, and why we should.

CHAPTER 16.

A LECTURER'S ALMANAC

KATIE ROSE GUEST PRYAL

MARCH

The hall of the department is a 1960s-era Bunker, molded of concrete and rebar, with tall, narrow windows to repel even the most determined activist. I watch my feet as I climb the lino-clad stairs so I don't stumble in my skinny high-heels, bought specifically to match this suit. The suit is black, with pale pinstripes, more fashionable than the *interview suit*.

I'd always sworn I would never buy one of those.

Dr. Comp and Dr. Rhet sit in a conference room. He directs the composition program; she's an assistant professor. I have a new doctorate in rhetoric and composition, the most marketable everyone on my committee swore to me. And it seems so, since Dr. Comp and Dr. Rhet want to hire me for this special position, crafted just for me or someone like me, for someone with special training in special disciplines. Plus, Dr. Comp says, it pays really well and comes with great research support. Sure it's still a contract position, but the contract is multi-year, and the Department Chair is really *committed to changing the lecturer paradigm.*

Dr. Comp says, when I ask about the possibility for contract renewal, *I promise we'll continue to exploit you as long as you let us.*

We all laugh.

APRIL

I moved here for him, for Mr. Tall. Like many women before me, I traded some super-bright job offers for a pretty darn shiny one and a bungalow with the man I love.

In late April, I get a phone call from the chair of another English department to offer me a position at a school far away, one I applied for weeks ago. I say I've taken a job at the Bunker, so I'm not available any more.

He says, *I'm not surprised. Talent like yours gets snatched up quick.*

I feel a twinge, thinking maybe I've accepted a job that isn't good enough, that I should have held out for something better.

Mr. Tall says he wants to take me to dinner near the Bunker. First, he suggests a walk around campus. He says, *I've always loved this place at dusk.*

A decade ago, my new institution belonged to him, a skinny kid with big round glasses. The coincidence across space and time suits my love of scientific anomalies. We stop outside my Bunker-to-be, and he pulls me into the foyer. We stop at the Board, black background with white letters, the long list of professors' last names with digits beside indicating the small rooms where genius happens. *Your name will be up there soon,* he says.

He drops to a knee, holding something round and shiny. *Now you'll think of me every day when you come to work.*

AUGUST

The syllabi are written. The readings selected and scanned. The bus schedule memorized. The keys placed on my keychain, the copy codes in my head. I am, I believe, ready.

My office, I discover, was painted pink and yellow, each wall a solid pane of color, by the graduate students who inhabited it before. Pink paint splatters the ceiling and the baseboards, yellow drips have dried on the desks and linoleum. I hang my four diplomas, hoping to distract visitors from the unprofessional colors with my professional credentials.

I visit Dr. Rhet's office, professionally painted a refreshing green. She reassures me the department pays to repaint offices. *You just have to ask.*

I learn that, because I am a lecturer, the department will not pay to repaint my office.

Every time a student comes for office hours, there's a funny moment when the shocking colors evoke an unintentional response, often pursed lips, or a sniff as though the colors emit a smell. Embarrassed, I lie, *The walls will be repainted soon. Don't worry.*

I learn my office is to be shared. My office-mate is also a lecturer, one of the special lecturers like me, hired as part of the *new model* for fixed-term faculty. Each week, she travels far to teach here, so she sits in the office a lot, lacking anywhere else to go.

I decide I prefer the campus coffee shop for my office hours and buy a new desk for the spare bedroom in the bungalow to have a place to do my writing.

SEPTEMBER

They've repainted the hallways of the Bunker. The windows don't open, so there's no fresh air. Near the mailboxes, I feel a bit lightheaded from the fumes. Dr. Cultural Studies stands next to me, fumbling with his mail, the same mail I've received, a tightly-packed tome of fliers, notices, and newsletters, each printed on a different shade of pastel office paper.

We stand, our rainbows in our hands, and I say, *The paint smell sure is strong, don't you think.*

He says, without a sign of recognition in his eyes, *You should just be glad they painted.* Then he turns and drops his rainbow in the trash.

I wonder if he talks to all faculty that way.

OCTOBER

I stand in the foyer of the Bunker, where Mr. Tall proposed to me, staring at the Board with its small white letters. My name still isn't there.

"Autumn Almanac" by Erich Ferdinand on Flickr; CC BY

[one year passes]

OCTOBER

My name does not belong on the Board, I'm told, because lecturers are *itinerant,* and because to purchase more small white letters would cost the department too much money.

NOVEMBER

I'm going to have a baby in June.

I hide in the bathroom when I feel sick, armed with a slick pack of lies: *I sure gained the newly-wed fifteen,* or, *Avoid the sushi in the Union today. It's a little off.*

DECEMBER

Faculty meeting. A new course scheduling policy. All Faculty must teach one semester of Monday, Wednesday, and Friday courses each school year, no exceptions. Many groans emit.

Then, Dr. Twentieth Century says, her voice high and sweet, *I don't see why we can't just have those lecturers teach three days a week.*

After all, they don't have to write. It's us researchers that should have the good schedules.

I remember some words my mother once said to me when I was in college. She said, *You grow up to be a doctor, do you hear me? Don't you grow up to be a nurse.* At the time, I'd just declared an English major, so her words seemed a little strange.

Now I know what she meant. She's been married to a doctor for thirty years, running the practice for twenty. But to some, she'll always just be a *doctor's wife.*

I became a doctor. But I'm still a nurse. Except nurses get paid more and have better job security.

JANUARY

My textbook proposal is accepted by a publisher. They send me a one thousand dollar advance. I sign my contract at a bistro with Mr. Tall, and he takes my picture with the pen in my hand.

The lecturers form an advisory committee and ask for promotion procedures. We want a senior title, with senior pay, and five year contracts. We form a listserv, start a newsletter with meeting minutes, and begin to plan.

Our push seems to be working.

FEBRUARY

My belly is starting to show, and I'm worried. I also majored in Women's Studies, so I can recognize my fear as an old one, one felt by working women for decades — that our bosses will resent the pregnancy, the promised leave from work (right there in contractual black and white), and the distraction that a child brings.

I've made friends with another lecturer, Dr. Cool. She's been in the Bunker for sixteen years. She invites me to sit in her office. It's hers alone, and it's bright, with pictures of her grown children on the walls.

Is your name on the Board? I ask her.

No, she says, *and it really makes me mad.*

I tell her I'm pregnant. It seems she already knows. She says, *Honey, you should tell everybody. Then they sure as heck can't fire you.*

I tell everyone.

I tell our new chair. She reassures me that not only will I have a job when I get back from parental leave, but that she'll do all in her power to make it as good a job as she can. She tells me she is happy for me, and I believe her.

I sign a form that gives me a semester's paid leave in the fall, and I'm really happy I work in the Bunker.

MARCH

An announcement to all lecturers: Due to budget shortfalls, all lecturers will be placed on one-year contracts for the foreseeable future.

We are reassured, however, that the department — the tenured faculty — will do all it can to *protect us.*

APRIL

All faculty receive a golden-yellow announcement in the mail, asking for proposals for University-funded small research grants, given to the most promising research projects proposed by any faculty member.

In boldface, like a black eye, the form letter says, *Adjunct professors are not eligible, nor are lecturers, instructors, or others of non-professorial rank.*

I wonder, if the grants are truly based on merit, why they choose to exclude certain members of the faculty.

I think of high school, when I was a young player on the junior varsity volleyball team. During a preseason scrimmage against the varsity squad, we kicked their butts. Our ever-pragmatic coach simply admitted his error and traded squads, placing J.V. players on varsity and benching his former starters. Ignoring their protests, he told them, *You just need to play better, folks.*

I'm starting to wonder about the meaning of merit in the Bunker.

MAY

My son comes six weeks early. His skinny, premature form lies in a plastic bin, tubes and wires tracking to machines that blip and flash. For one week he sleeps in that bin, and I forget the Bunker, the Board, the pink-and-yellow office, Dr. Cultural Studies and his disregard, Dr. Twentieth Century and her naive insults. I think, *If my baby comes home safe, nothing else will ever matter again.*

I sit by his bin and grade final papers for my four writing courses. Grades are due in two days.

SEPTEMBER

Home with my son, enjoying generous parental leave, I feel like a hypocrite. Sure, no one dreams of growing up to be second-class. But, I tell myself, second-class academia is better than most jobs.

The state budget is getting ugly. Our new chair comes to a lecturers' meeting, where we're finalizing our proposal for the creation of a senior lecturer position. She says, *The budget has been deeply cut. It's not certain that you will all be rehired next year.*

Suddenly, the promotion and retention proposal we've been debating, revising, and debating seems pointless.

After the Chair has left, a lecturer says, *We sure got put back in our places. The lecturers were getting uppity.*

DECEMBER

The senior lecturer promotion proposal comes up for a vote. Due to budgetary constraints, the bits in the proposal about higher pay and longer contracts are excised. After six years of teaching, a lecturer can put in for a promotion to Senior Lecturer. At least the title will be better.

At the faculty meeting, I point out what appears to be a mistake in the paperwork. It says all tenure-track faculty can vote on lecturers being promoted to senior lecturer. I think, a first-year assistant professor who hasn't even passed third-year review shouldn't be able to vote on a veteran such as Dr. Cool. That's absurd.

I raise my hand and the chair recognizes me.

I say, *Shouldn't this say "tenured" faculty? Do we want assistant professors to vote on senior lecturers? Do we really think that all Assistant Professors are a higher rank than Senior Lecturers?*

The room, stuffed with sixty faculty members, is silent for a moment. Then, Dr. Linguist turns around to look at me, except she doesn't really look at me, just toward me. She says, *Yes they are. I'm sorry, but that's just the way it is.*

The chair nods. The motion passes.

I go to the departmental office. One of the administrators has been holding my son during the meeting with the sure hands of a grandmother. His small body is draped across her, his fist tucked into his mouth. I see my small boy lying on her chest, sleeping, and I shut the office door and cry.

JANUARY

I come to the Bunker for the new semester, returning to teaching after a semester of leave. My textbook is in production. I did it all on my own, with no help from the Bunker. I'm proud of myself.

I walk into the Bunker's foyer, and the Board is down. Dr. Cool walks up to me and says, *Our names are going up. It's gonna happen today.*

I say, *Is it silly that I'm so excited about this?*

In a world in which we always lose, we have finally won something. I snap a picture of my name — well, Mr. Tall's name — on the new board, using my cell phone, and send it to Mr. Tall.

He writes back, *It's finally official.*

CHAPTER 17.

ADJUNCTIFICATION: LIVING IN THE MARGINS OF ACADEME

TIFFANY KRAFT

Unfair labor practices are commonplace in American higher education, public and private. Hardly anyone denies the problem of adjunctificaton and contingency, and, more epidemic, laborers on the fringe in any trade or profession recognize this deficit; yet we continue to work for less, essentially exploiting our worth, thus the possibility of a solution is vexed. And the issue is not unique to adjuncts, but many other university laborers, including students who are uniformly paid minimum wage for providing essential services. But how can a problem so transparent and pervasive fail to generate actionable change? Why can't I get equal pay for equal labor? And why is silence the norm? These are self-posed questions that warrant wider consideration.

Multiple labor hierarchies exist campus wide, all arguably fundamental to the operation of the university, and the adjunct problem begs reformation right now. I do not believe all adjuncts are qualified for tenure, and some tenured professors likely don't deserve it either. But many adjuncts who are every bit as qualified as those with tenure don't get equal pay for equal labor because we are powerless in a system that is indifferent to faculty working conditions. This was certainly the case for Margaret Mary Vojtko, as reported by Daniel Kovalik. Let's stop to remember Vojtko through Elie Wiesel's statement: "I believe that a person who is indifferent to the suffering of others is complicit in the crime" (Hirt-Manheimer). And this means, of course, that in our silence we are equally complicit in this problem.

Nigh 75% of us are complicit in this problem, so why blame the complicit elite, the other 25%? Because the majority of them are content and quiet? I believe we are stronger together, as one faculty, than pitted against one another. So let's question the hierarchy of the institution instead. Let's reevaluate tenure, for as James Wetherbe says, "tenure has hamstrung colleges' ability to fulfill their two fundamental missions of advancing knowledge and disseminating it." Let's also demand transparency and redistribute the top-down wealth, starting with the president of the university.

A realistic approach would embrace reorganization that values mutual interest in pay equity and job security alongside innovative teaching, research and publication, and continuing education. Though levels of teaching and/or research focus differ among universities and colleges, the stereotypical system holds ranked professors accountable for research and publication, but marginalizes the significance of teaching or vice versa. We need to find a new balance that values both teaching and research equally and imagine something other than the disparity of tiered faculty, a hybrid plane where both/and rather than either/or are equally valued and compensated. We should at least look to other models that manage to balance teaching and research pathways and roles more equitably.

In an interview by Moshe Z. Marvit, Dan Kovalik, senior associate general counsel of the United Steelworkers, says the two-tiered faculty model is "destroying the academy," and that our CEO-like presidents and administrators are not all to blame. Yet, even though the failure of our system is apparent to outsiders, we remain paralyzed. So why do we contribute to a fatally flawed and oppressive system when so many of us, like Vojtko, will die sick and penniless after years of service to our students and university? Why, when we are ripe for reorganization, do adjuncts fail to organize? For my own part, I am stuck in a spiraling cycle, afraid to lose what little seniority I have as an affiliate adjunct, and I am stretched thin juggling heavy course loads, which makes it hard to look for work elsewhere or dig my way out of this hole through publishing. As is, I know a tenure committee would not look at my file because I have been an adjunct for a decade plus now: I am branded. This stigma needs to change.

I can't say I've ever met a complacent adjunct, but I have met several who, like me, have both front and back burners on high. Sometimes I wonder how long I can sustain the workload without burning out or boiling over. Even after a decade of extreme adjuncting, what I find most oppressive is not the workload itself, but the cyclical fear of unemployment without benefits. And sometimes, though it seems a past life away now, I remember that I was a privileged housewife, married to an affluent periodontist with a house in Kings Heights. And I left that life to pursue academia, to contribute to society, to be something more socially and economically valued than a mother and a wife. Of course, devalued and un(der)compensated domestic laborers of all sorts have more in common with adjuncts than I anticipated. Reflecting on that privileged life now, knowing I left because he told me he could make more money in one hour pulling teeth than I could in one year teaching English, and he was about right, I don't regret my decision. And even though I found out the hard way that society does not value teachers either, I am proud to own both identities: mother and teacher.

So where do we start to reform and reorganize? I would like to see revised promotion and tenure guidelines, though this is an unlikely scenario unless the national academic consciousness revalues the teacher's role in education and its administration. The natural place to start this revaluation is with students. The classroom is not the place to politicize faculty working conditions, but asking students what they value in an education, administrative bloat or innovative teaching, technology, and facilities is an ethical way to approach the topic. Education should be mindfully pursued and questioned. Kovalik believes that once students and parents are savvy to the system's failures and abuses that they will begin to more thoughtfully question the value of a university education. If he is right, then we are sinking our own ship, and even those who feel most insulated in the upper echelons of academe will eventually drown.

I've lived in the margins of academe for so long that I am conditioned to inhabit the space without too much adverse reaction. When I do stop to reflect on my experience, it's maddening. But I don't want to become embittered by years of unfair labor conditions and compensation. I want to keep doing what I love: teaching. So far I've maintained buoyancy because I've adopted an attitude of submission and survival (denial), but in doing so I've compromised professional integrity and quality of life. And sharing my thoughts openly and publicly may put me at risk for reprisal, but what is the alternative? Going quietly into that good night? No, all of us need to stop doing what adjuncts do all too well: glossing over the problem, remaining anonymous, waiting silently for last minute appointments and course cancellations, and pretending we're free agents of our universities when in reality we are all bait on a hook.

Like Vojtko, I keep waiting for the guillotine, knowing full well that my life could shatter any minute if I get ill or lose affiliate status. In many ways, I am the model puppet flitting between jobs habitually and efficiently, only pausing occasionally to imagine myself a full professor in an office with windows, working on my book or waiting for the soft knock of a shy student with paper in hand for conferencing. But then I remember I have multiple courses at multiple colleges to juggle for the 3rd consecutive academic quarter for years ongoing. I am a well-oiled work addict.

The reason I am sharing my adjunct narrative is simple: I want to help break the silence of contingency and complicity. I want equal opportunity to research, publish, and teach with job security and fair pay. I am sick of living in the margins of academe. And this is not a white-collar problem; my woes are real and widespread.

I wonder how much my voice matters, but I fear cowardice more. I trust sharing my story here because I trust *Hybrid Pedagogy's* unwavering and un-egotistical ethos. They have created a safe place to share openly and honestly, wherein I feel insulated and empowered to talk. I value their moxy and willingness to tip the elephant in the room, and if enough of us join the conversation, here and elsewhere, our chances are greater.

Fortunately, there is a growing body of academic colleagues advocating for change and pinning their names on the unpopular Problem of Contingency in Higher Education, including Joshua Boldt, William Pannapacker, Jennifer Ruth, Karen Kelsky, the editors here at *Hybrid Pedagogy*, and more. We can no longer justify silence, denial, or complicity in the problem of contingency; rather, we have to work together toward an equitable solution.

It's not too ironic that I turn to bell hooks, who in *Yearning* reminds us that "marginality [is] much more than a site of deprivation; in fact … it is also the site of radical possibility, a space of resistance … It offers to one the possibility of radical perspective from which to see and create, to imagine alternatives, new worlds." The new world I imagine is not radical but just; it is closer to the romantic ideal that I thought existed back when I was an undergraduate, before I realized that the corporatization of higher education has fundamentally flawed the idea of the university.

CHAPTER 18.

LIBRARIAN AS OUTSIDER

NORA ALMEIDA

Academic librarians are worried about power. And powerless-ness. They are particularly concerned with the way power dynamics shape their identities as educators and inform their pedagogical capacity.

Recent library scholarship has introduced a number of com-pelling arguments for pedagogical alternatives to what Freire calls the "banking concept of education," which conceives of stu-dents as passive "receptacles," teachers as "depositors," and knowledge as capital (*Pedagogy of the* Oppressed). If James Elm-borg's seminal 2006 article "Critical Information Literacy: Impli-cations for Instructional Practice" is any indication (it's been cited more than 250 times as I write this), the banking concept of education doesn't work for information literacy instruction. Elmborg begins his article with a problem and ends it with a challenge: "the real task for libraries in treating information lit-eracy seriously lies not in defining it or describing it, but in developing a critical practice of librarianship — a theoretically informed praxis." This is a daunting task, particularly consid-ering the logistical reality of information literacy instruction, which typically happens in 'one-shot' library sessions. While a "problem-posing" approach is difficult to achieve in the context of the one-shot, a critical approach is not just an alternative but an imperative.

Here's why.

The push towards critical information literacy instruction, which is related to the critical pedagogy movement at large, reflects the fact that an authoritarian pedagogical orientation does not promote dialog about the social or political dimensions of information or engender students with critical autonomy. However, there is another, more fundamental reason why a banking approach to information literacy fails in the context of the one-shot: in this paradigm the librarian is an outsider. In the banking model, student receptivity relies on a power exchange; students relinquish power in order to reap the rewards of educational success, and teachers, representing the academy, retain the power to define the parameters of what constitutes success. In a society where higher education is viewed as a means to a lifestyle or as Cathy Eisenhower and Dolsy Smith have it in "The Library as a 'Stuck Place'", "the bottom rung of the corporate ladder," educational success isn't about knowledge but about measurable indicators: grades, accolades, job offers. Academic librarians, without the power to bestow success indicators, reside in liminal space. And since librarians don't have access to the insider power dynamics upon which the banking model relies, their limited agency is granted only at the directive of the teacher unless they manage to fundamentally shift the nature of the educational exchange through "theoretically informed praxis."

This is not to say that there is no critical pedagogy outside of the library, or that no students believe that education has intrinsic value, or that all faculty are authoritarian just because they maintain, by virtue of their position in a classroom and disciplinary knowledge, authority (as Freire reminds us in his "Letter to North-American Teachers"). The liminal position of the librarian is — in a best case scenario — rather, situational. And this may stem from the fact that information literacy, as Joshua Beatty argues in his compelling analysis of Freire, authority, and library instruction, "is interdisciplinary, or transdisciplinary, or part of a larger metaliteracy [but is not itself] a discipline." And a liminality based on disciplinary otherness rather than authoritarian oppression may actually be a helpful critical frame for librarians to adopt.

Beatty argues that information literacy can only be learned "via the subject matter" of a discipline. As a result, information literacy instruction is necessarily situated in a disciplinary context but it can still operate outside of disciplinary rhetoric. This is important because students often struggle with academic discourse and librarians, as disciplinary outsiders armed with knowledge of rhetorical genre conventions and an understanding of the ways in which disciplinary discourse relates to information organization, can invite students to examine their own subject knowledge and critically reflect on disciplinary conventions. In doing so, librarians are not only helping students find an entry point into scholarship but are also promoting awareness of knowledge production cycles and the relationship between labor and information.

The View from the Margins

Many librarians view themselves as outsiders by virtue of their roles in the academy and, too often, this outsiderness is conflated with marginalization. This is not to say that librarians aren't ever marginalized, but that marginalism and outsiderness are distinct forces that inform our autonomous capacity and pedagogical orientation.

In "Why Information Literacy is Invisible", William Badke argues, "faculty do not generally see librarians as full academic colleagues and, thus, have little appreciation for librarians as instructors," which is likely why librarians devote so much time, per Eisenhower and Smith, to "convinc[ing] the powers that be of their value." However, from the perspective of this long-time adjunct classroom faculty turned librarian, the margins aren't so bad, and they aren't so marginal either. The large majority of faculty at most academic institutions are adjuncts and they could be our important allies in the margins (read: trenches). And if we work to form a camp for the disenfranchised and collectively acknowledge what Eisenhower and Smith call "the labor of scholarship and our relation to the infrastructure and systems that discipline it [and us]," then we have already begun a productive conversation about information literacy.

But the question remains: is this conversation possible to have?

The perception of the librarian as a marginalized figure in higher education rests on a cultural precept of higher education (and academic work) as impermeable and somehow distinct from the labor (and laborers) that are responsible for its existence and continuation. This perception is problematically one that many academics — disenfranchised and otherwise — accept and the fact of its illusoriness does not make it any less potent. Marginalization is also the product of real stigmatization caused by social stereotypes. While Nicole Pagowsky and Erica DeFrain argue in their article, "Ice Ice Baby: Are Librarian Stereotypes Freezing Us Out of Instruction?", that librarians can do their part to defy stereotypes and resist polarized "warm/female" and "cold/male" dichotomies, we can only do so much to change the expectations of society at large. In their article, "Not at Your Service: Building Genuine Faculty-Librarian Partnerships", Yvonne Meulemans and Allison Carr identify the corrosive effects of a legitimate "lack of understanding of how librarians can contribute to student learning" on the part of classroom faculty and illustrate that marginalization not only feels personal but has real implications for a librarian's professional efficacy.

However, Meulemans and Carr (and others) argue that we can *begin* to change oppressive systems through resistance and by fostering genuine partnerships with faculty and engaging in "quality, collaborative teaching." This necessarily has less to do with transforming our own sense of critical agency than it does with systemically addressing the capacity of students to understand how information works and provoking colleagues outside of the library to consider how information literacy is intimately connected to the disciplinary rhetoric with which they expect their students to engage. This also means becoming more comfortable with the fact that (perceived) pedagogical subversion in the form of critical instruction and genuine resistance might be met with anger or further marginalization.

To Eisenhower and Smith, who more drastically conceive of attempts to "enter discursive communities on campus ... as allies in the struggle against 'oppressive formations'" as efforts ultimately "subsumed in [their] Foucauldian way into numbers that scaffold the very discourse we critique," collaborative engagement can be self negating. They also question the critical capacity of the librarian who, unlike faculty, have not "built the intimate public" out of which dialogic dimensions of knowledge might surface. However, Eisenhower and Smith's view of the librarian as educator is not entirely nihilistic; Ian Beilin notes that these "librarians [in 'Stuck Places'] may be in a position from which to exercise a greater freedom of action vis-a-vis the pressures to conform, by virtue of their marginal or liminal position within the academy."

Laurent Wallis, in her blog post series, "Smash all the Gates", argues that librarians play a role in "perpetuating [their] own marginalization" when they "uphold the status quo" in their approach to instruction but also believes that real resistance outside of the classroom is necessary to assuage the impotence of a librarian who is "dehumanized" by teaching faculty. Wallis, who also recognizes "the [critical] power inherent in our insider/outsider position" in the classroom is driving an important wedge between marginalization and outsiderness here. Outsiderness is a badge. But marginalization is a closed door, the interaction that makes you feel at the end of the day like "human garbage," a silencing and diminishing force. Outsiderness, Wallis and Beatty reminds us, is more than simply the product of marginalization plus empowerment. It is, rather, baked into what academic librarianship is and it comes with both critical responsibility and privilege.

The Outsider Paradox

When we mistake outsiderness for marginalization this is problematic because marginalization is defeatist and precludes resistance. And resistance is at the core of critical information literacy instruction because, as Beilin argues:

> Critical librarianship is at pains always to show that the existing information system [and the academy in many senses] mirrors the larger social and political order, which is characterized by a radically asymmetrical distribution of power, and is shot through, systematically and structurally, by racism, sexism, homophobia, militarism, and class oppression.

And what librarian wouldn't want to be outside of that system?

Resistance is an act of political positioning but it's also a helpful pedagogical foothold because a lot of students feel disconnected and marginalized too. The trick is to recognize that authentic critical (and pedagogical) power comes from a place of otherness, from a positioning against. And this outsiderness is not the same thing as marginalization and is, in a pedagogical sense, an inherently privileged position. Librarians, Michelle Holschuh Simmons asserts:

> are simultaneously insiders and outsiders of the classroom and of the academic disciplines in which they specialize, placing them in a unique position that allows mediation between the non-academic discourse of entering undergraduates and the specialized discourse of the disciplinary faculty.

Librarians, because they understand the socio-political underpinnings of information, because they are rhetorically limber and disciplinarily agnostic, and because they authentically want students to gain critical literacy skills and agency, can and should serve as mediators. If they can negotiate the space to do so.

And here we find the paradox: that we must position ourselves as outsiders in our approach to pedagogy even as we resist marginalization as an oppressive force that detracts from our own agency. We must also recognize that there are others in our institutions who we count among our oppressors who are marginalized in more fundamental ways than we are: who are grossly undercompensated and who do not have the privilege of publicly reflecting on "asymmetrical distribution of powers," as I am now, because it is too risky.

When we resort to the banking concept and cling to whatever residual power might remain in a podium, when we fail to acknowledge the particular situation of outsiderness that we find ourselves, when we fail to employ "theoretically informed praxis" and bow to those fictive and vicious forces that malign us, we are failing to demonstrate an understanding that knowledge comes from a fraught, disorderly, and imperfect place.

What does critical information literacy look like in a classroom?

It looks, more often than not, like a conversation.

CHAPTER 19.

CONTINGENT MOTHER: THE ROLE GENDER PLAYS IN THE LIVES OF ADJUNCT FACULTY

MARGARET BETZ

I am a mother. I am also a PhD in philosophy. And, finally, I am a contingent college professor at two universities. I am an example of how being a mother in that environment significantly affects a woman's academic career. In addition to the struggles faced by the average contingent faculty member, contingent teaching is for many women the only viable employment option in the academic world. Indeed, motherhood alone may be a significant reason why women end up in the non-tenure track as parenthood unequally affects female academics. Many have found the academic setting is entirely inhospitable to mothers. Fellow academic Miriam Peskowitz, for example, argues women who are mothers often carousel in and out of work and, for that reason, motherhood may funnel qualified female PhDs into the exploitative world of contingent academic positions.

One myth associated with those of us in the non-tenured world is that there must be something wrong with us, something "defective" — either we are too lazy, unmotivated, unambitious or just not qualified for one of the "many" tenure track jobs offered each year. In an effort to help personally dispel that myth,

I would like to mention that I have published a book, written both academic and non-academic articles, do at least four book reviews a year, present papers at conferences, develop new courses, teach three to four courses a semester, volunteer at my university — all while raising my two sons without the use of outside childcare. Hiding behind this "defective" myth, institutional power structures take the scrutiny off of why the academic system maintains so many part-timers and the way it might be culpable for that exploitive reality. In addition, most colleges and universities only benefit from the fact that many of the students before me have never heard of "adjunct professors." Our visible invisibility means universities sit in the comfortable position of never having to justify to parents the ever-increasing cost of a college tuition coupled with the reality that many of their children's professors may be making as little as $16,000 a year.

So how and why did I enter and remain in contingent teaching? I saw no other viable route. At thirty-three, less than a year after I finished my PhD, I became a mother. Little did I know at the time, but I was making decisions that put me on a more difficult path in the academic world. At the time, I thought I was making responsible decisions: my husband and I purposely waited until after I had finished my degree to begin our family. As a graduate student, I witnessed first hand the overwhelming struggle of a woman newly hired into a tenure-track job in my graduate department. Simply put, she failed miserably; mostly, I would surmise, because she was the mother of very young children, or, as Judith Sanders has put it, because of the fact that the academic model remains one of "men-with-wives." The department simply expected a higher level of output from a woman teaching full-time, finishing her dissertation, and trying to be a mother. She regularly revealed to me how frantic her life was and that she rarely slept or spent time with her children; yet, she was later let go. I made the deliberate decision not to repeat her mistakes. Because of this, once my own child was born, I stayed within the part-time circuit. In their article "Nontraditional Academics," Susan Bassow, Dana Campbell and Liz Stock-well write, "the tenure process is so rigorous and time consuming that many opt out of this path to pursue career alternatives that are more amenable to spending time with family" (179). As a result women like me become caught in a Mommy Crunch: as long as the university upholds the "men-with-wives" idealized academic, women academics who are mothers become caught in a bind that facilitates a secondary status as contingent faculty.

Contingent faculty are vital yet invisible in the contemporary university. Michelle Kern reports on the finding by the AAUP that in 2005, 48% of faculty were part-time. In an article on the "Abysmal State of Adjunct Teacher Pay," Jeff Nall estimates that non-tenured, part-time instructors comprise almost 70% of contemporary faculty. Data from the U.S. Department of Education shows 1.3 million of the 1.8 million faculty providing instruction are non-tenure track. This vital role, however, is not adequately rewarded. Despite often teaching the same exact courses as tenure-track professors, part-timers' pay and benefits are grossly unequal. Nall reports that the average salary for a tenure-track academic today is just under $66,000. In June 2012, The Coalition on the Academic Workforce (CAW) released a report which found that adjuncts were paid on average for a standard 3 credit college course $2700 in the fall of 2010. In Florida at community colleges, for example, it can be under $2000 per course. This would mean, Nall points out, that teaching 8 classes a year would yield a mere $16,000 income. A minimum wage worker makes a little over $15,000 a year.

The result of this overuse and underpayment of adjuncts on college campuses across the country has been that an unexpected sect of workers is growing in the U.S. — impoverished graduate degree holders. An ABC News report by Susanna Kim found in May 2012 that the number of people possessing a PhD who received some sort of public assistance increased three-fold between 2007 and 2010. As Nall notes, universities help perpetuate this reality by staying willfully ignorant through administrators choosing to refer to adjunct teaching as some sort of "side gig" instead of what it really is: the means through which most are making their living. Just as with the "defective" myth, the "side gig" trope allows universities to perpetuate a system that exploits contingent academics by willfully ignoring the reality of the situation in favor of protecting the status quo. In my own experience, I've never met a fellow adjunct who fit this "side gig" description. I know of one contingent academic who strung together enough "side gigs" per semester (ten to be exact) that he was able to afford to buy a home. Of course, he spent more time in his car than his new house as he raced between four different colleges to teach.

Contemporary literature confirms my anecdotal experience with the young mother hired then fired by my graduate department. Miriam Peskowitz bemoaned the sorry state of Higher Ed in 2008, discussing how poorly she was treated as a freshly tenured professor when she learned she was pregnant and turned to her university expecting a more supportive response. She argues in the forward to *Mama, PhD: Women Write About Motherhood and Academic Life*:

> For years the academy has been experiencing a brain drain of women — women who are highly skilled and who are expensively trained, and whom our society needs not to lose. We also have witnessed the well-documented personal challenges that mother-professors face — the incredible and extraordinary and overwhelming exhaustion of doing their academic jobs with children, in an academic culture that doesn't recognize how much labor is entailed in either.

Peskowitz writes of taking a leave of absence (because her university did not have a maternity leave policy) and the injustice of an academic system working against mothers. In the end, she left her academic job after finding the combination of mother and rigorous academic unsustainable and eventually moved into adjunct teaching for a while before turning into a full-time author, penning the successful *Truth Behind the Mommy Wars*.

Peskowitz said in an interview with Mothers Movement Online, "I loved being with my daughter. I was thrilled by my new life as a mother. And I couldn't believe the social price I was being asked to pay to incorporate her into my life."

Likewise, the editors of the book *Mama PhD*, Elrena Evans and Caroline Grant, report:

> Academic life is predominantly a man's world. Women remain on the periphery, and children are all but absent. American universities consistently publish glowing reports stating their commitment to diversity, often showing statistics of female hires as proof of success, but the facts remain: university women make up disproportionately large numbers of temporary (adjunct and non-tenure track) faculty, while the majority of permanent, tenure-track positions are granted to men... The disproportion between male and female university faculty, as in other work forces, is most striking among those who choose to be both professors and parents.

Evans and Grant's overriding point is that it is obvious why newly minted female PhDs are funneled into the non-tenure track world if children are at all involved. As the system is currently arranged to favor the "men-with-wives" academic model, something has got to give in this picture for mothers. As Evans and Grant state, "With no easy solutions for the struggles they encounter, women take a variety of different approaches as they attempt to reconcile family and academy. None of these solutions is perfect." In my own case, avoiding the nation-wide job search in favor of maintaining more flexible contingent positions at area universities became my "solution." Evans and Grant point out that, typically, instead of decisions like mine implying an indictment of the system, it is instead viewed by others as a personal failure (the above "defective" myth). Peskowitz suggests the true subject of our righteous anger should be business, governmental, and education leaders shaping today's workplace, not the women struggling in the workplace because they are unsupported after having children.

In an article entitled "Do Babies Matter?", Mary Ann Mason

and Marc Goulden report that women who have at least one child within five years post-doctorate are significantly less likely to achieve tenure than men who have children early in their career. In my own experience, at one university where I teach, there are ten full-time professors: six are men, four are women, and only one of these women has children, and they are grown. In 2001 Robert Drago and Joan Williams conducted a study they called The Faculty and Families Project and found that because women are still considered the primary caregivers in our society, the ideal academic favored in the university setting is therefore discriminatory towards women. Drago and Williams conclude succinctly, "American women, who still do the vast majority of childcare, will not achieve equality in academia as long as the ideal academic is defined as someone who takes no time off for child-rearing."

What solutions are there if any? Few exist, but those that do could help improve things. It is likely the shared conclusion of those doing contingent teaching that it drastically demands changes that restore the dignity and respect we as contingent faculty deserve. More than once, I've had to swallow hard as a full-time colleague has unconsciously made me feel like an outsider, an amateur, a failure, or just plain invisible. One part-time colleague once told me that after having taught Composition at a university for over ten years, the Chair of the department admitted she "forgot" about my friend when assigning courses for the next term. Perhaps the first step is making students more aware of the academic caste system that is often actively hidden from them, making the invisible visible, as Joseph Fruscione suggests. Another would be to demand the system look to increase full-time teaching positions instead of exploitive part-time ones.

Regarding mothers in particular, this problem represents the classic "having-it-all" difficulty all working mothers experience in the American workplace. Ample writing has already suggested that better support must be given to women who are mothers to end what essentially becomes one more expression of gender discrimination. As that relates to the academic world specifically, more than once while researching for this article, I witnessed criticism of what's referred to as the "free floating head syndrome," or the common failure to recognize academic instructors as real people with outside lives and responsibilities. An authentic attempt to combat this would involve sincerely valuing the contribution of women academics who become mothers.

If tenure track is bad for mothers, contingency as currently configured (although it offers more flexibility) is hardly a satisfactory solution, given the significant lack of leaves of absence, health benefits, and a living wage. One actual solution might be what Judith Sanders refers to as "dignified part-time positions," not exploitive adjunct ones that, as she says, pay Walmart wages. Sanders, in her chapter in *Mama PhD*, also calls for more flexible career paths, or a "willingness to allow people to proceed in the profession even if they have taken time away from it." And finally, perhaps most obviously, we in the academic world need to change our perception regarding parenthood and see it as a dignified and worthwhile choice for an educated person.

PART IV.

PEDAGOGICAL ALTERITY

"The story of identity in a learning space can't be told by one person, or even seven people, but only by a cacophony of voices, a gathering together — of sounds, of ideas, of pedagogical intentions."
~ Jesse Stommel and Sean Michael Morris, "CFP: Pedagogical Alterity: Stories of Race, Gender, Disability, Sexuality"

CHAPTER 20.

MAKING DISABILITY PART OF THE CONVERSATION: COMBATTING INACCESSIBLE SPACES AND LOGICS

RICHARD H. GODDEN AND ANNE-MARIE WOMACK

In a string of recent education articles, researchers have praised the benefits of hand-written notes and instructors have forbidden computers from classrooms. Frustrated with her student's technological fixation, Associate Professor Carol E. Holstead reports, "I told students they would have to take notes on paper. Period." In such a learning environment, Anne-Marie, who can't listen without pen in hand, would thrive. Rick, though, who relies on various technologies to supplement or replace handwriting, would struggle.

Holstead's preference for handwriting over technology is part of a recent trend to ban laptops in the classroom advocated by critics such as Hinda Mandell, Dan Rockmore, and Anne Curzan. Recently, National Public Radio's James Doubek even picked up the story, reporting that "there are still advantages to doing things the old-fashioned way." All describe common problems: student distraction and their reluctance to process information, perhaps the defining pedagogical concerns of the 21st century. As educators race to address these problems, though, disability has been noticeably absent from the debate.

This debate is about more than the best way to take notes. It is about the assumptions instructors make about students. It is about the narratives educators construct about learning. All too often, underlying discussions of appropriate student behavior and traditional best practices are narrow visions of students' abilities and classroom praxis. Seeing a study body as an undifferentiated group leads to strict rules and single solutions.

While many supporters of no-tech accommodate disabled students who present the required paperwork, for instance, they still cite handwriting as best practice. *Are people with disabilities, then, doomed to substandard learning? Can any pedagogy be sound if it doesn't fully incorporate people with disabilities?*

Planning for Disability

Jay Dolmage is frequently quoted for his observation in "Disability and the Teaching of Writing" that "too often we react to diversity instead of planning for it" (21). What would it look like to integrate disability into the screen debate, into pedagogical understandings of the classroom space and writing technologies?

Many students cannot handwrite notes and rely on assistive technology, so in no-laptop spaces they would need an accommodation. These might include giving the student copies of the teachers' notes, providing the student with a peer note-taker, or allowing the student to use assistive technology in class. With the first two, if the student is still denied a screen, then the student may end up with a set of notes, but during class will be denied the ability to record their own thoughts, to communicate ideas. The end product of the communication, the notes, would counterintuitively trump the ability to communicate, to write in whatever form that takes.

If an instructor honors official accommodation requests and lets the student be the exception with a screen, it forces students to out themselves as a person with a disability, which can come with considerable stigma. Ramona Paetzold et al. studied students' perceptions of people with disabilities — specifically individuals granted longer test time — and found that "granting an accommodation was seen as less fair than not granting one" (27). With that kind of social pressure, it is unsurprising that many students don't report, and as a result, instructors then think they don't have many disabled students and don't need to plan for their inclusion. Exclusive policies could deter students from taking the course from the outset.

The issue of screens, though, does not only affect those denied them. Students with Attention Deficit Disorder and Obsessive Compulsive Disorder might find the distractions of a large lecture space difficult to overcome, and these distractions are likely increased by the screens of fellow students. So what's the answer?

There is no *one* answer even within one classroom. In contrast to singular best practices such as a universal ban on screens in classrooms, disability studies promotes multi-modal options and flexible design. When information and tasks are presented across multiple modes, it opens choices for users about how best to access that information. So, a lecture video would contain captions as well as verbal descriptions of any visual information, such as a graph. This seemingly basic principle is far from simple, though, because, as the notes debate shows, our tendency is often to choose the "best" mode *for* students. This foreclosure of choice is investigated in Yergeau et al.'s webtext "Multimodalilty in Motion." Six disability scholars demonstrate the many ways that digital space, which is often assumed to be accessible, excludes disabled readers, and they advocate for creating more choices. Individual users are better equipped to make decisions about their own abilities than authoritative requirements, and so we return to the choice lying with students.

Building Inaccessible Spaces

It is not lost on us that our experiences with small writing-intensive classes are markedly different than those of instructors with hundreds of students in lecture halls. These spaces, themselves, maximize numbers and to do so make big assumptions about the kind of people who work within those spaces: the ability to climb stairs, see and hear across long distances, maintain focus amidst large crowds, stay awake in a room darkened for a presentation, etc. These spaces, which seemingly make information more accessible to ever greater numbers, make it less accessible to many, many individual students.

Instructors, too, note their drawbacks. These spaces make students feel anonymous and hidden enough to spend the class checking social media or texting friends. That's what the screen ban policies are supposed to help. But this approach takes an inaccessible space and makes it less accessible. It follows the same logic of the underlying classroom architecture by assuming students are the same and by treating them in one limiting way instead of in multiple and flexible ways. It does not question the limits of the pedagogical and institutional setting, but rather "solves" the problem by further feeding into it.

These kinds of rules envision a learning environment in which any student can be dropped in and function well without an instructor having to negotiate space, skills, or learning with those individual students. Disability scholar Stephanie Kerschbaum notes that "access will always require the hard work of negotiating among all members of a classroom community, and teachers cannot know, predict, or assume who those members will be nor what moves will be needed." Spaces like large lecture halls often lock teachers into inaccessible pedagogy but could more productively lead us to push back, to hack these spaces, to cooperate with students to make them more accessible. This will inevitably look different for different populations.

Building Inaccessible Ideologies

When new social science experiments demonstrate that a majority of participants do well with a particular learning tool, instructors may feel pedagogically justified in requiring that method.

However, mandating a universal use of tools does not plan for diversity in the classroom but rather treats it as an afterthought. There are several normalizing leaps involved in moving from "65% of students succeed with this tool" to "All students must use this tool to succeed."

Certainly instructors don't mean to suggest that the disabled are doomed to inferior educations. That is the implication, though, when students cannot implement the quickly hardening conventional wisdom that handwritten notes (or the next throwback to no tech) are superior.

The ideologies underlying many of our traditional spaces and traditional practices often fail to take disability into account. As uniquely disabled instructors teaching a population of uniquely disabled and abled students, we offer not one answer, but rather a way of thinking about the problem — one that focuses on disability and accessibility, one that looks outside traditional ableist logic to make classes more accessible to all students.

By making disability a part of the conversation — or perhaps, more pointedly, by acknowledging that it is always an integral part of any conversation about learning and pedagogy whether we explicitly acknowledge it or not — we encourage instructors to evaluate classroom spaces and pedagogical practices for accessibility. Do your practices privilege one sort of body-mind over another? Would contingency plans for accommodation be better integrated into teaching methods as a choice rather than an exception? Identifying the potentially ableist logic of our pedagogies is only the first step, however. Designing inclusive learning spaces is a process, one that must be reevaluated on a continual basis, and one where our students need to be invited into, rather than be treated as the recipients of, "best practice" authoritative models of teaching practice.

CHAPTER 21.

AMPLIFYING INDIGENOUS VOICES

SUE RENES

It is not too hard to recognize that educational institutions, to a large degree, determine the process of engagement with learning and engagement with the learners. It should come as no surprise that unrepresented students might be tentative about actively participating in this process when their previous experiences with other schools or other social institutions might not have been positive. What underrepresented students are often asked to do, whether it is recognized or not, is leave their true identities — their true voices — at the door. According to Joe Kincheloe, "anytime teachers develop a pedagogy, they are concurrently constructing a political vision. The two acts are inseparable" (*Knowledge and Critical Pedagogy: An Introduction*). As institutions and teachers, the way we set up our classrooms either makes space for students or ignores their identities.

In "How to Build an Ethical Online Course," Jesse Stommel says teachers need to be cognizant of the physical space(s) and the virtual spaces(s) the teacher and the students will occupy and also create pathways between what happens in the various physical spaces and what happens on the web, either with each other or by ourselves. To that I would add that teachers need to create pathways among students' "voices" (students' cultures, backgrounds. and experiences) to enhance the learning environment even further. Hybrid learning should not only involve combining the physical classroom with the web and other environments outside the classroom, but also combine western viewpoints, experiences, and ways of learning with those students who are often asked to leave these attributes at the door.

After spending several days with Indigenous scholars from the United States, Canada, New Zealand, and Australia, Alaska Native students who were part of a three year Alaska Native Teacher Preparation Program (ANTPP) gathered with the faculty from University of Alaska Fairbanks (UAF) School of Education and the University provost in 2011 to share their experiences. One Alaska Native student stated, "This world of higher education: it's a whole new animal for us, and it is not a friendly one." A doctoral student shared, "I have to give up being Native in school, and at the end of the day it is exhausting." The Provost approached the ANTPP Project staff after the presentation to ask if she could meet with Project participants to discuss some of the issues raised at the international gathering. Project participants, staff, partners, and evaluators engaged in a candid conversation with the Provost the following day where she committed to tracking down data on Alaska Native retention and completion of teacher education programs at UAF in order to determine the extent of the issues facing Alaska Native students in the School of Education. The comments from the Alaska Native students prompted me and others to ask, "Are our underrepresented students dropping out of our colleges and universities, or are they being driven away?" and "How do critical digital pedagogues use the 'environment' to amplify Indigenous voices and the voices of other underrepresented students to achieve a more inclusive learning classroom?" As teachers, the way we set up our classrooms either makes space for students or continues to ask them to leave their identities at the door. This is a political act; one we will make whether we realize it or not.

Believing that the higher education system has for centuries marginalized Indigenous cultures and peoples, Ilarion Merculieff, an Aleut elder from the Bering Sea's Pribilof Islands, and Libby Roderick, a white professor from the University of Alaska Anchorage, jointly directed the Alaska Native Ways of Teaching and Learning project with faculty from the University of Alaska Anchorage. Alaska Native people from across the state spent a week with non-Native faculty to introduce the difficult dialogues of science and racism and help non-Native faculty learn in a setting profoundly different from their western experiences. In the introduction of their book *Stop Talking* that resulted from the project, Merculieff and Roderick write, "Before we could meet in a place of mutual respect and understanding, the privileged voice of academia [had] to yield some ground to Indigenous voices that have long been silenced or ignored." There are numerous Indigenous voices waiting to be heard.

Indigenous peoples are typically thought of as the first people to occupy a land, and they have a strong connection to a land base and the environment. Indigenous people have their own forms of language, their own laws, and their own cultures. A shared aspect among Indigenous peoples is a shared experience of this connection to the land and the experience of colonization. Historic and contemporary forms of colonization bring Indigenous peoples together whether in Canada, Norway, New Zealand, Australia, Hawaii, Alaska, or other parts of the United States. Q'um Q'um Xiiem (Dr. Jo-ann Archibald), a member of the Stó:lō First Nations in Canada, is Associate Dean for Indigenous Education and Professor of Educational Studies at the University of British Columbia. Her book *Indigenous Storywork: Educating the Heart, Mind, Body, and Spirit* uses the metaphor of Indigenous basket weaving to introduce readers to Indigenous ways of understanding knowledge. Q'um Q'um Xiiem suggests such questions as "Who is indigenous?" and "What is indigenous knowledge?" are important questions to answer to create a place of mutual respect and understanding. To understand Indigenous knowledge requires looking at the nature of knowledge, the sources of this knowledge, the ways Indigenous people come to know this knowledge, and the ways the knowledge is passed on to others. Indigenous knowledge can be a guide to help us learn and teach and understand that our interactions with others are a continual process of learning through shared experience. Q'um Q'um Xiiem describes how student retention following her Indigenous tradition would center on seeing new students as extended members of the University family. Seeing students in this manner could better guide us in determining how best to help students succeed. Q'um Q'um Xiiem suggests, "Let it be okay to have an Indigenous heart and mind."

At the 2014 Alaska Native Studies Conference in Juneau, Two Tlingit elders, Ḵaayastaan Marie Olson, and Kingeistí David Katzeek shared their views of education and describe how they actively work to ensure Indigenous voices are heard in the classroom and ensure Indigenous languages are not lost, especially in the academic setting. Ḵaayastaan Marie Olson says, "My language is my intellectual property and no one can take my intellectual property." As Ḵaayastaan Marie Olson's pupil, University of Alaska professor Lance Twitchell often says, "We are not looking to save our languages; we are looking to our languages to save us." Ḵaayastaan Marie Olson was born in Juneau and in her earlier years spoke only Tlingit. She is a member of the Wooshkeetaan (People of the Houses Facing Each Other) Eagle clan of Áak'w Kwáan and her Tlingit name, Ḵaayastaan, was the name of her maternal grandmother. She graduated from the University of Alaska Southeast and currently works to preserve the Tlingit language, culture, and history.

Shangukeidi Clan Leader Kingeistí David Katzeek began his talk at the conference by putting a can of the soda Dr. Pepper on the podium and stating that his only Ph.D. is Dr. Pepper, a fact he is proud to claim, as he introduced the beverage to Southeast Alaska. Traditional Indigenous scholars, such as Kingeistí David Katzeek, are elders who are given the same recognition in their communities as Ph.D.s are given in the academic setting. By saying his only acknowledged Ph.D. in the western world is Dr. Pepper, he was interjecting humor into the beginning of his talk. Kingeistí David Katzeek told the story of "Eating from each other's mouths" as an essential part of their learning process. He spoke on the traditional Tlingit Educational System, and how it used stories to teach about weaving baskets, making Chilkat Robes and canoes, as well as impart knowledge on salmon, biology, hydrology, and other disciplines. Tlingit people have lived in Southeast Alaska for 10,000 years or more, and their traditional educational system is built on four primary pillars/corner posts based on the foundation of respect: (1) Lingít áwé wa.é. Kaa x'éide kukg_ees.áax. (You are a human being. You are to listen.); (2) Lingít áwé wa.é. Yaa keedzigéi. (You are a human being. You are Intelligent.); (3) Lingít áwé wa.é. Yáa at yakg_eenéi. (You are a human being. You will respect all things.); and (4) Lingít áwé wa.é. Wóoch.een yéi jigaxyeenéi. (You are a human being. You are to work together.)

In their statement, "Teachers should not be the gatekeepers for student voices, and once we suppose we are, we miss half the conversation" ("Listening for Student Voices"), Chris Friend and Sean Michael Morris echo the voices of Merculieff, Roderick, Q'um Q'um Xiiem, Kaayastaan Marie Olsen, and Kingeistí David Katzeek. Chernik's description of ethical hospitality supports the amplification of Indigenous voices, as it supports welcoming those who have not previously been welcomed and doing so unapologetically. In doing so, ethical hospitality aids in transforming the higher ed. classroom to a more inclusive learning environment. Diversity of thought and experience does not hinder a learning community; the learning community actually benefits from the variety of experiences of its members, making it a more supportive learning environment to women and minorities. There are approximately 60,500 residents among 150 small communities in Alaska's remote, rural villages, many with no roads or highways connecting the villages to Alaska's more populated areas. The rural villages are often accessible only by water or air. Many students from these communities thirst for education from the the state universities but often do not find the environment one where they can claim a comfortable space. We must waste no time in adding this to our list of what constitutes hybrid learning, for every day we do not practice this, we lose valuable, vital, and engaging knowledge.

The top of my syllabus reads:

> When groups of people who share a social and cultural context work together to learn, a culture or community of learning develops with everyone's participation supporting a collective effort to learn something new. The shared objective, combined with the diversity of expertise offered by each member of the group and sharing what is learned while learning how to learn, all play a significant role in a learning community.

The specific actions I take in the classroom include decreasing teacher power and increasing student voice, asking for both academic and personal reflection, and asking for participation in open dialogue to share these academic and personal reflections. My hope is that these actions in the classroom lead to action taken outside the classroom once class is over and the semester is done. To me, this is simply education at its best.

CHAPTER 22.

FINDING MY VOICE AS A MINORITY TEACHER

CHRIS FRIEND

As a high-school teacher, I kept quiet about my sexuality because I didn't want to draw attention to it. Instead, I created a deafening silence, a vacuum that tugged on everything around it and demanded attention by its absence. I was silent because I *thought* my sexuality shouldn't matter. I was also silent because I live in a state that has no protection against termination of employment due to sexual orientation. It's not called "discrimination" here; it's an employer's prerogative. Because a few administrators at the school where I taught were Good Ol' Boys, I was afraid. I was afraid that, as a new teacher, my sexuality would become an issue, a liability, or a pretense for joblessness. I was afraid the school's small surrounding community, transitioning from rural to suburban and demographically divided by which church everyone went to, would question my fitness as one who works with children to get them to think bigger thoughts and question the status quo. I imagined protests to the principal. I imagined parents saying awful things about the person teaching their children. Being two years younger than Matthew Shepard, I imagined suffering a fate similar to his. The county where I worked had a history of acceptance and inclusion that was tarnished at best.

So I silenced myself. As an introvert, that came naturally. I didn't tell students about my home life. I never mentioned my boyfriend as anything other than a friend. I placed no adorable photos on my desk and never shared my personal life with my students.

Curious, that phrase: "personal life". It suggests that there's only a portion of our lives that is ours, and the rest belongs to someone or something else. Perhaps our jobs dictate what happens in our "work life", but who's actually doing the living then? Isn't that life still personal?

While I taught high school, I sure wasn't living a personal life. I cared about my students. I connected with them. I listened to them. I supported them, and they confided in me. But the olive branch I offered the outcasts was extended with timidity: I merely co–sponsored the school's gay-straight alliance, letting a straight peer's name appear in any publicity because I didn't want my name associated with it. It met in my classroom, but the announcements that played on campus used my peer's room number from across the hall.

I know now that the only one I was hiding anything from was myself — students on campus had already figured out I was gay. They saw through my denial and avoidance, turning my efforts into a highlighter, pointing out exactly what I didn't want them to see. As a result, I was blindly broadcasting an aura of fear, of unacceptance, through the very efforts that were intended to accept and support the students. Students who were like me, who needed support and acknowledgement in a potentially hostile environment. It's not that the campus was violent. Kids at that school didn't get beat up for being gay. But the only time sexuality was discussed by anyone was for derisive or offensive purposes. And because I never brought up my sexuality on campus, I continued the discrimination. By hiding, I not only expressed my fear but also directly contributed to the problem I wanted, in my own feeble way, to provide relief from. I wanted students to feel safe in my classroom. Instead, I showed them that even I was not.

I had to miss work for a day; I forget why. But I knew in advance, so I was able to plan ahead and choose the substitute I wanted to take over my classes. My then-boyfriend happened to be registered as a sub, and he happened to be available that day. He knew how I worked, he heard me talk through my classroom policies, and he heard me complain about problematic situations and challenging students. He knew how my classes ran better than anyone else. Picking him as my stand-in was a no-brainer.

He subbed for me for one day. Days after I returned, several students asked if he was my brother. They commented on how we spoke alike, how we shared mannerisms, how it was almost like I was still in the classroom despite being gone. Those weren't the only similarities he and I considered before my absence. This particular substitute and I had to make sure he wore a tie to class that I had never, and would never, choose to wear myself, thus revealing our domestic connection. To the students, the substitution was a combination of eerie and amusing. But it worked. They did what they needed to do, and my class continued without missing a beat. By all accounts, the day went smoothly for everyone. And by all accounts, when the day was over, the substitute locked the classroom door before he left.

We're pretty sure the vandals didn't have a key. But they got in somehow. By the time the custodian got around to my room, it had already been trashed. Instead of cleaning any of it up, he wisely left it exactly as it was, knowing it was a situation that other people needed to see. That mess greeted me (with a student in tow for extra help before classes started) the next morning when I unlocked the classroom door and entered.

I don't have a photograph of the whiteboard because my immediate reaction — to get rid of what I saw — kicked in before I realized the scene was worth documenting. But scrawled across the three adjoining boards in the front of the room, in huge lettering written with black marker was something along the lines of "FRIEND IS A FAGGOT." It was probably a little less polite than that, but I don't recall the exact wording. As I looked elsewhere around my classroom, those words blurred into an overall scene of disorganization.

I want to say it was a scene of "destruction", although nothing had been physically broken. The neat, clean, organized arrangement of desks, tools, and supplies got destroyed, and it took my confidence and sense of control right along with it. So while it's accurate to say the scene was disorganized, I felt suddenly destroyed.

The contents of my desk had been strewn across the classroom floor, creating an atmosphere of post-tornado disaster in the room. That left room for the vandals to use a dry-erase marker to write threatening, obscene messages on its surface: "Mr. Friend is a fucking fag who deserves to fucking die!"

I somehow managed to teach that day. I don't remember what I thought we were working on, but I went through the motions. That still amazes me. What now infuriates me is this: I maintained my policy of silence, distance, and separation. I didn't explain what had happened, what it did to me, why I was so shaken by it, or why it happened in that community. The only unmistakable sign of trouble was the pile of disheveled papers I had collected on one side of the room during first-period plan; I told those who asked about it that my room had been vandalized, but I omitted the details about why or the messages I had found.

My silence had persisted all the way until third period (a whole hour!), when I decided to use the overhead projector. Earlier that morning, I had removed all the threatening language from the projector's surface so that I could use the machine as intended. I never thought to check the screen, which had stayed retracted into its housing. I pulled it down to use it, with a full class of students watching. Rather than a blank, white surface, the screen was filled with another message left in marker: "Kill the gays!! Dicks are for chicks!"

I immediately rolled the screen back up and used the whiteboard instead, apologizing for the glare. *The glare.* I acted as though the writing — the actual problem that was hurting me and disrupting my ability to function and feel safe — wasn't there. Of all the "teachable moments" I've encountered in my career, this was probably the one moment that most needed to be taught. Yet it was the one moment I tried hardest to cover up because I was uncomfortable with being gay at my own school, with being who I was while at work. I wasn't ready to stand up for myself because I believed speaking up risked more damage than remaining silent. I didn't want to stand out as "the gay teacher", but my attempts to silently hide drew just as much attention. It seems I needed that teachable moment more than my students did.

Well, more than most of them. One student, upon seeing the writing on the screen, started laughing. I gave him the fiercest look of death I could manage, but my voice wasn't able to cooperate at that moment. I was angry, embarrassed, and choked up, effectively mute.

Another student took up my cause and told the laughing student that his actions were inappropriate, etc. I don't recall exactly what she said or how the conversation proceeded, but I recall how much I immediately loved the student who spoke up, saying what I was physically unable to say. The one student who gave voice to the problem and who openly admitted that something was wrong. The student who drew attention to a problem while her teacher was too shocked, unwilling, and frankly terrified to draw any more attention to the issue. I admired her courage in speaking up on my behalf.

———————

I've spent time — on *Hybrid Pedagogy*, on my personal blog, and in conference presentations — talking about the opportunity for and benefits of bringing the outside world inside the classroom walls using online technology. I believe a hybrid approach to education helps open the door to learning that matters in the world outside school. Looking back on that vandalism, I've started to see that the "outside world" also includes the personal. Pretending my personal life and my educational practice can be separated denies the validity and relevance of both. I am a gay man who teaches; I am a teacher who is gay. I cannot be only one of those things, and I cannot expect my students to interact with only one of them, either.

Those of us in this invisible minority have an obligation to speak out, most especially as teachers. I'm not talking about any "agenda" or political assertion. I'm talking about identification. We must make our existence less invisible and less silent. Not only will greater visibility help students who might be in less-accepting environments feel a connection with others, but the visibility will also speak directly to those in the majority, letting them know we exist and showing that we are not afraid to be heard.

I now believe the exact opposite of what I did when I started teaching in that high school. I want to draw attention to sexuality, to make it matter, to end the silence. My sexuality is not a liability, and it should not be a reason to sack me (though my local laws still offer no protection). Instead, my sexuality offers perspective and experience, both of which I can only give my students when they're first aware I possess them. To teach as myself, I must let my students see who I am. I must use my voice and end the silence. We all must stop hiding, stop perpetuating the shame, and stop pretending sexuality is a non-issue. We all must find our voices.

So let me re-live that day. Let me stop my routine and talk to my students. Let me come out to my classes. Let me show that I can shake with combined anger and embarrassment. That I can shed tears from being overwhelmed and caught off-guard. Let me point to the vandalism and say that I live in a society that allowed such an act to happen, that allowed the perpetrators to go unidentified, and that trapped me into being silent. With this article, I am ending that silence and committing to use my own voice. I will use it to speak up on behalf of those caught without the ability to speak for themselves. I will use my voice to speak more loudly when others hope for silence. And rather than hoping the problem of discrimination will simply go away, I will give my voice to the problem and say that the problem is both very real and very destructive. Because no matter how loud the silence may have felt, using my voice makes me louder.

CHAPTER 23.

CORRECTIONAL PEDAGOGY: PRISON REFORM AND LIFE-OR-DEATH LEARNING

JOSEPH STOMMEL

Education cannot just be filling an empty brain, but must be as Paulo Freire says in *Pedagogy of the Oppressed*, "the means by which men and women deal critically and creatively with reality and discover how to participate in the transformation of their world." Learning in prison is about the future that is at stake and the society at large. Prison rehabilitation should be based on process not content — should be focused on learning to make good moral decisions in a variety of situations and not a single dogmatic code of right behavior in our society. This must mean making prisons places of rehabilitation not *imprisoning*. The programs described in this piece may reside within prisons, but any of them can (and do) reside also within communities, both residential and non-residential. Over many years working in corrections, I have found that rehabilitation is at odds with the aims of contemporary prisons.

A pedagogy of rehabilitation is a life-or-death pedagogy. If even one inmate becomes a responsible, contributing member of society, there is a potential reduction of hundreds of new crimes and their potential victims. To the offender this means a life of integrity, new and positive relationships, a sense of peace and belonging, and a new self-efficacy. If the offender does not change, then it could be death on the streets, death in addiction or overdose, or a long slow death by the revolving door in and out of prison.

We need more nuanced, less polarizing, perspectives on prisoner learning. There are experts on the one hand who believe criminals can never change, and those on the other who believe a quick and easy solution is available, a conversion or instantaneous rebirth. A belief in quick solutions feeds the criminal mentality that makes the mere appearance of "going straight" the most valued outcome. I've heard this quick-solution thinking — "if only I stayed off the booze, or stop dealing drugs, I could live a good life and avoid re-incarceration" — many times from prisoners themselves, their jailers, and so-called rehabilitation experts. I've worked for decades as a provider, developer, and administrator of prison programs. Substance addiction is often underestimated as a whole-person condition, and it is just as often used as a black hole to sink our blames and fears inside.

Many believe criminals never actually change, even after many years of responsible action and living. A single offense from one former inmate can confirm the cynical view that "old habits never die" or "a leopard never loses its spots," which I've heard from corrections executives and program administrators alike. What is worse is that this feeds a lurking despair and demoralization in the minds of the offender, that confirms "I can never change" because "I have failed too many times." I have seen suicides committed over this pervasive belief. One man named Patrick completed treatment as a role model and leader in two of my programs, one in prison and one on parole. But he struggled with mental illness and relapse. He ended his life in the desperate belief that he was doomed forever and his children would be better off without him.

I believe the primary measure of correctional institutions is whether they foster real learning and growth in the lives of the inmates. Many prisons claim to have an orientation or a mission to support rehabilitation, recovery, or reintegration into society. But few provide significant and effective opportunities for offenders to truly change their lives. There may be token funding and resources, but they are limited at best.

Sadly, most institutions provide only a secure housing arrangement. They are merely warehouses for people. The simple fact is that prisons hold people and do not work to change them. They may stop them, but only temporarily.

In the learning environment of a prison, staff and peer influence is often negative. An inmate code exists, where criminal and irresponsible norms control actions beneath a façade of respectable and orderly inmate behavior. Most prisons have a peer culture where an 'us vs. the man' philosophy is the norm, and exploitation of others is a mark of status among offenders and jailers.

Most prisons and jails have either a custodial or clinical model, setting up a jailer/prisoner or doctor/patient dichotomy, respectively. Both models are autocratic. According to these models, jailers control inmates, and doctors and social workers cure them. In *Pedagogy of the Oppressed*, Freire critiques a "banking" model of education, in which "knowledge is a gift bestowed by those who consider themselves knowledgeable upon those whom they consider to know nothing … The teacher presents himself to his students as their necessary opposite; by considering their ignorance absolute, he justifies his own existence." Both the custodial and clinical models place the staffers in the position of "teacher" described here by Freire. Neither the custodial nor clinical models lead to comprehensive change.

Program Models for Prison Reform

Most correctional institutions have rehabilitation programs in work, education, mental health, and substance abuse that don't talk to each other. They are silos with administrators often fighting each other for funding. They value one or more "magic bullets" that singularly hold out wonderful and amazing benefits to change the lives of offenders. Or sometimes an institution will provide more comprehensive programming that is ill-coordinated. Progress in one area does not necessarily lead to progress or change in another:

- Education or school programs can provide useful skills for reintegration into society. Their message to the offender is "here is some information you're going to need to make it." However what is important is not what inmates know but what they do with it. If prisons don't focus on a comprehensive change process, then educating criminals will make for smarter criminals. Schooling needs to be part of a broader rehabilitation program. It's good to liberate inmates, but we must work with them to use that liberation in healthy ways.

- Self-help programs like twelve step groups help offenders understand what addicts and alcoholics go through and offer positive models. This appears necessary for change but is also insufficient on its own.

- Treatment groups help offenders work through what is going wrong with them. But these groups rarely reach the intensity and frequency that would be ideal, hence group members are often shy to voice significant challenges to each other. There need to be ample opportunities to practice changed behaviors and verify change on a daily basis, something unavailable in most treatment groups. In-group role playing is also insufficient. Treatment groups have been researched with positive results. But most often the target populations are low risk and self-selected for a strong motivation to change. Failed outcomes with countless group programs are rarely published.

- Community supervision with urinalysis, day reporting, and sometimes electronic monitoring will help watch offenders, but here the goal is to verify appropriate behavior without attention to whether the behavior is more than a ruse.

- Work programs teach responsible habits and the ability to contribute to society, but employment can also be a front for continued criminal and arrestable activities. In fact, work and/or schooling are the façades of respectability that every probationer/parolee knows they must show to their supervision officer.

What is needed are rehabilitation programs that are comprehensive and make use of positive peer influence. Comprehensive programs are multi-dimensional and effect change in all attitudes and behavior, including substance abuse, mental health, employment, education, leisure time, and most of all personal relationships. Comprehensive programs treat the whole person with a range of modalities.

Therapeutic Communities for Whole Person Change

Therapeutic communities (TCs) offer an alternative model that is comprehensive and peer-oriented with self-help methods of programming where the community of peers are seen as the vehicle for change. When incorporating comprehensive cognitive-behavioral and educational programming, TCs have significant empirical data (from the U.S. Department of Health and Human Services) supporting their effectiveness, particularly for hard-core offenders with substance addiction and mental illness. I have developed TCs in six different correctional facilities in the Colorado prison system, and I'm honored to witness the personal growth in those who appear hopeless to both society and self.

TCs are currently operating in over 100 correctional facilities in the US. They are staff-led programs where the participants communicate the program elements and change process to each other. The peer culture develops as a positive influence on daily behavior. This becomes a culture antithetical to the usual prison code and is insulated from the rest of the prison society, since TC units are separated physically from the general population in most daily activities.

Comprehensive programs have breadth, depth, intensity, and duration. The therapeutic community functions as a 24/7 program which typically lasts from 6 to 18 months. They incorporate educational, therapeutic, and work activities into daily living. But the real force of influence happens in community meetings. For example, there are morning and close-of-day meetings where members motivate each other and relay important community business. The community interrelations are familial; community members are like brothers and sisters in recovery.

TCs are a healthy family-living situation and also a school for moral development. For much of their lives (and especially while in prison), many offenders have not been a real part of anything, and TCs require close involvement. Behavior becomes public and is subject to intervention by the rest of the community. Groups meet weekly to develop learning experiences in response to problem behaviors, which facilitates the peer-driven environment of the program. Frequent "pull-ups" and "push-ups" are key tools, formalized activities that members use to encourage and motivate each other.

Education groups are often co-led by members of the community, requiring greater learning but just as importantly a willingness to teach others. As Freire writes in *Pedagogy of Freedom*, "Whoever teaches learns in the act of teaching, and whoever learns teaches in the act of learning." This is the community view of real education for life change.

Therapy groups are also peer-directed. As an expert and teacher in group therapy, I've often felt the urge to intervene. But in TC groups I've marveled at how skilled members in the group seem to always make the best interventions before I would even consider jumping in. That is the way group therapy or *learning in any environment* should work.

TC life also provides structured roles and responsibilities for each of the residents. All are expected to be role models to the others; and each are given sophisticated responsibilities. Roles change frequently. All are expected to be leaders, and also to follow others' lead. This provides an environment for peer support, the acquisition of leadership skills, identity change, and increased self-esteem.

A big key to effectiveness in TCs are shared norms and values. Let's be clear what these are. They are not dogmatic propaganda. They are not a code of strict and "perfect" conduct. They encourage simple and necessary values for good citizenship — honesty, accountability, work ethic, and community responsibility.

The above program elements have contributed to a record of empirical research that shows TC to be an effective correctional program reducing drug use and return to prison, and improving the mental health of the participants. These programs have been researched extensively and have been recognized within the Department of Human Services SAMHSA National Registry of Evidence Based Practices for "Corrections Therapeutic Community" and for "Modified TC for Persons with Co-Occurring Disorders." (This is a credit to Tania Garcia, Managing Counselor of the Colorado DOC Therapeutic Communities, whose developmental work and daily leadership made this possible.)

Reintegration

The vast majority of criminal offenders are or will be living in our neighborhoods. We must advocate for comprehensive programs of recovery and rehabilitation so that they can be positive contributing members of society. We lock offenders in prisons and jails, but we also must be willing to welcome them back into our community of citizens and supportive groups of recovering people.

This is exactly where school reform and prison reform intersect. These are not separate and distinct movements. Our schools can't be prisons. And our prisons must be schools.

We must believe in and recognize a positive process of personal transformation from irresponsible exploitation of others to personal responsibility and value to the community. Personal agency is not a simple decision or conversion. It is a complex and lengthy path to responsibility and growth. Hassan Latif is an ex-inmate and graduate from one of my TC programs in the Colorado prison system. He has a lengthy and serious criminal past and was initially denied entrance to the TC as too high risk. He says in his book that change starts with "owning your own crap" and becomes "a vision, a desire to achieve, the willingness to be guided, the discipline of dedicated efforts, and the patience to see it all come together."

Since I wrote the original draft of this article, Hassan has continued to advocate in the field and has now developed and built the Second Chance Center in Denver, CO, which provides services to ex-inmates, including non-residential programming and housing. Hassan's efforts epitomize the reform work we need to be doing in our correctional systems.

CHAPTER 24.

THE PLEASURES, THE PERILS, AND THE PURSUIT OF PEDAGOGICAL INTIMACY

DANIELLE PARADIS

Intimacy lacks a satisfying definition. It is, according to the *New Oxford American Dictionary*, a "close familiarity or friendship...; a private cozy atmosphere; an intimate act (especially sex)." To be intimate with someone means you're closely acquainted. These are not satisfying descriptions, as they fail to describe the emotional ferocity and pleasure that the proximity to someone we esteem brings. There is nothing more soothing than an intimate conversation — the kind that lasts until three in the morning, leaving you glowing with warm satisfaction. It leaves you aching for more. These are often the best ways of learning, about someone else or about yourself. These conversations have the capability to transform ideas. They are moments for teaching, and for learning. Intimacy between friends or lovers is seen as a good thing.

There is a further point to be considered, and that is the matter of intimacy in another setting — a classroom. Intimacy in an adult classroom, is a rather sticky subject: is it allowed, and to what extent? In transformatory education, we must explore what Paulo Freire calls "the distance between the teacher and the taught." The liminal space of possibility and uncertainty. Why must we mess up pedagogy with intimacy? Because when working between order and chaos we can produce either with a simple action.

When we talk about intimacy in the classroom, we do so in a sort of dualism, either fully embracing all of what intimacy entails or politely skirting the idea that sex and attraction happens in post-secondary environments and focusing on the "pseudo-intimate" nature of classrooms. Katie Rose Guest Pryal (2010) describes intimacy as something all students and professors battle in the classroom. If not cisgender, heterosexual, white, and male we may attempt to adopt a raceless genderless persona so as to broadcast that we are as competent as our colleagues who make up that shopping list of perfection. Pryal then defines intimacy in the classroom as the moments that the careful façade breaks down — when we, students and teachers all, become aware that we are bodies as well as minds in the classroom.

Intimacy is a qualitative subject, and so often explored through the lens of personal experience. Here there is only one student's experiences with intimacy and gender in the classroom — my own. I regret therefore that my personal experiences provide a limited scope — they are both largely cisgender and heteronormative. However, to attend to intimacy with the nuance the subject deserves requires mining personal experience. It means reflection on the very personal ways desire and learning work together.

Where am I going with this? I asked myself the same as I typed, and how much to let you know. A writer and her reader is, after all, an intimate connection too — reader and author are as bound by a link that is every bit as intimate as the connection between teacher and student. I could answer some questions and dodge the others leaving your mind to wander on the academic and his protégée. There's a deliciousness in the unspoken, but there's a horror too. There was an English teacher I had in my first year of University that really focused me on what it's like to connect closely with someone whose job it is to teach you. I think often of the impression my English 101 teacher left on me. He wasn't a pedant. He didn't wear tweed. I never wrapped my arms around him and tilted my head upward, coquettishly, so he might kiss me. But nonetheless, I was immediately taken with him. I was fascinated by his ability to deconstruct poetry and his knowledge of story. To me, with my lack of experience in post-secondary education, it was eye opening to be around someone with the ability to interpret text the way he did. He was my first academic crush.

When bell hooks wrote in *Teaching to Transgress* about the inequality in relationships between students and teacher, I wonder if she knew that Jane Austen agreed with her. Austen writes in *Sense and Sensibility* that "it is not time or opportunity that is to determine intimacy; — it is disposition alone. Seven years would be insufficient to make some people acquainted with each other, and seven days are more than enough for others." As fascinated as I was by the English teacher, he was mostly indifferent. Like Alcibiades to Socrates, I longed to find a way to seduce the wisdom from him. Something about him made me want to spend hours talking to him. He stirred all manner of emotions with divine conversation. After this first class, I immediately sought out a chance to be taught by him again, but wasn't able to until my second year. I never quite fell to the level of Alcibiades, who punctuates a lecture by Socrates on the beauty of souls over the beauty of bodies by stumbling in drunk and complaining that Socrates is a tease — but my restraint was only because I doubted this would be well received.

In *Symposium*, Plato presents the love of wisdom as the highest form of love. In pursuit of that love, I often kept the English teacher company during office hours. Happily, they lined up with my breaks in-between classes. Slowly, and very reluctantly on his part, something endearing formed. I have three artifacts from this intimacy, improved punctuation (a playwright does not mark grammar and diction lightly), a long-standing friendship, and a very keen recollection of Gothic horror. I hope that the intimacy of the relationship — forged by hours of conversation — has also proven valuable to him. My attraction was both to his physical presence, which always made me calm, and to the way his mind worked — these things could not have existed separately. I never felt vulnerable or coerced into being attracted to him. The feelings were entirely my own.

At least, I always thought they were. Dziech and Weiner don't quite agree — or rather they wouldn't if the relationship had transgressed physical boundaries. They declare quite firmly that in areas where power differentials exist, there can be no "mutual consent." They assert that the discussion of sexual intimacy in the classroom is a broken discussion that speaks "in the abstract as if it were unrelated to real life human beings." But they then go on to make generalizations about the types of men who will take advantage of young victims, dividing them into adolescent crisis, professional crisis, and midlife crisis. Dziech and Weiner correctly assess that a predatory male professor would not be a glitch in the software of a patriarchal society, but a feature.

Still, defining all intimacy between male teacher and female student as coercive or abusive troubles me because it is so out of scope with my own experiences. I worry that policing human interactions so closely continues to prevent women from participating as equals socially. Young women are often not able to access the help that their male peers may via the Old Boys Network. Policing interaction sends the message to young women that not only are they not allowed to claim their own sexuality, they are also not responsible for it.

With this conundrum in mind, hooks deconstructs the Cartesian ideology of splitting the mind and the body in a classroom in *Teaching to Transgress*. To thwart intimacy, argues hooks, is to teach with the "false assumption that education is neutral, that there is some even emotional ground we stand on that enables us to treat everyone equally, dispassionately." This ignores that "special bonds between professors and students have always existed."

Cultural misogyny is the root issue of sexual harassment. There is a myth of personal accountability for women in a rape culture. There's a tendency to discredit victims, to insist — blinded by a societal belief in the just world fallacy — that surely the victim led the perpetrator on. Sexual harassment is a component of sexual violence, and women coming forward need to be believed and dealt with fairly by a University administration. The cornerstone of the issue is not preventable by paternal policy. Trust women. Trust women to make their own choices — and mistakes and regret will be a part of that. There're many questions to explore. Can we accomplish any closeness if post-secondary pedagogy shuns intimacy, and when do we risk intimacy being a cover for harassment? People who argue that there is no nuance in a discussion around sex and power dynamics erase a lot of the conversation. It is true that the power imbalance in life can't help but follow us into intimate settings, but once there perhaps there is no better place to work on subverting patriarchy, and making a space more egalitarian.

In my narrative, my agency didn't fall to a lecherous professor. I wasn't a doe-eyed innocent. I was the one pushing for a relationship to exist. Again, I turn to hooks for her ability to be at once both definitive and nuanced. She explains that the only way teachers can begin to think about how to make the world a better place is to fully understand the authority they wield over their students. We always think of sex when we think of eroticism, but like intimacy, that isn't the entirety of the definition. As hooks argues, the erotic can extend to anything you are passionate about. In *Back to Reality*, hooks mentions that whether in white or non-white classrooms we are too eager to continue to deny the body. Too quick to agitate towards repressive structures that dehumanize us. Our classrooms are messy because they include people. In the book, hooks recalls her own experience with wounding a student through her attempt to deny her erotic charge with him — leaving her seeming indifferent and brusk. She realizes that her desire to be professional overrides her desire to be compassionate and vulnerable in the classroom. She had to unlearn the defence mechanism that is the mind/body split. It is not transformative, it is repressive. When we can leave a classroom and hardly remember the physical presence of either student or teacher we do each other a disservice.

The Perils

William Deresiewicz speaks about eros and intimacy in pedagogy, asking if in our Western culture we could possibly be less set up to explore this liminal space. Perhaps without my even needing to prod, your mind has moved towards an academic stereotype — that of the young female student and the older male professor. He, and it is always he, was perhaps once young and creative, but now is narcissistic and creatively sterile. Deresiewicz writes a brilliant exploration of the trope of the lecherous professor in popular culture. The professor is depicted as a mean wife-and-children neglecting inebriate. He appears in Baumbach's *The Squid and the Whale*; Hanson's *Wonder Boys*; Parker's *The Life of David Gale*; and as a "self loathing, suicidal Proust scholar" in Dayton and Faris's *Little Miss Sunshine*. Why this trope? Well according to Deresiewicz,

> The existence of academia, an institution predicated on intellectual hierarchy, irritates Americans' insistence on equality, their feeling that intellect constitutes a contemptible kind of advantage. At the same time, as American society has become more meritocratic, its economy more technocratic, people want that advantage for themselves or their children.

While the popular imagination has yet to notice that increasing numbers of women too have become instructors, our pop-culture collective unconscious is also suspicious of intellect and intimacy. Socially there isn't a lot of room for a relationship forged by a young student and a young English teacher.

The presumption that the pronoun of the professor accused of sexual harassment will be male is not always true. Distinguished professor Jane Gallop is no stranger to challenging this paradigm of intimacy in post-secondary, she herself having been accused of sexual harassment by two students. In the beginning of her book, *Feminist Accused of Sexual Harassment,* she notes the deliberate use of a tabloid-style headline. Click Bait. This is, after all, how professorial peccadillos are written about. Filled to the brim with scandal. It is fascinating how the writing exploring intimacy in the classroom would make for a dissatisfactory erotic novel, and yet nearly always reeks of prurience. I prefer Gallop in her refusal to infantilize women who engage in tense relationships, sexual or not, with their teachers. As either teacher or student it doesn't serve us well to presume a young adult has no ability to make decisions for herself.

Whenever the news cycle picks up stories about professor-student relationships, there are inevitably those who slam their fists on the table and declare that *there ought to be laws!* The administration agrees. There are many policies forbidding adult student and teacher relationships. While on the surface this seems inherently practical, hooks describes in *Teaching Community* the experience of working on a committee of professors drafting a sexual harassment policy. She found that the professors on the committee were not interested in engaging in real intellectual feminist thinking. They were more interested in working with simplistic stereotypes, writes hooks:

> I was met with a complete lack of interest in brainstorming about ways that would empower students to protect themselves against unwarranted advances ... many of these women really were more interested in reinforcing the idea that men are always and only sexual oppressors, and that females, especially young adults, are always and only victimized by sexuality. They were not interested in empowering female students, in preventing them from being hurt; they wanted to identify and punish perpetrators.

The focus for sexual harassment, Gallop believes, must stay on the harassment and not the sex. Gallop notes that her problem with academic sexual policy is, "precisely that it isn't academic enough, that it has not been formulated according to "academe's own rigorous standards of inquiry."

The pursuit of intimacy in a classroom, or even intimacy *in pursuit of us* in a classroom, is terrifying for far more reasons than sex, but that seems to be the reason on which we harp. As Deresiewicz so beautifully writes, "in our sex-stupefied, anti-intellectual culture, the eros of souls has become the love that dares not speak its name." A mentor once told me that the student-teacher relationship never really evaporates. That depends on the people involved. The English teacher and I haven't occupied the same physical space in years. Our friendship deepened when I finally let him off the pedestal.

I'm speaking at the very edge of what I'm trying to say. Learning is uncomfortable, and the trouble with letting someone teach you is that it leaves a mark — an impression. You can come to either love or hate someone, but what lessons they have taught you will linger. Pedagogy is inextricably bound up in this because it's an ecology, a community. We must see education as hooks does, as a form of praxis. As constant reflections on action in the never-ending reinvention of both theory and practice in a movement towards liberation. We can no more shun intimacy in the classroom than we can elect to create a sexless and genderless space and expect anyone to thrive within it.

CHAPTER 25.

PRACTICE AND PERFORMANCE: TEACHING URBAN LITERATURE AT THE LESS THAN LIBERAL ARTS

AISHA DAMALI LOCKRIDGE

"Literature can be our teacher as well as our object of investigation"
~ Gayatri Chakravorty Spivak

To say that being the only African American woman professor at a small, liberal arts college in the rural United States is a series of racial microaggressions (and macroaggressions) waiting to happen is something of an understatement. And still, you are hopeful that the aspirational institution that sent for you will be able to support you on its campus. Initially, you may ignore being regularly mistaken by your colleagues for the other (only) Black woman on campus, or be willing to patiently explain that the institution's expectation that you mentor every Black student is not only unreasonable, but not conducive to successful tenure and promotion. By the time you encounter the catch-22 of seeming uncongenial, in part, because you carefully consider the social spaces you inhabit and very few of your colleagues notice the confederate flags that casually drape the windows of cars parked in front of too many local watering holes, you begin to feel less hopeful.

In that American outpost, teaching became my refuge. With very little interference, I began to create courses which integrated canonical material from my subject areas of African American Literature, African Diaspora Literature and Black Studies with urban fiction, Hip Hop music and other forms of less traditional Black literary expression. These types of courses on a stodgy, rural, liberal arts campus encouraged a faithful student following, and that following felt like protection against the racist and sexist campus community outside the classroom. But it was not real protection; it couldn't be. Through the experience of teaching Black urban literature, I soon came to realize that continued innovation cannot thrive in hostile spaces and that students' goodwill cannot substitute for professional collegiality. For as bell hooks argues in *Teaching to Transgress* "'engaged pedagogy' ... means that teachers must be actively committed to a process of self-actualization that promotes their own well-being if they are to teach in a manner that empowers students." (15)

The first time I taught urban literature, it was Sister Souljah's memoir *No Disrespect*; it did not go well, and I was not prepared. I was teaching Introduction to Black Studies, and along with traditional texts, my approach included autobiographies, music, and narrative film. We read Richard Wright's *Black Boy*, which they loved, and Rebecca Walker's *Black, White, Jewish* which they met with curiosity. The films, Spike Lee's *School Daze* and Marshall Curry's *Street Fight*, engendered much interest and debate. The music project was so popular I have included it in every subsequent version of the course; I presented my version of Black music in the US, playing music chronologically from work songs to contemporary rap and then invited students to add music they could not believe didn't make my list.

Midway through the semester, we began reading Souljah's memoir and my lively and engaged students disappeared. In-class discussions became one-sided and students rarely, if ever, referred to specific passages in the text, something they had regularly done in the past. Their books sat on the tables in front them unopened. When I finally just asked the students to account for themselves, they lambasted the text. They spoke not of the subject matter which at times is deeply problematic, but on what they considered to be the poor quality of her writing, her questionable vocabulary, and the aggressiveness of her tone. In stark contrast, Wright's memoir caused them to express an appreciation for the racism and social injustice his text revealed, but they felt no such connection to Souljah's text. Using coded language they dismissed not the substance of her writing, but the subject position from which she wrote. In what was unfolding, the race and gender makeup became as central to our discussion as the text under review. The class consisted largely of upper-middle class students, was almost exclusively male, and of those male students, most were white. Their rejection made clear that the race, class, and gender bias that supported the institution outside the classroom was taking over inside it; I intended to restrict its creep into my classroom.

I did not urge these students to reconsider their points of view, to relish the opportunity to read a life often closed to them — the experience of a once impoverished rapper's unlikely journey into the educated middle class. Instead I righteously lectured them on how their privilege prevented them from seeing the world. Referring specifically to their interest in Black music, I pointed out their eagerness to ignore the socio-political injustice, educational disadvantage, racism and prejudice that served as historical backdrop and subject of the music that laced through their iPods. I told them that in rejecting Souljah's text they were participating in the continued cultural appropriation of Black culture, taking, using, and understanding nothing. When I was done, the class was cowed and I smug. Their privilege was theirs to manage, and so while they were required to finish reading the text, I made little effort to help them find a way back into it. I do not regret the lecture I gave that day, but I do regret not doing more to facilitate a re-engagement with the text on its own terms. Their resistance signaled the need for me to have made a different teaching choice. Now that I have left that college, I know that I did not make the effort to help them because I did not have anything left to give them; my teaching goals were becoming more impossible to realize. Surviving the college outside the classroom, the community outside the college, narrowed the spaces I could remain an engaged teacher.

The geographic location in which I taught, a place sometimes derisively referred to as Up South, and the image I had of myself there — as a pioneer in the wilderness of whiteness bringing African American literature and Black Studies to those who had never seen a Black woman professor up-close — very much limited the potential outcomes for that class. The institution had very few racially diverse faculty and my partner and I would become the second and third African American faculty members as part of a long term plan to racially diversify the current faculty. My refusal to acknowledge that recruitment is not always tethered to retention and that aspirational benchmarks have little to do with actual people, led me to look for support in places where I could have been providing it. I was a popular teacher on a small campus and the students' collective goodwill led me to ignore signs that my own supply lines were drying up.

Until this failed teaching experience students who had signed up for my clearly identified Black-centered courses, while usually uninitiated, were excited. Reading *No Disrespect*, however, proved to be different; the memory of that class and the coded language students used to discuss Souljah's memoir, stays with me even now, years later. It seems that reading it required students to look at themselves in a way they had not expected in a course entitled Introduction to Black Studies. *No Disrespect* deviated from their literary expectations and seemed to make them ill at ease with themselves. Unlike Wright's older text, Souljah was writing about poverty and racism in the US during the 1980s and 90s. Wright's anger they understood as righteous indignation, a man fighting against his times. Anger about more recent social injustice however, meant that the fight for civil rights was not over and that fact, like no other, made them uncomfortably aware that even if unknowingly, they benefited from systems of privilege. In that time and space I could not perceive the specific tonalities of their resistance, could not recognize that while it was rooted in class, gender and race privilege, it was rooted there in a very particular way. Ultimately, my battle-scarred response obscured the teaching possibilities of that text with those students.

I eventually left that college because I was no longer able to be the teacher I aspired to be in that space. The classroom was operating as a place of refuge for me, but not often enough as one for students.Teaching less conventional material successfully, requires more labor: more preparation, more flexibility and as result a safe space in which to do so is not a luxury, it is a requirement. Finally recognizing that my former institution was incapable of providing that and, in the interim, leading me to undermine my own teaching goals, I made a decision that meant leaving behind likely tenure, unsolving a two-body problem and starting over again in a small office with no windows. It remains one of the best decisions I have ever made.

I now work at a different type of Predominantly White Institution (PWI), this time an urban university with a Catholic affiliation. It is not without its problems, but there is a real cohort of tenured and untenured faculty of color. The institution has moved beyond perpetual aspiration and has managed to integrate its diversity goals into its culture with both clear successes and failures. Now, I am, more often, asked to do something because I am qualified to do so and not just because I am a Black woman. In short, I am no longer a pioneer in every public space. With the time, flexibility, and space to consider the potential outcomes for introducing urban literature into the classroom, I developed a comprehensive strategy that did not depend solely on students' goodwill for success. What follows is the evidence of an engaged pedagogy which was only possible to create in a place where supply lines are practical rather than performative.

In a contemporary African American women's literature course, I designed a section of the syllabus entitled "Keeping it Real?" in which students consider literary interpretations of the prison industrial complex, sexuality and the politics of respectability, the role of education. I selected "Unique", a novella in the *Girls from Da Hood* series by Nikki Turner, as the centerpiece of the section and invited students to consider the cost of keeping it real. I planned for the class to interrogate the life that underlines the text; that is, how does Nikki Turner imagine and narrate the life of a poor, single, undereducated Black woman getting by on her feminine wiles? Rather than like my first attempt at urban literature, I chose fiction designed to give students more space and tools to investigate the text. I also defined very specific lines of inquiry to frame our in-class discussions.

My previous experience teaching this material prepared me to expect resistance and, liberated from the search for protection, I knew that comments about writing style, vocabulary, tone, and perhaps even subject matter would likely reflect class, gender, and race bias. So rather than having students read this book as a standalone text, I sequenced "Unique" with more traditional forms of literature with similar themes by established authors. Students read the title story from Z.Z. Packer's *Drinking Coffee Elsewhere* followed by "Speaking in Tongues" from the same book, then "Unique" and finally Suzan-Lori Park's play *In the Blood*. Earlier in the semester students read sections of Hazel Carby's critical text *Reconstructing Womanhood* and in preparation for non-literary questions, I consulted Angela Davis's work on Blacks in the prison industrial complex, *The Meaning of Freedom*, and Beverly Tatum and Jonathan Kozol on educational inequalities in the U.S. I placed urban fiction within a literary tradition and suggested by doing this that it was as deserving of the same level of inquiry.

Instead of beginning with a text like *Black Boy* and continuing with *No Disrespect*, which was alienating to privileged majority students in my previous experience teaching this material, I began this section with "Drinking Coffee Elsewhere", a story about a young Black woman negotiating her unease as a first-year student at Yale University, mirroring the privilege these students sometimes express. Students come to this story with strong beliefs about affirmative action as an unfair panacea for poor Black students. The story quickly reveals however, that while race and gender are salient to the protagonist, they are not the primary basis for her alienation. We read "Speaking in Tongues" next in order to interrogate the potentially devastating effects of the politics of respectability and examine how help can come from unexpected places. In this text, we focus on how the absence of sexual knowledge because of an insistence on sexual purity, puts its protagonist directly in the hands of a predator. Students respond well to these two stories in part because it is what they expect to find in a literature course. They have been selected because they do and because they raise similar critical questions they will encounter in "Unique". I do not just expect the students to follow me, I prepare them to do so.

Putting urban fiction to work in the classroom involves an active pedagogy that insists on anticipatory practices. There is a push-pull as we read "Unique" because students have been trained to have narrow expectations of literature courses; as this text fails to conform to those expectations, I am prepared to meet that resistance. This kind of flexibility is not possible when you are harnessed by environmental constraints that inhibit mindfulness in the immediacy of the classroom. "Unique" begins with a collect call from prison and drawing from Angela Davis's work, I ask students to consider what the existence of prisons say about non-prisoners. I do this to immediately trouble preconceived notions about incarceration. I use this same strategy for the same reasons when they learn that Unique drops out of school. Knowing that many students at the University participate in service learning opportunities at racially diverse and underserved schools, and drawing on Tatum, and Kozol, I attempt to re-orient them from easy assumptions about education as a panacea. I ask them to consider why the experience of attending a school in an underserved and underprivileged environment may make school seem disconnected from success. As sexual prowess is the trait Unique values most, we spend a lot of time discussing how she chooses to express her sexuality. Students react most strongly to this. They want to count up her sexual partners and sit in judgment; Instead I ask them to consider the agency involved in transactional sex. As we read each section of the novella, there is pushback for every decision Unique makes and I rely heavily on the next text, Park's "In the Blood," to reaffirm some of the claims I encourage them to make about "Unique." While it is important to push students to reconsider their uninformed opinions, they must find their own compelling reasons to do so. In this place, I can read the room with a wider lens and each moment of dissent becomes an opportunity and a challenge I am better able to meet.

By the time we get to "In the Blood," students are not yet convinced that Unique is anything other than her own worst enemy. But this retelling of Hawthorne's *Scarlet Letter*, as a homeless mother of five so mishandled and abused by the safety nets most Americans imagine to be firmly in place, that she snaps as a result of sheer abjection and murders her son, leads to quiet questions of indignation. In those moments, I think I have found the success I failed to find the first time I tried to teach urban literature. Students express muffled outrage at the utter exploitation Hester experiences by those designated to help her and it is then that I ask them to reconsider Unique's attempts to control her life. Only then are they more able to consider Unique's pursuit of agency and perhaps, her ingenuity.

Successfully teaching Black literature in innovative ways demands an engaged pedagogy and an engaged pedagogy requires time, space and freedom. Unfortunately, this means that many students will never read beyond the canonical texts in a Norton Anthology because teachers like me: Black, feminist, women, who will speak truth to power in ways that do not always conform to the expectations of majority cultures, come to realize that we can only do this kind of work from places where the performance and practice of diversity meet. Those kinds of places are often more difficult to locate than they seem. Once I was in a place that better facilitated that union, I could do more than observe and name the seeming failures of my students, I was able to help them work past them. By becoming the kind of teacher who structures pedagogy to penetrate through gender, race and class privilege, I created avenues through which students could find a way to read difficult material and learn from it.

People of difference often find themselves at the outposts of America clinging hopefully to jobs at aspirational institutions. Like pioneers and early settlers, we are unsure if those who sent for us will continue to provide the provisions we need to survive, or those who came with us will be able to continue to weather the isolation. In those places, we must pay careful attention to any sign that supply lines are collapsing or that railway tracks are being diverted from our town, and if those things happen, we must be willing to leave. No institution's aspirations should supplant our own. Teaching urban literature has taught me that safety is not a luxury and that pioneering can only continue to function in its presence.

CHAPTER 26.

A PEDAGOGY OF KINDNESS

CATHERINE DENIAL

In the past two years, when I've been asked to sum up my approach to pedagogy, I've said "kindness."

I didn't always think this way. My graduate education encouraged me to think of students as antagonists, always trying to get one over on their instructors. I was urged to be on the lookout for plagiarism, to be vigilant for cheaters, to assume that the students wouldn't do the reading, and to expect to be treated as a cog in a consumerist machine by students who would challenge their grades on a whim. I was once advised by a senior graduate student to "be a bitch" on the first day of class so that my students never wanted that version of myself to show up again, advice that I dutifully repeated to several of the graduate students who came after me. I was a stickler for deadlines, and memorably once refused to excuse the absence of a student who was battling a burst pipe in his house when class was in session. I look back on that now and wince.

I gradually learned, through a great deal of trial and error, that this combative way of approaching teaching was counterproductive at best, destructive at worst. Students didn't communicate with me easily, since many of them didn't see the point. They knew (I realize now) that I approached them with suspicion, and so returned that sentiment in kind. It quickly became clear to me that I needed to build relationships, not defensively prevent them from forming, and that trust was a vital part of creating the circumstances under which learning could happen. There was no space for trust to grow in the learning spaces I'd been trying to create, and so I learned to ease up, to let go of rigid control I'd tried to impose upon the classroom, and to make room for the unpredictable and unexpected. I thought, twenty-three years into my teaching career, that I was doing a pretty good job. And then I went to the Digital Pedagogy Lab Institute at the University of Mary Washington in the summer of 2017.

The entire Institute was predicated upon the concept of kindness. From the pronoun buttons available at the registration desk, to the probing questions of the session leaders, to the time people took, one-on-one, to talk about syllabi and assignments, there was an ethos of care running through the whole four days of my residency. I had signed up for the Intro track, and had expected to spend my time evaluating digital tools to bring into my classroom. I did do that, but first I was asked to think about why I needed those tools at all, whom they would serve, and how I would build in accommodations for students with disabilities. My fellow attendees and I were constantly asked to consider why we were doing things the way we were, and what subtextual messages we were sending to our students about who *they* were. I took a good long look at my syllabus, and realized I had communicated everything in it from a position of absolute authority. The language I used to describe the college's Honor Code, for example, expressed the suspicion that everyone was going to commit some awful academic offense at some point, and my attendance policy made no room for the idea that my students were adults with complicated lives who would need to miss a class now and again.

Why? Why did I posit my students as passive novices who couldn't contribute to their own learning? Why did I require students to jump through hoops to prove that they deserved an extension on a paper? Why did I dock points if my students missed three classes in a term? No one had ever asked me to defend my pedagogical choices before, and once they did, I found much of my pedagogy indefensible. I felt regret and no small amount of embarrassment. My teaching was undone by the presence of a question that was never articulated quite this directly but was everywhere around me:

Why not be kind?

And so I chose kindness as my pedagogical practice. Telling people this has often elicited a baffled response. Kindness is something most of us aspire toward as people, but not something we necessarily think of as central to teaching. In part this is an effect of the pressures that are brought to bear on our classrooms from outside them, symptomatic of a nationwide clamoring (in some circles, at least) for standardization, testing, and rote assessment. Instead of kindness, we're more likely to hear about standards and rigor. (The national professional organization to which I belong, the American Historical Association, says that "good teaching entails accuracy and rigor," but never mentions compassion, for example.) And when we are urged to be kind within an educational setting, it's too often to make up for a lack of institutional support for students and faculty in need, asking a particular service of women and non-binary individuals of all races, and men of color. Kindness can be a band aid we're urged to plaster over deep fissures in our institutions, wielded as a weapon instead of as a balm. And too often people confuse kindness with simply "being nice."

But, to me, kindness as pedagogical practice is not about sacrificing myself, or about taking on more emotional labor. It has simplified my teaching, not complicated it, and it's not about niceness. Direct, honest conversations, for instance, are often tough, not nice. But the kindness offered by honesty challenges both myself and my students to grow. As bell hooks memorably wrote in *Teaching to Transgress*, "there can be, and usually is, some degree of pain involved in giving up old ways of thinking and knowing and learning new approaches."

Yet in practice, I've found that kindness as pedagogical practice distills down to two simple things: believing people, and believing *in* people.

When a student comes to me to say that their grandparent died, I believe them. When they email me to say they have the flu, I believe them. When they tell me they didn't have time to read, I believe them. When they tell me their printer failed, I believe them.

There's an obvious chance that I could be taken advantage of in this scenario, that someone could straight-up lie and get away with it. But I've learned that I would rather take that risk than make life more difficult for my students struggling with grief and illness, or even an over-packed schedule or faulty electronics. It costs me nothing to be kind. My students have not, en masse, started refusing to meet deadlines, but the students who *are* struggling have had time to finish their work. My students have not, en masse, started skipping class, but they're not required to undergo the invasive act of telling me personal details about their lives when they can't show up. My students have not, en masse, started doubting my abilities or my expertise, but they have stepped forward to direct their own education in meaningful and exciting ways that I could not have thought of.

That's believing students. But what about believing *in* students?

Believing in students means seeing them as collaborators — believing they have valuable contributions to make to the way in which syllabi, assignments, and assessments are designed, and life experiences that should be respected in the classroom.

In Fall 2017, I asked both classes to give me questions about the topics we'd be covering — American Indian history in one class, and the history of gender and sexuality in the U.S. in the other. I was then able to craft a syllabus for each class that wove together my own sense of important historical context together with answers to the questions they had posed. The students were offered a sense of ownership in the course, and I was alerted to things I might not otherwise have considered — basic terminology around which there was confusion, for example, or, say, a strong interest in understanding changing concepts of masculinity over time.

I drew on the wisdom of teachers who had gone into this 'kind space' before me, and made significant changes to the way in which I graded work in those classes. Rather than distributing a finished list of grade requirements, I shared some suggestions, and refined those with my students' input until we'd reached a consensus about meaningful assessment. When my students turned in a paper, they also filled out a self-evaluation of their work that asked them what they'd do differently next time, how pleased they were with what they produced, and what they learned about themselves. These adjustments are possible in any class, be it one like mine, with twenty-five students, or a much larger lecture course at a different kind of institution. Both approaches give students greater ownership over their grade and the way that it's awarded; grading becomes, to whatever degree possible, a collaborative venture. In smaller classes it's possible to go further; my students and I sat together and talked over the answers on their self-evaluation, and I asked my students to give themselves a grade. Together, we entered into a conversation about why that grade felt right to them, and why it did or didn't feel right to me, before reaching a consensus on what grade they'd earned.

I've also begun to think of my classes in terms of universal design. For many years I taught with the idea that there was a well-established, academic norm that was fair and impartial, and my job was to make accommodations available for those students who had particular disabilities, or faced particular challenges in meeting that norm. I no longer believe in such a practice. My job, as I see it now, is to make my classroom accessible to everyone. I've begun the long work of redesigning my lessons and assignments so that everyone is a full participant, and no one needs ask for extra time or a note-taker, because those needs have already been addressed. Because I don't believe students with disabilities should have to out themselves, I no longer ban laptops in my classroom, or have quizzes that some students have to take across the hall to get their necessary time-and-a-half. Instead I've experimented with take-home quizzes, options for students to record videos as well as write papers, and final project guidelines that allow students to create anything that will demonstrate to me what they've learned over the term. This, too, is about belief in my students, and believing that by designing my class to accommodate all types of learning I'm demonstrating something important about the ways in which we should be creating a more just world.

I feel more comfortable as a teacher now than I ever have. The subconscious sense that students were antagonists lingered inside me for a long time — long enough that it has been a marvel to teach these past two academic years and experience a teacher-student relationship without that default expectation. I was less stressed; I didn't have reservations about walking into the classroom. My students rose up to meet every new challenge I presented to them, and vocally affirmed that they appreciated the new approach to grading. Crucially, they articulated that when I looked them in the eye and told them what they had done well in a paper, they believed me, whereas when the same info was written at the end of a paper, they didn't. They saw it as pablum — something that I had to write before I delivered the bad news of what they could still work at (which they interpreted as "what I did wrong.") I see that shift, from their exasperation and disappointment to them becoming partners in the assessment of their work, was emblematic of the fruits of a pedagogy of kindness. It was, and is, transformational for all involved.

A pedagogy of kindness asks us to apply compassion in every situation we can, and not to default to suspicion or anger. When suspicion or anger is our first response, a pedagogy of kindness asks us to step back and do the reflective work of asking why we're reacting in that manner and what other instances of disappointment or mistrust are coming to bear on a particular moment in a particular student-teacher interaction. This can transform the student-teacher relationship — but it's not only on an individual-to-individual level that it can alter our working world. To extend kindness means recognizing that our students possess innate humanity, which directly undermines the transactional educational model to which too many of our institutions lean, if not cleave. Transactional models of education identify students as consumers and teachers as retail workers who must please their customers (an inhumane model for retail sales as well as the world of learning). Administrators become managers in this model, looking for cents they can save rather than people they can support. This drains the entire system of its humanity, and leads to decisions at every level where the personhood of a student, teacher, or administrator is diminished.

To value and practice kindness is to resist such models. Even where institutions are leaning away from investment in personhood in favor of hedge funds, we as teachers have the ability to insist that individuals matter. We have the means to hold a line, to see the student without shelter — or food, or safety, or a laptop, or an internet connection, or health, or confidence, or a support network — as someone who matters exactly as they are and even because of the challenges they face. We can refuse to dehumanize our students and presume an adversarial stance. We can prioritize kindness.

PART V.

THE SCHOLARLY AND THE DIGITAL

"Digital scholars do not only risk causing sparks — fireworks, conflagration — when we do our work, we risk dismissal of the validity of that work. We are told to take risks later in our careers, after securing a job, after tenure, after promotion, after earning the approval of our less-digital peers; yet to delay is to hazard the ossification of our ideas, our creativity, and the ingenuity that makes us good scholars in the first place."

~ Chris Friend, Sean Michael Morris, and Jesse Stommel, "CFP: The Scholarly & the Digital"

CHAPTER 27.

BEYOND RIGOR

PETE RORABAUGH, SEAN MICHAEL MORRIS, AND JESSE
STOMMEL

Intellectually rigorous work lives, thrives, and teems proudly
outside conventional notions of academic rigor. Although institutions of higher education only recognize rigor when it mimics
mastery of content, when it creates a hierarchy of expertise,
when it maps clearly to pre-determined outcomes, there are
works of exception — multimodal, collaborative, and playful —
that push the boundaries of disciplinary allegiances, and don't
always wear their brains on their sleeves, so to speak.

Hybrid Pedagogy focuses on creating conversations within and
outside institutional structures that often eschew multimodal,
collaborative, playful work. Through projects like MOOC
MOOC and Twitter vs. Zombies, we've begun to explore a new
sort of communal rigor for the networked learning landscape,
which depends on engagement, reflection, and curiosity.

As Pete and Jesse have said, "Play is critical inquiry."

The voices that decry collective, playful learning, often do so
from the soapbox of rigor: How can this sort of wild learning —
that doesn't aim at specific objectives, that focuses on dialogue

and creativity instead of content mastery — ever pass muster as meaningful academic work?

In truth, it cannot. But not because the product of playful learning isn't meaningful, but because our notion of academic rigor is *irrelevant to that product*. We must move past our traditional definition of rigorous academic work, and recognize that a learning experience or a pedagogical methodology can be both playful and also have the qualities of the best academic work, if not the reagents of traditional rigor. We hear "rigor," and the word feels vague and unnerving; or worse, exclusionary. The work we're describing here is expansive and not exacting — experimental and not insoluble — the moment before (and even anathema to) understanding. This is work where excellence is measured by exception.

Neurologist and teacher Judy Willis states in her book, *Research-Based Strategies to Ignite Student Learning: Insights from a Neurologist and Classroom Teacher*, "The highest-level executive thinking, making of connections, and 'aha' moments are more likely to occur in an atmosphere of 'exuberant discovery,' where students of all ages retain that kindergarten enthusiasm of embracing each day with the joy of learning." Play, experimentation, and collaboration can all lead to important discoveries and deep intellectual inquiry. Yet the results of play are often overlooked because the process leading to them can't be evaluated within traditional academic models for assessment. (In these cases, the problem is wrongly assigned to the experiment or approach, instead of to the assessments designed to measure the outcomes of a less playful approach. We faced this issue with MOOC MOOC, when outcomes were unpredictable due to the extemporaneous learning that took place. How do you "objectively" grade a word cloud?)

An unhealthy attachment to outcomes discourages experimentation. In *Deep Play*, Diane Ackerman writes, "We may think of play as optional, a casual activity. But play is fundamental to evolution." At its best, play functions not as a methodological approach toward a set of outcomes but as the outcome in and of itself. (A similar argument about community can be found in "MOOCagogy: Assessment, Networked Learning, and the Meta-MOOC" by Jesse and Sean.) What is rigorous, then, is not process but our curious examination of the (unforeseen, unexpected) results and their effectiveness.

We must redefine rigor (and find practicable alternatives to rigor) for the connected learning environment. If we begin to parse the learning environment itself, we can determine where rigor lies outside academic standards, and this may help us understand how to revise our digital pedagogies.

Rigor in a networked learning environment emerges when that environment is:

Engaged: Meaningful work arises from genuine inquiry. When we inspire learners' interest, their work bears the marks of higher critical thinking precisely because the subject resonates with their own concerns and preoccupations.

Critical: We can't be afraid to critique our own circumstances, our own context. In MOOC MOOC, for example, we saw participants playfully deconstruct not just the MOOC, but the systems we were using to examine the MOOC (our online learning environment, Canvas, and the digital tools we asked participants to compose with).

Curious: A rigorous curiosity underpins the most fruitful work scholars do. However, we often forget that our interests, as those thoroughly enculturated by academia, don't need to be grafted on to students. Better that we model our passion *to know something thoroughly* than to merely transmit content or knowledge.

Dynamic: A genuine process of inquiry invites unexpected outcomes — indeed, it does not assume outcomes other than a resolution to the inquiry (which may look a lot like the need for further inquiry). The work we do is framed but also emergent, crowdsourced during and not prior to its unfolding. The rigor is apparent in the framework, in the expectation of what can or may be learned and discovered, but is no less apparent in the creative ways that framework is interpreted and reinvented.

Derivative: A rigorously derivative work is aware of its sources but does not handle them with excessive reverence. (In mathematics, a derivative measures the rate of change as one variable influences another.) A derivative learning environment is attentive and alive, responsive not replicative. It emerges, like the Twitter Vs. Zombies community, across a series of iterative experiments.

In his Introduction to *On Critical Pedagogy*, Henry Giroux writes, that a commitment to critical pedagogy "provides tools to unsettle commonplace assumptions, theorize matters of self and social agency, and engage the ever-changing demands and promises of a democratic polity." Giroux's assessment is apt for anyone wanting to address the changing landscape of online education; it also speaks to connectivist scholars and digital pedagogues interested in digital literacies. We are, when we are at our best, meant to unsettle assumptions, to reorganize our ideas of agency, and to push the boundaries of what is possible in a connected learning environment. How to do this without framing education the way it first appears to each of us: bounded by playgrounds and punctuated by bells for recess?

It's impossible to ignore that new media practices are changing (have changed) the collaboration and knowledge sharing within and outside of institutions of higher learning. In "Rhizomatic Education: Community as Curriculum", Dave Cormier writes, "the foundations upon which we are working are changing as well as the speed at which new information must be integrated into those foundations … Information is coming too fast for our traditional methods of expert verification to adapt." New media practices — of researching, composing, testing, surveying, and publishing — are developing so quickly that waiting on the traditional publishing cycle to verify knowledge is insufficient. Scholars of digital culture and practitioners of digital collaboration must resort to new methods of knowledge creation, including relocating that creation to spheres outside their own. Vast pools of knowledge are being filled by non-experts (for example see eternagame.org). Cormier suggests rhizomatic education — constructing and negotiating community knowledge through a series of interdependent nodes — as a pedagogical solution within quickly changing fields of information. In other words, by connecting to each other, no matter our expertise or station, knowledge grows.

Stephen Ramsay argues, in "The Hermeneutics of Screwing Around; or What You Do with a Million Books," "there are more books, more ideas, more experiences, more relationships worth having than there are hours in a day (or days in a lifetime)." What this means for learning is that a new kind of order emerges when we consider the *content* of a course to be the connections that form within and beyond that course. We may provide the content, but this is no different today than scattering LEGO bricks on a table: what happens next is not up to us. Both the content and the practice of our teaching must shift from a traditional model of schooling to one more compatible with the realities of the digital landscape. Experimentation, inquiry, and play are both the research tools we must use to create online and hybrid classrooms, and also the methodologies best employed within those classrooms.

As educators, the three of us have worked to acclimate students and colleagues to social media environments (and to critique and subvert those spaces), encouraging a breaking down of the divide between the work we do in classrooms and the work we do in the world. Testing and canonical content are less vital to the new media landscape than interactivity, play, and relevant application. The online class portal and the brick-and-mortar classroom each have valuable lessons to teach the other, and both must adapt to the developing principles of 21st century education. Online teaching practices *especially* should encourage these principles — that students "show up," be curious, collaborate, and contribute. The digital has reminded us that learning happens unexpectedly, and so should our approach to learning be unexpectant. We must return play to education, to pedagogy, and to all scholarly practice.

CHAPTER 28.

CONVERSATIONS: INSTRUCTIONAL DESIGN, TRUST, AND DISCOVERY

SEAN MICHAEL MORRIS AND JOSHUA EYLER

Sean Michael Morris and Josh Eyler recently sat down for a conversation to set the stage for MOOC MOOC: Instructional Design. Sean had been dipping into *A Pedagogy for Liberation: Dialogues on Transforming Education* by Ira Shor and Paulo Freire — a book they call a "talking book" — which was written as a kind of textual vérité. It's less formal, and we presume less edited, than most pedagogical or academic texts, which makes it more interesting to read. As Josh says, dialogue is one of our best tools for collaboration, for working together to move our understanding of pedagogy forward. As an homage to the style of Shor and Freire's text, and in the spirit of collaborating on developing pedagogy, we are presenting the conversation between Sean and Josh in its original, conversational format.

Sean: It strikes me that the most important pedagogical maneuver is dialogue. Unless we are willing to sit down and talk to one another, even the most critical, generous pedagogues can seem to bluster and strut.

Twitter in particular is one modern, digital platform for that kind of solo runway walk. It's satisfying to see all the "likes" and retweets, the chorus of "amens" that follow a short rant like the one I had the other night. But I have to say it's more satisfying when I see a response like you delivered:

> .@slamteacher I'm not sure I follow. Many evidence-based practices (PBL, inquiry-based learning) are designed specifically for discovery.
> — Joshua Eyler (@joshua_r_eyler) January 11, 2016

Which is why I asked for this conversation.

I want to agree that project-based and inquiry-based learning offer more opportunities for learner discovery. Unfortunately, I see both of these as still ultimately teacher-centered, authority- and mastery-driven approaches. From what I understand, inquiry is a controlled substance in inquiry-based classrooms, and projects are delimited by the requirements of curriculum and learning objectives. To me, discovery is like wandering into a forest where you've never been and choosing a path (or no path) through the woods. In the wandering that follows, you may discover that you are fascinated by mushrooms, or that the height of the trees stirs you, or that slugs are the most interesting thing ever. But PBL and inquiry-based learning feel much more like an invitation into the teacher's garden. Yes, you can discover, but there are parameters for that discovery, and they've been set long before you ever arrived.

In "MOOC MOOC: Instructional Design," I wrote recently that,

> Student agency arrives in the form of open inquiry, which relies on learner autonomy at a foundational level. This is not just the teacher constructing opportunities or scaffolding for agency, leading the students to discover that they have certain, limited ownership of their learning. Student agency is an assumption built into the pedagogy, and comes from an integral trust of learners' capabilities.

I would be curious as to your thoughts about how PBL and inquiry-based learning are or are not built upon student agency?

Josh: Like you, I firmly believe that curiosity and discovery are the foundation for learning. Students need to wonder; to be puzzled; to try, fail, try, fail, and try again in order for them to build knowledge and make meaning. Much of the discussion here, then, probably comes down to the issue of terminology. For me, PBL and inquiry-based learning are large umbrellas under which sit a variety of strategies. Certainly, as you say, there are some courses where activities might be rooted in discovery, but the discoveries are either already predetermined by the instructor or there is so much structure that it inhibits the process itself.

On the other hand, in just a few minutes I am heading over to take part in a pitch session for our ENGI 120 course. ENGI 120 is a Freshman Design course in the School of Engineering. At the beginning of each semester, the students listen to pitches from folks at Rice and the larger Houston community. They then vote on the projects they would most like to work on and spend at least a semester trying to design a solution. In the past, they have developed mechanical limbs, housing for birds at the Houston Zoo, and a device (featuring a regular old mousetrap!) designed to treat dehydration in children in African countries. Students work in teams, and they receive guidance from Ann Saterbak and Matthew Wettergreen, two of our faculty. The answers are unknown, and there is no guarantee that the projects will be successful. Students are simply given the freedom to explore and create with the goal of making real change. This, to me, is PBL at its finest, but I am also aware that many courses look far different from this.

So it seems like the answer to your question about student agency depends on just how much an individual instructor is willing to give up control, to allow the inquiry process to unfold, to help when asked. Another way to put this would be that so much depends on the degree to which an instructor embraces the notion of constructivism, a theory of education that emphasizes the importance of students shaping their own learning.

In order to embrace pedagogies like these, though, there needs to be an extraordinary amount of trust between instructors and students. Trust is such an important part of teaching.

Sean: I love the idea of students voting on the projects they want to work on! That's a wonderful example not only of learning through projects, but also that learning ties so intimately to the work these learners would be doing in the field. I assume with such a project that invention is welcome, that it would be possible for learners to come to a solution for a problem that even their instructors might not foresee? I'd be curious to know how much guidance — or, more popularly, "scaffolding" — instructors provide learners for these projects? Any at all? Or is their role more supportive?

You raise the issue of control, that surrendering control may be not only an individual choice but, perhaps, even a personal one. Teaching is a highly personal craft, I think, the way that parenting can be. Few teachers like to be given suggestions — "Oh, in that situation, I would do it this way", or "Have you tried…?" or "What I do is…" — and I think the suggestion to let go some authority and control is one that's very hard to hear. I recently wrote to a colleague that "you can't hand over all the responsibility and then take away authority". Teachers usually consider students responsible for their grades, their performance, their learning, but don't give them the authority they require to actually manage that responsibility. Do you see what I mean?

Designing for discovery is tricky business without that surrender of authority. It's not a surrender of leadership — at all — but it is a surrender of that mantle most PhDs-who-teach waited far too long to wear: the mantle of "expert". Perhaps this is also related to the issue of trust. Can we, as teachers, trust students to be authorities in their own learning, without giving over their trust in us as guides? The guide-learner relationship feels a lot friendlier than the teacher-student relationship. Do you think that PBL or inquiry-based learning, done well, can open up that friendlier relationship?

And also, how do we avoid uncritical application of PBL and inquiry-based learning, especially when the two methods have earned their place among today's education buzzwords?

Josh: For the particular projects I was discussing above, the instructors simply provide guidance. No one knows whether or not the projects will be successful, but all work together towards a common goal.

As I said earlier, though, trust is an essential component in this model. I actually think that there is a great deal of vulnerability at the heart of any interaction between teacher and student. Students make themselves vulnerable when they say, either explicitly or through their actions, "I don't know this. Please help me to learn." This takes a kind of courage on their part that we don't often recognize or take seriously enough. That space of vulnerability is almost holy ground as far as I'm concerned, because it underscores how much trust students implicitly have in their teachers. The only way to truly honor that trust, then, is to trust them in return: trust them to be autonomous; trust them to take the tools you can provide and build knowledge that surprises us with its originality; trust that they are in our classrooms because they genuinely want to learn, not because they want to be preached to or condescended to.

For most instructors, this yielding of, as you say, the "mantle of expert" can be unsettling at best and terrifying in other cases. But it is necessary, perhaps not for the wheels of the university to keep turning, though certainly to further the process of transformational learning. As advocates for education, we will have failed if we cannot help others to see this.

So your point is well taken, Sean. Any application of what we call PBL or inquiry-based learning (or any discovery-based pedagogy) must move past the jargon and embrace these notions of trust and respect. Otherwise, courses that purport to have discovery at the root will simply be teacher-led rather than teacher-guided.

Sean: I think at this point, if it's okay with you, I'd like to return to the objection I originally voiced about evidence-based practices. As I think of them, these are teaching approaches that seek to use "proven" methods, or at least "best" practices, and that rely on sociological and psychological research as "evidence". My bias is that teaching from evidence dehumanizes teaching, leaving teachers at a distance from learners. I'm reminded of a quote from *The Qualitative Manifesto* by Norman K. Denzin: "Qualitative research is a moral, allegorical, and therapeutic project." Which reminds me of bell hooks from *Teaching to Transgress*: "To teach in a manner that respects and cares for the souls of our students is essential if we are to provide the necessary conditions where learning can most deeply and intimately begin."

Does evidence-based teaching seek to care for the souls of students? Is it a moral project?

Since the onset of online learning, I've perceived a growing distance between teachers and learners (and already there was a significant divide). Having just finished a year working at an educational technology company, I've also seen from that side how learners become quantities on a spreadsheet, numbers on an infographic. I worry that *researching* learners and learning is not the same as *knowing* learners and learning. Can you respond to that? Can we consider this in terms of inquiry-based learning and PBL? Do those methods seeks to close the distance between teacher and learner? Do they address (also from Denzin) the "practice, politics, action, consequences, performances, discourses, methodologies of the heart, pedagogies of hope, love, care, forgiveness, healing"?

Josh: I would answer "Yes" to all of these questions, but there are a few qualifiers here. Evidence-based practices are simply those pedagogies that we have found to be effective after substantial research. I think as teachers and scholars we seek evidence for all kinds of things — evidence that supports our hypotheses, evidence that students are learning what we hope they are learning — so it makes good sense to me that we would also look for evidence about some teaching approaches that are better for engaging students and helping them to learn than others.

One issue, then, is this: where do we look for evidence? The research literature is a starting point, but we need to approach it with a wary eye. Isolated studies can show effects, but that doesn't mean they are broadly applicable. I prefer meta-analyses like what Freeman et al. wrote for the Proceedings of the National Academy of Sciences. They evaluated 225 studies and determined that evidence-based active learning strategies were more effective than lecturing from start to finish. The work done by John Hattie in his Visible Learning resources is similar. Now, we can certainly intuit some of these findings, but I strongly believe that this evidence gives many teachers confidence that they are at least pursuing a path toward helping students that has some support behind it. I would be skeptical of an approach that advocated for choosing a strategy that was not supported by evidence (in Derek Bruff's terms, "continuous exposition") over one of these other, evidence-based practices.

That said, we also find evidence in our own classes with our own students. We see what works with and for them, and we test new pedagogies as others seem to be falling flat. I just think it's important to start by trying out strategies that have been found to be effective by folks who have been studying these questions for the breadth of their careers.

The problem, to my mind, is if a teacher employs evidence-based teaching approaches *only because they are evidence-based* without paying attention to what is actually working for students. Evidence-based strategies can be just as morally focused, just as interested in caring for the soul, as any other pedagogy. We absolutely must get to know our students, empathize with them, and understand fully and completely that each one is a human being who brings her or his cares, worries, hopes, and fears into our classroom. But, beyond this, we just as surely need to think about the ways in which these students will learn and the techniques we can try to help them. Evidence-based strategies are an important starting point for this.

Sean: This is a great conversation. Thank you for engaging with me so frankly. In the interests of "time", if you will, I just have one more piece I'd love to hear your thoughts about.

If, as you say, discovery-based learning must "embrace these notions of trust and respect" with regards to learners, where along the line do teachers learn to trust and respect themselves? In other words: how do we teach discovery when our teaching is heavily informed by evidence? "Best practices" flow outward, I think. If we employ them, we teach them. If our work as teachers is not exploratory, if we cannot trust ourselves and our own (unverifiable, anecdotal) evidence, how will we help learners do that?

What do you think?

Josh: In *The Courage to Teach*, Parker Palmer says something that I think applies directly to your question:

> Authority is granted to people who are perceived as *authoring* their own words, their own actions, their own lives rather than playing a scripted role at great remove from their own hearts. ...Authority comes as I reclaim my identity and integrity, remembering my selfhood and my sense of vocation. Then teaching can come from the depths of my own truth — and the truth that is within my students has a chance to respond in kind. (33)

Although I don't necessarily agree with everything Palmer says in this book, I find this passage to be so important. The notion of individual truths responding to each other, for me, lies at the core of what it means to be a teacher. We need first to understand what we value as educators and what we, uniquely, can bring to our students. This acknowledgment then leads to the kind of connection you were discussing earlier, as we use our "sense of vocation" to help our students achieve the extraordinary things of which they are capable. As we discover our own best teaching methods, we can model for students the discovery process, which — in many ways — is a kind of intuition that needs to be built over time, just like effective teaching. Such authentic interactions should stem from our own observations, but they need not be impinged by external evidence. Indeed, that evidence can give us an added bit of the courage Palmer writes about.

As you indicate, I think developing this trust in ourselves can be difficult. We try out new approaches, and we learn, little by little, to trust our instincts in working with students. We observe which strategies students respond to, and we learn how to make small or large adjustments to maximize learning. None of this is mutually exclusive from adopting evidence-based pedagogies. I still believe that these should be a starting point. But, in the end, discovering how to trust ourselves and — by extension — our students takes time, takes patience, and is absolutely necessary.

I really appreciate the opportunity to talk to you about these issues, Sean. I've learned a lot.

CHAPTER 29.

LEARNING AT THE INTERSECTIONS

AMANDA LICASTRO

I started writing this article on the day the Trump administration announced they were bombing Syria. A dark coincidence. The announcement came via my *New York Times* alerts just as I finished responding to Bonnie Stewart in regards to an article I sent her about the prejudice Canadians harbor against Muslim refugees — an article she immediately added to her keynote that evening. Bonnie and I were in correspondence because she recently Skyped into my Introduction to Digital Publishing class at Stevenson University to speak about her involvement in a Kickstarter campaign to fund refugee families on Prince Edward Island where she lives and teaches. Bonnie's experience resonated because my students were working with Asylee Women's Enterprise (AWE), a local nonprofit that offers resources to asylum seekers in Baltimore, Maryland. The students were building web content for AWE as our final project. My class was paired with AWE in the spring of 2016 — before Trump, before the travel ban, before the bombings — when the Director of Service Learning, Christine Moran, reached out to me to create a collaborative experiential learning opportunity for my course.

As Christine proved when recruiting me for this project, service learning is a "high impact practice" building the communication, technical, and professionalization skills employers look for in new graduates. Students would be applying the concepts of digital publishing to a real world, client-based objective. As demonstrated in the reflection letter of student Ryan Roche, "having a client to work with helps give the class a direction and helps to really show the 'behind-the-scenes' action that takes place in the digital publishing field." Additionally, my 200-level Intro to Digital Publishing class partnered with a 300-level Interactive Advanced Design course in order to produce a professional product for the client. This collaboration created an interdisciplinary, team-based learning environment that involved design thinking and project-oriented learning objectives — digital pedagogy at its finest. However, this plan also involved attempting a collaboration across physical space and political divides, a complex feat that had the potential to fail on multiple fronts. In my experience, innovation involves "failing forward," but in this case failure involved disappointing a client that was counting on the results of our experiment. Needing to produce a viable website for AWE reframed the way I think about risk in the classroom.

Digital Citizens

As a professor of digital rhetoric I frame my pedagogy as a path to cultivating "digital citizens," or students who actively, critically, and thoughtfully participate in online spaces. Stemming from Kathleen Yancey's call to action in "Writing in the 21st Century," the intention is to "help our students compose often, compose well, and through these composings, *become* the citizen writers of our country, of our world, and the writers of our future" (1). This is why, at all levels, I ask students to compose in public spaces (for more on this see Mark Sample's "What's Wrong With Writing Essays"). Students write blog posts about course content, live-tweet their readings of novels, create multimodal projects, and perhaps most importantly, respond to each other's work in these digital spaces. Options for privacy controls and anonymity are always provided, but even writing within the "public" audience of their peers helps develop audience awareness and rhetorical strategy. Low stakes assignments of this nature prepared students for the work of writing content for AWE's website, but still the considerable stakes of composing for a client intimidated my students, and quite frankly, me.

The anxiety surrounding writing publicly was exacerbated by the fact that students were writing about and for asylum seekers in the United States in a particularly tumultuous political climate. Some students expressed feelings of inadequacy when confronted with this task, while others found the high stakes incentivizing. As student Taylor Barksdale writes in her final reflection letter:

> Having a real client gave us confirmation that the work that we would be doing was indeed meaningful. I know it gave me an increased amount of motivation to turn in the best work I possibly could because the work we turned in would actually be going live on a website for the world to see. More importantly, I knew the work we were doing was for a website with the incredibly urgent goal of getting people to help asylum seekers in America.

On the other hand, one student commented "[i]n redesigning Asylee Women's Enterprise's website, the burden placed on students was heavy, especially for an introductory course" (anonymous evaluation). That, of course, is true. Perhaps 200-level students should not be responsible for a professional website, even when paired with an advanced course? Or perhaps I needed to provide greater oversight and stronger critique throughout the process? I know in the future I would schedule the introduction to publishing course at the same time as the advanced interactive design course so that the students could meet during class time and collaborate formally under the guidance of both professors. But these expressions of inadequacy also stem from the difficulty in balancing the technical skills of the course and the content needed to teach students about digital publishing and the politics of asylum.

Because I teach students from a wide range of political backgrounds, I avoid revealing my political leanings in the classroom. Certainly, topics covered in my courses are inherently political — we talk about gender, race, sexuality, ability, and the freedom of information — but these are offered as launching points for discussion and debate. The invitation to work with AWE demanded I engage in the political directly. It felt imperative to ensure students had the space to grapple with this complex issue, while still producing content that offered support for the asylum seekers. Therefore, for the first time in my teaching history, I shared my personal immigration story with the class. As someone who rarely reveals personal information to my students, I took this risk in order to open a safe and confidential space for my students to share their stories. Although I acknowledge that, as Sam Hamilton argues, "taking risks as a instructor pales in comparison to taking risks *as just about anything else* (most notably taking risks as a student)," I felt the need to offer them a piece of myself — to demonstrate my personal connection to this issue — in return for their willingness to work toward a shared outcome.

Participating in this service learning course led me to reflect on the political rhetoric — both acknowledged and inferred — of my class materials. In this case, the success of the course was contingent on the students actively participating in public, digital citizenship. The students needed to be aware that the goal of this course was to aide asylum seekers in the United States. To emphasize this point, I used visual rhetoric in the header for our course site:

The imagery not only unveiled my politics, it also welcomed students to engage in a specific form of citizenship. Much like Amy J. Wan proposes in "In the Name of Citizenship," this course gave me an opportunity to question "what kinds of citizens" I was hoping to cultivate (29). I was asking students to share their stories; to connect to people and a cause that may be outside of their own experience. I was requesting not only empathy, but vulnerability. In highlighting the political nature of this course, I realized that empathy and vulnerability are often unspoken requirements we summon from our students — not only in service learning courses, but also in the undefined demands of our writing assignments. As Maha Bali writes in "Critical Digital Citizenship: Promoting Empathy and Social Justice Online," the aim is to "help young people become more empathetic critical digital citizens." This course forced me to make my intentions transparent, and to offer anyone who was not interested in participating the opportunity to drop the course. Bali's question from "On Whose Terms Are We (Digital) Citizens?," namely, "Do we recognize that sometimes, in our zeal to help students question, we may also be hampering their capacity to truly listen to the 'other' with an open mind?" replays in my mind. I did not want to discourage conservative students from taking this course when their views would be welcomed and valued. Despite having a right-leaning student body at Stevenson University, no one who registered for this course dropped.

High Stakes Learning

What started as a fairly typical service learning initiative quickly became a matter of life or death. Once Trump announced the travel ban, AWE extended their services to men and children, opening their doors to an influx of families fleeing from over 15 countries around the world. AWE provides legal counsel, housing, transportation services, hot meals, English courses, wellness activities, clothing and food donations, and above all a community center for their clients. The website the students created for AWE needed to present all of these important resources in a way that addressed an audience of asylum seekers, volunteers, and donors. Students faced the challenge of crafting content that was narrative and informative, well-researched yet approachable, and all with language simple enough to be translated by a web-based tool. Additionally, I was mindful that everything we created would be maintained by the overworked AWE staff. In order to accomplish these goals, I wanted to teach students rhetorical analysis, information architecture, editing, multimodal composition, social media writing, and somehow provide enough context to break down the stereotypes associated with refugees and asylum seekers.

It was important for the students to understand that AWE addresses the needs of asylum seekers, not refugees. Both my students and I learned about the significance of this distinction through our interactions with AWE and through the research students did to develop the content for the site. Yes, we have a refugee crisis. However, when refugees arrive to the US they are provided with resources to sustain their basic needs for up to six months. Certainly that is not enough, but because they are pre-vetted and approved they are welcomed into our country with somewhere to live and a caseworker to facilitate the process. Asylum seekers often flee from their homes with no warning, and therefore have no plan if and when they cross the border. Take, for example, the woman who was a business owner in good standing in her community who gave birth to a child with a disability and was accused of witchcraft and denied medical services for her at-risk newborn. Or the lawyer who provided counsel to citizens in support of the opposing political party whose 13-year-old daughter was kidnapped as revenge. These are professionals forced to leave their homes and businesses to come to the US with practically nothing and only a slim hope of proving they qualify for asylum through a grueling process that typically drags on for years.

During my visit to AWE, the lunchroom was filled with quiet young mothers and their less quiet babies. The women picked at plates of donated noodles, occasionally leaving to participate in a yoga class or use one of two computers to look for work. An infant slouched in a high chair that was too big, a puppy nipped at toddler pulling its tail, and a baby was passed from an elderly male volunteer to Tiffany who fed the baby a goldfish cracker as she continued to tell me about their need for "trendier" clothing donations. The place embodied the adage that it takes a village to raise a child. I felt ill-equipped to help. In an attempt to turn my feeling of inadequacy into action, I harnessed the spirit of that room and rallied my community of my female friends — many of whom have young children — to gather clothing and collected donations from colleagues at Stevenson. Similarly, as my students began visiting the center, they were inspired to give their time outside of our final project. For example, RISE, our women's group on campus, organized a drive to collect feminine hygiene products to donate. These are small steps, but the first in what I hope to be an ongoing mission to sustain this partnership.

The partnership between my class and AWE proved to be a learning experience for all of us. In "Developing Accounts of Instructor Learning: Recognizing the Impacts of Service-Learning Pedagogies on Writing Teachers," the authors argue that students *and* instructors engaged in service learning programs experience increased community engagement, reflective practices, and and critical engagement (Leon et al.). By visiting AWE and working together to create a website for the organization, my students and I have a shared experience that will resonate far beyond the general course concepts. Student Ryan Diepold articulated this in his reflection letter:

> Reading about asylum seekers and refugees only goes so far. Taking research and regurgitating it out into a research paper only goes so far. If I did not go down to Asylee Women's Enterprise and talk with the volunteers and asylee [sic] seekers first hand, I am positive that I would not have put forth the energy and time into this project that I did.

Perhaps this is the ideal outcome for a community partnership. My students developed an awareness that the content covered in class had real world applications. However, I learned that not every teaching experiment is entirely successful, and that I need to improve the structure and balance of my course content.

Sustainability

In this course students needed to acquire basic WordPress skills and gain knowledge of universal design, while learning to write for a translingual audience and provide reliable information. Final projects included a multimodal transportation map of Baltimore, video interviews with AWE volunteers, "day-in-the-life" narratives of AWE clients, and an interactive map of information about refugees from specific countries. Students learned to install plugins, communicate directly with a client, and vet highly politicized "facts." None of this could have been accomplished with a traditional learning management system, or without guest speakers with expertise in a variety of content areas. I wanted students to see this work as a contribution to a community project that would live on after the semester ended.

I admit to contributing to a vast digital graveyard of student artifacts in my prior teaching in the digital humanities. Since entering my first full-time faculty position, I have been working toward ending this cycle by creating long-term projects that students build upon each year. Not only does this create consistency across semesters, it also gives students a greater sense of audience and purpose. As student Brie Green puts it,

> Knowing there was a cause and people counting on us, and knowing that we were creating real content that was going out into the world made the process much more meaningful than textbook work that would only be retained for the time required — ultimately ending up in a recycle bin at the end of the semester.

The goal here is to offer this service learning course every spring so that the AWE website is updated every year by a new group of students. However, annual updates are not enough. Therefore, I also worked with the chair of my department to set up an internship for an English major to help design curriculum for the English classes at AWE, and ideally update the website regularly. This internship will offer English majors interested in teaching a chance to gain valuable experience without an education degree, and put their digital publishing skills into practice. It is also a recognized contribution to my career-oriented university, and thus makes sense as a faculty career strategy as well.

Looking to the Future

Nothing ever goes as planned. My best intentions for this course were deterred by emergencies, staffing shifts, and scheduling conflicts. Many students struggled to communicate with their partners, or failed to execute grandiose technical architecture, but all of them managed to produce thoughtful — and above all useful — content for the AWE website. Although from my perspective as the instructor, the final projects represented a wide range of ability levels and effort, the director of AWE was elated with the work presented by my students. Several of the projects went above and beyond my expectations and provided AWE with resources they can surely use for years to come.

As preparation for a new year begins, I am struggling to do my own reflective revisions to this course. In her work on global digital citizenship, Maha Bali states that "in higher education, one can promote social justice and empathy that develops critical citizenship in three ways: apolitical civic engagement through community service (which research has shown promotes adult political civic engagement), simulation of authentic political contexts in a safe environment, and intercultural learning experiences" (Critical Digital Citizenship: Promoting Empathy and Social Justice Online). In the future, I would like to work on the intercultural experience of this course. How can I create the space for authentic intersectional learning? I want to incorporate more of the voices of the population we are severing into my syllabus. First, I am going to assign *Americanah* by the Nigerian author Chimamanda Ngozi Adichie. But while this novel is relevant and raw, it is still fictionalized. What I hope to do is present the uncensored narratives of asylum seekers and refugees in a way that does not usurp or fetishize the stories, but rather engages the student in honest reflection and revelation.

CHAPTER 30.

IN PUBLIC: THE SHIFTING CONSEQUENCES OF TWITTER SCHOLARSHIP

BONNIE STEWART

The idea of publics is central to scholarship. Scholarly pursuits are financed in part through public purses, and scholarship — in its idealized form, at least — contributes back to publics. Research. Knowledge. The public good. These are the returns through which scholarship justifies its place in society.

Yet scholarship has never been particularly open to the public. It operates, in increasingly-rationalized incarnations, as a carefully-managed ecosystem of gatekeeping measures: the prestige hierarchies of academic credentials and the academic publishing system comprise a powerful inside-baseball discourse. Contemporary scholars have tended to be far more accountable to the system itself than to actual publics, except in rare cases where the scope or consequence of the work — as in the cases of McLuhan or Milgram — has been rendered public by media.

Until now.

Over the past decade and more, digital networked communications have crept into scholarship. List-servs, then blogs, then social networking platforms crept into corners of scholarly practice. Twitter in particular has become a means by which many scholars create and curate public identities and share their work and that of others. But open networked scholarship is, by definition, open to those who choose to participate; the price of admission is not a degree or an accolade or a particular number of publications in the *right* journals. The price of admission is the willingness to engage, in public, over time, in sustained and iterative discussions over ideas and knowledge and what counts as the public good, among other things.

And that price is getting a little higher — and a little more public — all the time.

This week, I defend a dissertation on networked scholarship; an ethnography, based in extensive participant observation, document analysis, and interviews. It's odd, this point of supposed closure. When I look back on the nearly two years in which I've been embedded in envisioning, conducting, and writing this research, my days look little different at the end than they did in the middle, or at the start. I am still on Twitter, watching and contributing and trying to make sense of things, much as I was on Twitter throughout the thesis process and for years before I ever even imagined this dissertation. I am still reading and learning and sharing in broader networks, though my neglected blog — spurned for months as I tried to discipline myself to the craft of publishable academic papers — might beg to differ. My study has ended, and my Research Ethics Board approval has expired. But there has been no particular sense of closure or leave-taking in the process. I have not left my ethnographic field.

Yet if there is minimal change in *me*, the field itself — the water in which I swim as a networked identity and a networked scholar — has altered. I have had the privilege and discomfort of researching and analyzing my small subset of participants through a period of relatively dramatic shift in Twitter as a participatory culture.

Sure, since networks are distributed rather than monolithic or centrally-controlled, the social norms and memes that constitute in-group behavior within academic Twitter (and Twitter more broadly) shift constantly. But occasionally, these shifts alter the way the platform operates as a public.

The increasingly public consequences of academic Twitter may be, in the end, among the most important things I observed during my research... even if they weren't what I thought I was studying all along.

It was New Years Day, 2014, when I first realized academic Twitter was changing in front of me. I was smack in the middle of three months of daily ethnographic observation, looking at the Twitter practices of 14 highly-networked scholars from various disciplines and various parts of the globe. Since academia runs on the Christian calendar and the majority of academics are neither teaching nor grading post-Christmas, I'd expected the final week of the old year to be busy-ish but banal. I hadn't expected my research timeline to erupt in fraught and widespread back-and-forth exchanges around adjuncts and advocacy and how tenured academics should — and should not — speak to the untenured. And I hadn't expected that the eruption would signal a permanent shift in what it meant to be a public scholar. Looking back through my research data from that day, though, I think it did.

Commentary, response, analysis, re-tweets and further contributions spread out from initial volleys to constitute more than half the discussion in my research feed during the week leading up to New Years 2014. And I screencapped more than 50 tweets related to the debate — from a research sample of only 14 — on New Years Day alone.

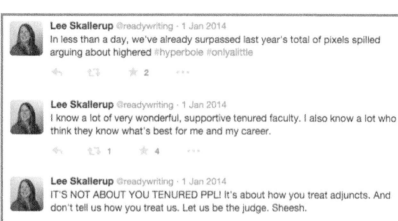

Lee Skallerup @readywriting · 1 Jan 2014
In less than a day, we've already surpassed last year's total of pixels spilled arguing about highered #hyperbole #onlyalittle

↩   ⟲   ★ 2   ...

Lee Skallerup @readywriting · 1 Jan 2014
I know a lot of very wonderful, supportive tenured faculty. I also know a lot who think they know what's best for me and my career.

↩   ⟲ 1   ★ 4   ...

Lee Skallerup @readywriting · 1 Jan 2014
IT'S NOT ABOUT YOU TENURED PPL! It's about how you treat adjuncts. And don't tell us how you treat us. Let us be the judge. Sheesh.

↩   ⟲ 4   ★ 16   ...

Lee Skallerup @readywriting · 1 Jan 2014
Like I said that other night, stop making it all about you and your hurt feelings and discomfort. Let the adjuncts SPEAK and you listen.

↩   ⟲ 2   ★ 6   ...

Dr Raul Pacheco-Vega @raulpacheco · 1 Jan 2014
Academic Twitter is about to implode with great scholars agreeing and other equally great ones disagreeing with points of blog posts.

↩   ⟲   ★ 1   ...

Dr Raul Pacheco-Vega @raulpacheco · 1 Jan 2014
Nobody, tenured or non-tenured, adjunct, post-academic, or else, is going to say exactly what you're thinking. That's why you speak up.

↩   ⟲ 3   ★ 5   ...

Dr Raul Pacheco-Vega @raulpacheco · 1 Jan 2014
Speak up so you let your own voice make the arguments. These past 3 weeks have been brutal in academic Twitter and I'm out of energy. HNY.

↩   ⟲   ★ 2   ...

I am not here for a recap of the old wounds of that week's controversy. It scabbed over, inevitably; the key parties worked out the rancor in their own ways. The larger issues of inequity, precarity, and respect remain... unsolved. What lingers, though, is not the content of the fracas so much as its markers. A year down the road and a few dozen rodeos later, these markers are familiar as what I now think of as Call-Out Culture in action:

1. the **vitriol was public and sustained**

2. it was generated not by pre-existing factionalism but by **specific public statements and responses made online**

3. it **aligned a group perceived to have power and privilege against a group without**

Specific scholars were called out by name, on record, for the implications of their words and positions, and in turn called out others; because the dispute had its origins in a public conflict between two individuals, it was difficult to engage without effectively "piling on" to a heated and highly-personalized debate. Yet the conversation was so pervasive, amplified through re-tweet and commentary, that to be present within the network almost demanded a public staking out of position, at risk of otherwise appearing oblivious or insensitive to the issue at hand.

I was a newly-fledged Twitter Researcher. I made notes.

"Speaks to an alteration of academic Twitter's implicit social contract?" — ethnographic research note, January 1, 2014

"If one does not participate or signal, can one still belong?" — ethnographic research note, January 1, 2014

"The people on the power side don't seem to realize they're on the power side." — ethnographic research note, January 1, 2014

To be an engaged and aware participant in academic Twitter at that juncture was to be embroiled — whether willingly or not — within a contested realm of speech, and one with public, ethical implications. The debate expanded and trended to the extent that silence and the refusal to engage publicly began to take on the appearance of an intentional signal, rather than the absence of a signal. Thus the calling out extended beyond those engaged in the conversation to those whose lack of engagement was seen as tacit support for the status quo.

In short, it ran like this: some people were called out in public for their speech. Some people were called out in public for their lack of speech. Some people reacted to being called out by defending their good intentions rather than owning their effects on others.

New Years 2014, in short, was a harbinger of the year to come.

———————

Looking back over the year and more since, I now recognize that the way in which the adjunct controversy played out had its roots in changing norms around public speech and speakability. Twitter, as a platform, had already begun to shift — academic Twitter was simply catching up. Mikki Kendall's August 2013 hashtag #SolidarityIsForWhiteWomen and Suey Park's December 2013 #NotYourAsianSidekick, among others, had called out implicit racism, exclusion, and inequities in representation, had raised consciousness of the implications of public speech on Twitter, and had opened up the platform as a site of concentrated political action around issues of identity and speech.

Relatedly, the now-infamous firing of Justine Sacco in December 2013, framed by Jon Ronson in the *New York Times* as "How One Stupid Tweet Blew Up Justine Sacco's Life," had demonstrated the capacity of mass Twitter outrage to generate swift real-world effects.

These newly-tactical uses of Twitter were fresh and reverberating in January 2014, and their capacity to catapult small-scale tweets to extremely large publics was just beginning to have effects on the participatory culture of Twitter more broadly. I'd been watching, all of it. But I hadn't expected it all to land on my quiet academic Twitter doorstep with quite such an immediate *thud*.

As Ronson's recent NYT headline shows, the effects of tactical Twitter have been taken up predominantly in terms of victimization. One stupid tweet can ruin your life, goes the dominant narrative, and open you to pillory and career carnage. This frame, however, fails to interrogate the operations of racism, sexism, and other forms of privilege in determining what kinds of "stupid tweets" lend themselves to viral outrage, and ignores the ways in which Call-Out Culture operates to speak for those whose identity markers are regularly silenced or smeared in "stupid tweets." As Tressie MacMillan Cottom notes, framing Sacco as a mere hapless victim of the collapse between (intended) private speech and mass publics contributes to reinforcing the sorts of casual, privileged dehumanization of others that many tactical uses of Twitter push back against:

> I get why people would not like that. Being stripped of your personhood to stand in the gap for a group of people against your will is rage inducing...You are ceaselessly primed for every implication that you have become another tick mark when you were busy living and laughing and being a wholly fallible human being. It is horrible to lose a job for that. It is a privilege to have never before lost a job for that. ("Racists Getting Fired: The Sins of Whiteness on Social Media")

I seldom stand in the gap, online. My experience of academic Twitter prior to New Year's 2014 had been one primarily marked by the intersections of my whiteness and my gender performance and my in-network centrality and my relative obscurity everywhere else. I am not the target of "stupid tweets." And thus, when I think about changes in academic Twitter and its tactical uses and effects over the past year, then, the question I focus on is "changes for whom?"

Tressie points that for many people, standing in the gap is nothing new. Yes, Twitter's increasing tendency towards calling people out lends alarming scale and reach to that experience of identity reduction, and this collapse of public and private is not something to be taken lightly. But when it is framed, as in Ronson's NYT piece, primarily as a spectre haunting unmarked bodies, threatening supposedly-innocuous white people like Justine Sacco with standing in the gap for reasons that amount to little more than schadenfreude, something is missing from the analysis. Twitter as a tactical public allows for abuses, and for defenses of power and privilege. It also allows for bodies marked by race, gender, class, queerness, disability, and intersections of these and other identity facets to publicly resist being made to stand in the gap. It forces a reckoning with the ways that casual, even ephemeral public speech can reinforce the marginalization of others. It has become a space less tolerant of speech unwilling to account for its own power relations and assumptions.

This matters for scholarship, and for the ideals of knowledge and the public good that scholarship espouses.

What has changed in the year and more since January 2014, I think, is that networks' capacity to turn into full-scale publics at any moment has become increasingly visible. Where academic Twitter once seemed quietly parochial and collegial almost to the point of excess, it is now thrust into the messy, contested business of being *truly* open to the public.

What has also changed is that the conversation on adjuncts shifted a bit, in academic Twitter. Consciousness was raised. Initiatives emerged. It is a little less acceptable, now, to speak from positions that deny the experiences and voices of contingent academic employees. Does this solve the problem? It does not and it cannot. But it changes the shape of the public scholarly sphere, and makes it just a little more open to those who stand in the gap for higher ed. And this is something.

CHAPTER 31.

THE RULES OF TWITTER

DOROTHY KIM

Twitter is an incredibly dynamic digital tool that can create spaces of flattened hierarchies. These spaces can fuel inclusive pedagogy. But before teaching with Twitter, instructors have to think about how to use it together with students. What are the rules — particularly in relation to ethics?

Twitter as a Digital Mediated Public Space

Several recent posts have considered participatory culture and the potential demise of social media. In "Something is Rotten," Bonnie Stewart writes, "they're multiplying, these narratives, just like the fruit flies in my kitchen." Academics and tech programmers have imagined Twitter has changed from the porch to their homes to now becoming Broadway the street. And in so doing, people like Alan Jacobs have declared the demise of the social media microblogging platform. This is not new. The spatial frames discussed by the four white men cited in Jacobs' piece (academics, writers, and tech programmers) are of a certain brand of tech culture — male, white, upper-middle class. So when lamenting Twitter's end, they believe it is the end of conversations "on the porch" where they can "have a nice chat with friends and neighbors." But the porch is located in a white, single-family home clearly either in the suburbs or further afield, but not in an urban (racially mixed) public space.

The lament is that now Twitter feels as if they've walked onto Broadway. Suey Park and David Leonard in "In Defense of Twitter Feminism" explain the white fear about Twitter, "By not being a segregated space, Twitter is marked as an unsafe space for the white middle-class user who has to share a platform with people of color, especially when whiteness and privilege are made visible." In other words, porch in the suburbs = white, upper-middle class life, while Broadway in the middle of urban public space = multiracial, multiclass mass.

The relocation of Twitter — from the bucolic image of conversations with neighbors in the "American Dream" single-family neighborhood to loud Broadway (clearly envisioning New York City) — is a statement about digital white flight. However, the neighborhood in the eyes of these white male pundits was always imagined as safe, suburban — by default — white, and upper-middle class. Basically, these pundits are blind to their own white privilege in discussing a digital space. And this is the issue: Twitter was never a porch, it has always been a mediated public space, a hacked public space.

Mediated Public Space

By understanding how Twitter is a mediated public space, students and teachers will understand the rules and etiquette this space demands. What is a mediated public space? Eunsong Kim and I discussed this briefly in "#TwitterEthics Manifesto." Working on the definition from danah boyd: "Social network sites are the latest generation of 'mediated publics' — environments where people can gather publicly through mediating technology. In some senses, mediated publics are similar to the unmediated publics with which most people are familiar — parks, malls, parking lots, cafes, etc." Likewise, if one thinks of these familiar public spaces — parks, malls, parking lots, cafes, etc. — one realizes that some might, in fact, be owned by private companies, but still function as public spaces.

When I say that Twitter is a mediated and hacked public space, what I mean is that Twitter, the medium as a microblogging platform owned by a corporation, was never intended to become such a vast "public" digital space. Rather, its aims were likely about networking for information and commerce, not for the goals of political and social protest, the vocalization and amplification of minority voices and points of view. Nor was it imagined as the digital space most conducive to the actual mingling of a huge multiracial, multi-bodied, multi-abled population. If Robert Jones's *Atlantic* article is right, most white Americans do not have any friends of another race. However, when they use Twitter, that changes quite drastically. Privately owned spaces can be hacked to become ersatz communal public spaces.

The best example I have of this is a small park/large lawn in front of a high rise office building on Wilshire Blvd in Koreatown. Los Angeles's urban landscapes are notorious for their lack of centralized public spaces; instead, there are many more spaces owned by corporations and seen as private property. Though technically Griffith Park is larger than Central Park, it does not function as a centralized public space. Urban geographers, city planners, and critics have discussed Los Angeles's dispersed geographies as well as its battles over private control of public works including the closure of the functioning subway system in 1963 (See Mike Davis's history). In Los Angeles's Koreatown, the central node of mediated public space is a patch of grass on Wilshire which is the small lawn/park owned by an office tower. But because of its location and the fact that the next building has a massive jumbotron on its side, it has become a hacked public space. There are public festivals; there are middle of the night viewings of World Cup games where the city shuts down Wilshire because of the crowds; there are more civic-minded political protests. In a city without a defined center, this mediated public space has at the moment become a central node for a minority population.

Likewise, Twitter is a corporate-owned digital medium that has become a hacked public digital media space. The medium has been bent to the purposes of its users. A large percentage of minority and women users are on Twitter according to a Pew Research Center study. As Sydette Harry has written in "Attacking the Stream," for groups who do not have or have never had the power to control conversations, Twitter works because "we don't expect technology to conform to our consumption habits; we adapt to the platforms we're given and make them our own." She discusses exactly how a hacked digital media public works and functions even within a government, academic, neoliberal surveillance climate:

> For those of us in marginalized communities, surveillance is a part of life that we have long been accustomed to. We know we are being watched and measured. Unlike many who bemoan a more innocent era of tech, we have come to accept those conditions because they were practiced on us first. So rather than falling into a fight or flight mentality, we find the cracks in the infrastructure and break through them.

So within a frame of understanding how Twitter functions as a hacked digital media public, instructors and students can work out how to create digital communities with lively dialogue and debates while also thinking about how mediated publics function and what sort of affordances and limits this particular medium allows and also breaks down.

Twitter Basics

What are the ethics and legalities of free speech, respectability, and "civility" in these contexts? In considering this question, start with Zeynep Tufekci's "Social Media is a Conversation Not a Press Release". Then, look at the aforementioned "#TwitterEthics Manifesto".

These begin to create a framework for how Twitter functions

as digital publics. From here, we can consider Twitter's multiple pedagogical functions. If Twitter is a public square, many kinds of activities can happen on it: business advertising; public protests (#Ferguson, #SolidarityIsForWhiteWomen), public lectures (and conference hashtags), public art installments and performances; rants on soapboxes of all sorts; hanging out with colleagues and friends; public grief; public information exchange; and public education conducive to open discussion (#SaturdaySchool, #DecolonizeSAAM, #MillenialsOfColor).

Twitter as a Mediated Public Protest Space

Twitter receives a lot of mainstream press about its function as a mediated public protest space. Hashtag Activism is a valid and important node in organizing, encouraging, disseminating information, and archiving public protests. For example, there were over 1 million tweets before #Ferguson got coverage from mainstream media. The #Ferguson protests have effectively mobilized the country with #BlackOutBlackFriday and #HandsUpWalk-Out. Likewise, Alicia Garza's #BlackLivesMatter has become a powerful node over the last several months. In the end, Twitter and other social media sites have usurped mainstream media as the main and primary source of on-the-ground, archived, filtered, and live information about police brutality, antiblackness, and #JusticeForMikeBrown. The power of social media, but particularly Twitter's rhizomatic (i.e. multiple, non-hierarchical exits and entry points), flattened structure, has created pushback and even #TwitterPanic. You can see this as recently as Bob McCulloch (Ferguson's District Attorney's) statement that social media and particularly Twitter were causing the problems in #Ferguson (rather than police brutality and anti-blackness). Of course, this particular charge is racialized since the trending, spread, and public protest and outcry over #Ferguson and #JusticeForMikeBrown were driven by #BlackTwitter.

Exploring Social Power Relations on Twitter

Some resources for instructors and students who want to explore these topics further:

- For discussions of the hashtag and its aggregating powers, begin with with Suey Park and Eunsong Kim's "Hashtags as Decolonial Projects with Radical Origins."
- Follow this up with Sophia Seawell's "#NotYourAsianSidekick: Rethinking Protest Spaces and Tactics."
- Finally, to delve deeply into the methodologies, pitfalls, affordances, and possibilities of doing analysis of Twitter as a social media protest space, I would recommend looking at a trio of articles by Zeynep Tufekci:
  - "Big Questions for Social Media Big Data: Representativeness, Validty and Other Methodological Pitfalls";
  - "'Not This One': Social Movements, the Attention Economy, and Microcelebrity Networked Activism";
  - "Social Media and the Decision to Participate in Political Protest: Observations From Tahrir Square" by Zeynep Tufekci and Christopher Wilson.

For pedagogical resources on #Ferguson on Twitter, see how #FergusonSyllabus was created and consider Marcia Chatelain's resource list in The Atlantic.

As a protest space, the point of Twitter is to boost the signal so that others and eventually mainstream media, local officials, politicians, and the world at large notices and adds their voice. It can also be an organizing space for international protest coordination as we saw after the Mike Brown murder when @FeministaJones organized #NMOS14 as a vigil reaching nearly all 50 states, Europe, and Canada.

However, analysis that requires harvesting data or visualizing data requires consideration of Tufekci's and Wilson's point that the big data modeling does not actually tell the whole story. In fact, as Tufekci has argued, the best approach to this work is to get the narratives from the communities and be scrupulously ethical about how this is done. Twitter is a multivocal platform, so it's important to talk directly with communities to see how they want their narratives told, archived, discussed. As Eusong Kim and I wrote in "#TwitterEthics Manifesto," the American Folklore Society has guidelines and statements about this, where they reject the term "human subjects." The main rule of working with students and Twitter is to realize that ethics should be emphasized above all else. Harvesting, quoting, and using others tweets without consent, attribution, discussion, or compensation/credit is a major problem. The odds are that if people are protesting using a hashtag, they are willing to speak about why they are protesting so interview them and ask permission about quoting a tweet. Likewise, if you are running a Twitter teach-in, you might as the moderator just say that you plan to storify the tweets in an archive and if people would just tell you up front if they want their tweets left out.

A subcategory of the Political/Social Protest is the Political/Social Rant. Yes, very much like a public space, people on Twitter can decide to tweet a rant while standing on a soapbox about a whole range of topics. This is completely standard in public spaces. As an undergraduate at Berkeley, I and everyone else on campus knew that between the hours of about 11am-3pm in Sproul Plaza, people would literally get on boxes and discuss socialism, Jesus, why we should all ask the Regents to divest in Big Oil, etc. There were also a cappella groups, jugglers, slam poetry, and step troupes performing. Feel free to retweet and boost whichever public event captures your interest. However, if they have a sign that says no photography, no recording, and no live-tweeting, you should know what that means.

Twitter as a Space for Public Community Grief

#Ferguson has made the public acutely aware about what public community grief can look like. This is also true on Twitter, people want to turn to this public digital medium to grieve as a group over local, national, and global events. But there are rules on how one should behave during these times of collective public digital grief.

1. Communities that are affected by tragedy should always be centered in grieving. They are most affected, bearing the largest burden, and dealing with the most public scrutiny. In so doing, be polite, show support, but do not take over the conversation by tweeting what you think of said tragedy for more than a handful of tweets. In fact, in such situations, and especially if there is a hashtag, follow the lead of the community, boost their signals by retweeting what they are saying (do not quote the tweets), and do what they ask including boosting certain hashtags. This is also known as staying in your lane. It is an incredibly difficult time, be mindful of your privileges and your inability to speak for the group grieving.

2. Along with this, if the group has asked to not post triggering images, video, or posts that they feel will harm them further, do that. Listen to the community. Do not discount their requests. Otherwise, you are basically creating more harm for them in this difficult time. Again, it is the community who should decide what they want to do in order to grieve.

3. In tweeting during moments of community grief, do not take things too personally if you accidentally make mistakes and are told off by the community members grieving. In particular, if you have to tweet someone to ask

basic questions about what happened and the narrative. Remember, this is labor that you have asked the community grieving to do that also triggers the trauma of the tragedy. Instead, go back and read people's timeline or the hashtag's timeline.

4. Always support the community who are dealing with the tragedy. Be polite, ask if they need things, or just silently retweet. This is about respecting community grief at all times.

5. If you want to do some sort of discussion and/or article on the grieving community and a particularly hashtag, please wait some time and be very careful to respect the community. Ask politely for permission to use their tweets, explain what you are going to do, and do not get angry if they say "no." The individuals in a community get to decide if they wish to have their grief publicized. Just thank them for replying and move on politely.

6. Never tone-police and tell the community grieving that they should grieve in the way you, as an outsider, feel is appropriate. It is not your place. Communities can decide how, when, and in what forms they wish to express their grief over their communal tragedy. Respect their rights to choose how to grieve.

Algorithms and Social Media

If students want a more in-depth consideration of the technical platform and its algorithms, functionality, and problems, they can begin by reading these two pieces by Zeynep Tufekci: "What Happens to #Ferguson Affects Ferguson: Net Neutrality, Algorithmic Filtering, and Ferguson" and "Why Twitter Should Not Algorithmically Curate the Timeline." Then, consider the many complaints that have been discussed on Twitter regularly by women of color users about privacy, stalkers, the functionality of the DM, the mute button, the issues of abusive twitter users, etc.

An excellent assignment would be to read Aja Romano's article about the #AskCostolo hashtag and look at the #AskCostolo hashtag. The students will undoubtedly notice that for a question and answer forum, Costolo never answered the majority of questions asked to him that related entirely to abuse issues on Twitter. Again, as a multivocal medium that talks back, Twitter makes it difficult for CEOs and others to "control" the conversation and the sound-bytes.

Academic Twitter and Live-Tweeting Conferences and Talks

The rules of live-tweeting academic conferences and talks have been specifically explained in numerous articles: Ekins & Perlstein in *PLOS Computational Biology*, Steve Kolowich in *Inside Higher Education* (The Academic Twitterazzi), Menachem Wecker in the *Chronicle*, and Ernesto Priego in *The Guardian*. I have written about it myself for my own Medieval Studies discipline in "#MedievalTwitter." An interesting assignment for students would be to read one of these and consider what their majors or academic disciplines' Twitter feeds look like, what they are most interested in topically, and what the varying reasons to use Twitter are in those disciplines. The academic etiquette surrounding Twitter is that live-tweeting is permitted unless the speaker and/or moderator says that the presenter does not want any live-tweeting. Though, one should, just to be extra polite, ask for permission to quote whoever you are tweeting if you publish something on a blog, article, or in other more formal ways.

Twitter Teach-Ins function similarly to public lectures but with more participants and more interaction. The point is also to signal boost to attract more participants and discussion. An interesting assignment for instructors and students would be to organize a teach-in on a specific topic and then to have the students advertise it on Twitter, possibly contact Rhonda Ragsdale (@ProfRagsdale) who does #SaturdaySchool to boost that signal or even collaborate, and try out a teach-in with your class. Likewise, I have seen #DecolonizeSAAM from the Save Wiyabi

Project, who regularly hold live-tweeting on varied topics accompanied by video conversations and discussion. Or look at #MillenialsOfColor who also work with a similar format. They advertise times for a live-tweet chat plus include Google+ video discussion. Likewise, you can see this happen with #Ferguson-Fireside which are chats with the organizers on video and in conversation on Twitter.

Twitter as a Social Space

Twitter is also a mediated social space. Friends and colleagues hang out, discuss politics, entertainment, how hot Alexander Skarsgård is on *True Blood*, how Apple's iPhone is too big or too small, the best recipe for chocolate cake, etc. These are semi-private conversations happening in a mediated social public. Therefore, when journalists, academics, and MRA activists from 4chan decide to use this digital space to harvest tweets without consent, permission, discussion, interaction, or credit/compensation, it is a form of harassment, stalking, and violent aggression. It can be compared to having the government come in and record your conversation without your permission or consent. Or how it would feel if unsanctioned pictures of you in a public space got sold to the National Enquirer. Again, this is not ethical and is a form of violent aggression. Be mindful. Public, as I hope this article shows, means many things. Do not blithely use the arguments so many white politicos, media pundits, and academics use: "Twitter is Public." As we can see, Twitter is a very complex, organic, and mediated public space. There are many rules in relation to many kinds of public situations.

In addition, when friends and colleagues are having specific conversations in groups that aren't necessarily about the political/social protest, part of a political rant, teach-ins, or live-tweeting a conference discussion, there are etiquette issues. Yes, it's fine to retweet things that you find interesting in the conversation, but please as you would in a social group at a public plaza that you do not really know and they do not know you, introduce yourself and ask politely if you can join in the discussion because you are very interested in x and y topic. Also, make sure you know what the conversation has actually been about before just jumping in. Be informed, be polite, and listen.

Twitter Abuse and Twitter as a Radically Inclusive Public Space

Finally, understand that like so many public spaces in the world and particularly in the Anglo-speaking world, certain kinds of digital bodies get more harassment, stalking, abuse, and violent aggression thrown at them than others. Digital bodies are an extension of bodies in real life. Therefore marks of race, gender, disability, religion, and sexuality make Twitter both a medium of possibility and a medium where the same sorts of surveillance, abuse, control, and silencing happens to these divergent bodies as in real public spaces. During #RaceSwap, for example, prominent black and other WOC feminists switched their avatars to white men and the number of threats, trolls, violent aggression, and harassment dropped substantially. Again, digital bodies and how they are marked matter tremendously in public mediated spaces.

For students and instructors to explore what this means, I would suggest reading the entire *Model View Culture* issue about Social Media, as well as Andy Smith and Miriame Kaba's great piece "Interlopers on Social Media: Feminism, Women of Color, and Oppression."

Twitter as a Space for Learning

Teachers and students alike need to understand that this particular social medium has become a space of activism and justice, which means that abuse will not be tolerated and that people and their friends and colleagues will fight back. Apologies are perfectly fine on Twitter especially if you've realized only after the fact that you have committed ethical and/or etiquette infractions. If Twitter is a space for learning, discussion, and thoughtful interaction, we need to consider how much particular forms of privilege will inform our positionality on this medium. Do not immediately expect to have "respect" and "authority" because you are a college student or a college instructor. Rather, understand that you will earn respect by what you say and what you do; by who you defend and who and what you fight for — by how much you have reflected on one's position and privilege in the world.

Twitter is not a one-directional medium. It's a complex, every-changing, rhizomatic digital medium. And this is entirely why Twitter is a wonderful learning space. Enjoy. Tweet. Interact.

CHAPTER 32.

SOCIAL MEDIA, SERVICE, AND THE PERILS OF SCHOLARLY AFFECT

LEE SKALLERUP BESSETTE

I am not a scholar, at least not in the traditional sense.

Almost 5 years ago, I wrote the blog post "How Higher Ed Makes Most Things Meaningless". It also appeared on *Inside Higher Ed*. It remains one of the most-read pieces on my old blog. And even though I don't post there anymore, my old Blogger site still receives over 2,000 hits a month. Five years later, I'm still left wondering whether the work I do online counts. It matters, but does it count?

Recently, William Thomas, Chair of the Department of History at the University of Nebraska-Lincoln and the John and Catherine Angle Professor in the Humanities and Professor of History, offered a typology for digital scholarship. He breaks it down to three types: Interactive Scholarly Work, Digital Projects / Thematic Research Collections, and Digital Narratives. What strikes me in these categories' descriptions is that they are all still deeply embedded in traditional forms of scholarship and scholarly expectations: theory, rigor, methodology, evidence, citation.

Scholarship, even in its digital form, is still narrowly considered. We are conditioned to accept old rigor in new clothing.

But my work, what I do on Twitter and through my blog and elsewhere, has become a kind of *Thematic Research Collection,* one that other scholars are mining for their own scholarship, but lacking in some of the other features Thomas describes. He defines Thematic Research Collections:

> Combining tools and archival materials framed around a historiographically significant or critical problem, these projects are sprawling investigations into a major problem ... Scholars embed interpretive affordances in the collection and use these affordances to open up new modes of inquiry and/or discovery ... Often traditional peer reviewed scholarship is derived from the thematic research collection. The next phase of thematic research collections might feature interpretive scholarship embedded within and in relationship to the collection.

My "sprawling investigation" includes (but in no way is only about) contingency, gender, and digital labor and affect. My network, my RT's are my curation, my pulling from various sources and formats. But my work through social media is also highly personal, history as it is happening. This is the natural progression of working "out loud" the way I do, and in fact I celebrate and embrace the deepening and understanding of evolving fields. However, that my work is considered secondary, in terms of its scholarly rigor, is problematic — who really benefits from the work I'm doing?

Perhaps the resistance to my work as a legitimate scholarly exercise comes from the simple fact that I didn't set out to create something "scholarly" when I began tweeting; however, I always tweeted as a scholar, academically trained and practiced, and I did and do always tweet with a purpose. Maybe not an explicitly stated thesis, like an essay or book (although I have tweeted and blogged enough for at least two scholarly tomes), but a purpose informed by my positionality as well as my evolving scholarly understanding and knowledge. I have informed and inspired scholars and scholarship; for examples of studies that heavily rely on my work on Twitter for their research and conclusions.

Maybe it's because *I* haven't yet made the final step, which is turning my work into peer-reviewed journal articles. In "'Who Do You Think You Are?': When Marginality Meets Academic Microcelebrity," Tressie McMillan Cottom has a powerful example of turning her own experiences and work in social media circles into an important journal article. But should I have to? Should anyone have to?

As a result, I am, for lack of a better term, having an impact. I am being cited. But the work being cited and where it is having an impact are outside of traditional models of scholarship. I am embodying the challenge of dual relationships and context collapse in higher education. Except the institution doesn't recognize much of the work, and the context collapses into an abyss of work that isn't seen as work, scholarship that isn't really scholarship.

There are those who are trying to articulate the argument for Networked Learning and other Digital Scholarship to "count" — scholars such as Bonnie Stewart ("In Abundance: Networked Participatory Practices as Scholarship"), Deb Verhoeven ("Doing the Sheep Good: Facilitating Engagement in Digital Humanities and Creative Arts Research"), and Martin Weller ("Reward and Tenure") are pushing open the definitions of scholarship. I want to argue, however, that coupled with the non-traditional appearance of digital scholarship, how digital work has been described and named within the academy remains a serious obstacle to its full legitimacy.

It has been largely agreed upon that blogging is not scholarship, at least not in consideration of peer-reviewed scholarship that we typically consider in hiring, tenure, and promotion. In fact, blogging should instead be considered service. Service, the most maligned of the pillars that academia is built upon, even more so than teaching. Service, the most gendered and racialized of the pillars. We can never do too much research and scholarship. We are warned against teaching too much. But we are often punished for too much service. Except when we are also punished for not doing enough.

At MLA 2015, Leonard Cassuto, Vanessa Ryan, and David R. Shumway presented a session on these tensions between teaching, research, and service, and the unequal nature of the conversations around them. While it isn't captured in the Twitter stream, there was an observation from the panelists that there is serious intellectual work, research, and synthesis in many of the service duties imposed by administrative responsibilities within the institution. This kind of service work could and should be seen as a form of scholarship.

Can we then also think about the serious intellectual work, research, and synthesis involved in the so-called service work many of us are gladly partaking in through Twitter and blogs and other forms of digital engagement? These kinds of skills, of transferring knowledge and communicating with different audiences, of collaborating and developing networks in a variety of circumstances, are valuable to our institutions as well as to our students.

I am, in very real ways, a primary source, one that is being used in scholarly research. I am also a better pedagogue because of what I have learned through my social media work. One of my hypotheses is that social media work involves a great deal of affect, of emotion, which is again, a gendered and racialized concept, particularly when considered alongside traditional scholarship, typically understood as unbiased, informed by fact and not feeling. Scholarly networks of trust and of collaboration that rely on affect to be effective, as well as traditional scholarly research and dissemination.

But then, how do we reward or measure or acknowledge this form of work in an environment that typically only rewards dispassion and "neutrality," where passion, as bell hooks notes, or *"excitement ... was viewed as potentially disruptive"* (*Teaching to Transgress*). hooks is pointing to how she is to appear in the classroom, but this excitement, these emotions, are even further excluded in the treatment of our research, particularly through our writing — to show emotion is to be unprofessional, unserious, unworthy. To be a professor is to be a professional and to be a professional is to limit affect.

Aimée Morrison recently wrote about her coming to terms with the emotional nature of teaching and learning:

> Real learning is transformative — and all transformations are fraught with fear and excitement and loss and gain. The crucible of the new self is necessarily hot; it burns. Teaching, I find, is as emotionally and personally wrenching as learning is, and I need to find new ways to incorporate this reality into my work, even as I create some boundaries for myself and my students. …When I teach, I necessarily make myself incredibly vulnerable to my students, by reaching out to them with ideas and sources and methods and assignments and illustrations, and asking them to hold on.

The title of the post is "Teaching and All The Feels", while I could have just as easily titled this essay, "Research and All The Feels." The work I do on social media, the research, the teaching, the learning, all involves a great deal of emotion, of vulnerability, of excitement, of disappointment, of affect. This is work that is not particularly valued in higher education, work that is seen as feminized, as irrational, as less-than. My affective, intellectual work, my service-through-social media are not valued.

But how do you measure the impact, the rigor, if my blogging and social media presence are, in fact, a form of scholarship? Four years ago, I wrote a blog post about contingent faculty issues, as they related to my disciplinary organization ("Taking Action for Contingent Faculty"). The post lead to a pretty intense discussion on Twitter with then-incoming MLA President Michael Bérubé about the importance of tenure, and was followed by another blog post ("Killing Two Birds with One Giant Stone: Tenure"). Four years later, *The Humanities, Higher Education, and Academic Freedom* by Bérubé is set to come out.

I bring up this example for a number of reasons. Although it lacked the trappings of more traditional scholarship, my blog posts and subsequent discussion on Twitter were deeply informed by both personal experience, observation, and research. I had an impact, I helped reshape someone's, a very important someone's, view on contingent faculty issues, tenure, and academic freedom. I was involved in the "conversation" at the highest level for my particular profession, a conversation however that was as filled with strong emotion as it was sound research.

But I doubt the exchange (and subsequent blog posts and conversations) will show up on the Works Cited page. Who gets cited, acknowledged, named are all important considerations when it comes to the reward system we have set up in academia. If we aren't cited or show up in citation indexes, we sometimes quite literally do not exist. These formal academic networks of citation are about the livelihood of aspiring scholars and academics. But they are also about respect, about recognition, about being included.

These are preliminary thoughts, the start of something that I hope turns into a much larger conversation. There are still things I haven't read, people who know more than me whom I haven't spoken to. But, what started as a feeling, for me, of something unrewarded, unnamed, unspoken, informed five years of being immersed in social media and networks and my own embodied experiences within and without, has become a tentative place to start having a larger conversation around the critically affective work being performed by scholars who would not be called scholars.

CHAPTER 33.

TEXTUAL COMMUNITIES: WRITING, EDITING, AND GENERATION IN CHICANA FEMINISM

ANNEMARIE PÉREZ

When I first proposed the research title "Editing Chicanas," one of my mentors, Alice Gambrell, commented that it was a good title, partly because it prompted such anxiety. I was surprised, as anxiety wasn't what I had intended. I was referring to the act of editing — how was this anxiety-making? As we talked, I realized she was thinking of the act of *being* edited. Being edited, like the process of peer review discussed so well by Sean Michael Morris ("Collaborative Peer Review: Gathering the Academy's Orphans"), is generally intimate, sometimes to the point of violation. Academic editors often serve a gatekeeping function, one that can allow them to define, or help define, a field of study. While writing, especially its myth as a solitary act of creation, is examined, deified and debunked, editing, so central to publication, is rarely discussed. The history of the book is figured as a triad relationship between authors, publishers and readers, with the role of editorship either subsumed under publishing or left invisible. Yet my research on the relationships and writings produced by Chicana print cultures demonstrated that editorship and editors were and are frequently a catalyst for writing and the "making" of theory. Editors can serve as gatekeepers, yes, but they also solicit writing, contextualize it, help refine it and, ideally, put it into conversation with other voices.

Peer review, frequently both blind and anonymous, is itself a form of and part of the process of academic editing. For me, one of the most interesting and sad conversations I've witnessed on Twitter, following the articles "Peer-Review Jerk Survival Guide" and "Revise and Resubmit!," both by Rebecca Schuman, was the discussion of blind peer review. In tweeted responses there were some defenses of the system while, at the same time, academics across disciplines shared the negative and often cutting criticism they had been offered. Sometimes, it seems, anonymous peer review more closely resembles Internet trolling than anything pedagogical. Ironically, within the Slate comments following Schuman's "Revise and Resubmit," peer reviews are frequently defended as a test by fire of the research and writer. Yet this process can result in work being lost, not only to the journal where it was originally submitted, but ultimately to any reader, as the author shoves the rejected article into a virtual file.

While readers may perceive the authorship of collected works, whether journals, newspapers or anthologies, as autonomous and absolute, the content is actually the result of individual and collective editorial decisions. Within a text, editors are seen, to the extent they are seen at all, as serving a generally administrative or organizational role. In reality editors act as facilitators, filters and/or gatekeepers — albeit sometimes uncomfortably — deciding who and what is included and excluded, encouraging writing that otherwise might never be published or even written. Editors also decide, in the case of a movement's newspaper, journal, or anthology, what constitutes the inside and the outside. By making these decisions, they decide whose thoughts merit inclusion, which ones belong and which do not, controlling how and if a subject or author will be presented. Still further, editors decide through which point of view or lens an artistic, social, or political movement will be viewed. Lien Chao comments on this in her discussion of the emergence of the Chinese Canadian anthology. She notes that minority-voiced anthologies frequently carry "larger-than-life" titles and roles. This was the case with the foundational text *Aztlan: An Anthology of Mexican American Literature* by Luis Valdez and Stan Steiner, which was the first (and for a while only) anthology of Chicano writing published by a popular press. This same point is made more bluntly — though doubtlessly tongue-in-cheek — by Norton editor Alane Salierno Mason, who writes in *Boston Review* that "editing a literary anthology is like forming a social club — you get to decide who are 'your' kind of people." Anthologies have the authority to speak with the collectively powerful voice of an otherwise mute community, and can end up being a movement's primary or even solitary voice.

The rhetoric of the 1960s-1970s Chicano Movement focused on manhood with leaders like Cesar Chavez galvanizing crowds by exhorting them in speeches that "...we are not beasts of burden, agricultural implements or rented slaves; we are men." While the rhetoric focused on manhood and nation, the Movement itself opened up opportunities for women to write and edit. From this grew a questioning of gender roles in the Movement. Chicana writers and editors of the late twentieth century split the single "divine soul" by pointing out the contradictions and flaws in a discourse on the nation (U.S. and Chicano) which presumes only masculine subjects. Their writings created textual communities as sites for feminist, cosmopoetic and cosmopolitical interventions into U.S. print culture. At the same time, like African American feminists of the same period, writers like Elizabeth Martinez and Anna Nieto Gomez resisted the essentialist and universalizing tendencies of white feminism, forging in its place a U.S. differential feminism of color. The publications of the Chicano Movement themselves became communities that were, to a degree, bound together by the intersections of their texts, as essays, poetry and reports were published and republished by one community newspaper after another.

The textual community created via Chicana editors are ones created as imagined communities — that is, the editors bring together authors who became a community as they imagine their own connections (whether or not they know each other face-to-face). The early Chicana textual communities, as Blackwell's research on *Hijas de Cuauhtémoc* demonstrates, were actual physical communities. Likewise, many of the contributors to *This Bridge Called My Back* were part of the same community of San Francisco Bay Area lesbians of color, something reinforced in the anthology's history, which recounts how Anzaldua's lack of money for postage meant that she handed out copies of the call for contributions in person. By the time Lopez, Davalos, and Alicia Partnoy restarted *Vocas* as *Chicana / Latina: The Journal of MALCS* in 2003, the community of Chicanas and Latinas is separated by geography but virtually real, through its connection with MALCS (Mujeres Activas en Letras y Cambio Social, a Chicana / Latina / Indigenous women's organization). This meant, and continues to mean, a community physically forms and reforms each year at a summer institute. As part of this annual institute, the journal's editors and former editors sponsor an intensive two-day workshop to help prepare first-time authors and their work for submission to the journal, helping to demystify the journal's conventional blind review process.

Discussing early African American periodicals in her 2005 article for *American Literary History*, Frances Smith Foster commented that "sometimes, the identities of editors, publishers, and financial backers are more important than the names of the literary contributors." Chicanas on the frontiers of the Chicano movement, such as writer, newspaper editor and publisher Elizabeth Martínez (editor of movement newspaper *El Grito del Norte*), used their position to create a collective community, supporting Chicana authorship. In the years that followed, Chicana activists and scholars, such as Teresa McKenna at *Aztlán*, edited Chicana/o chapbooks and journals, doing editorial labor and opening the Chicano scholarly publication to Chicana voices. In the early

1980s, writers and editors Cherríe Moraga and Gloria Anzaldúa used their anthology, *This Bridge Called My Back*, for a similar purpose, creating a textual community / collective of writers which participated in the project of developing and defining a specific new feminism by women of color, as well as Anzaldúa's border theory. Moving from the twentieth into the twenty-first century, academics such as Chicana historians Deena Gonzalez and Antonia Castañeda have edited the Chicana Matters series for the University of Texas Press, promoting texts by both young and senior Chicana scholars. At the same time, scholars Tiffany Lopez and KarenMary Davalos restarted the MALCS journal (which became *Chicana / Latina*), building the journal into the field's flagship, while in the process developing and defining a Chicana feminist editorial praxis. What even my preliminary research has demonstrated is that Chicana editors have shaped the emergence of Chicana feminism as a discipline. Lopez speaks of "citational footprints" within Chicana feminism, a feature of the journal during her and Davalos' editorial partnership. The history of Chicana editorship is to a significant degree the intellectual history of Chicana feminism.

Editing, at its best, is generative. The story of the publication of the anthology *This Bridge Called My Back*, told through a series of introductions, are a testament to that. The book began, as Gloria Anzaldúa recounts, with an act of her painful exclusion by a writing workshop. Channeling her hurt and anger at this rejection, Anzaldúa wrote a call for submissions, requesting writing speaking back to white feminism. As the works came in, were read, and were shaped by the two co-editors, the project and its context changed, its focus becoming not feminists of color talking back to white feminists, but the more resistant idea of feminists of color talking to each other. Researching *Bridge*, one of the things that stood out to me is that for many of the book's contributors, this was their first publication. Some went on to publish more; for some this is their only published work. The history of *Bridge* is a fraught one. Without Anzaldúa's initial call, would they have ever published their piece? More importantly, would it ever have been written?

Although I was not aware of the fact when I began this project, the term *textual community* is neither new nor original, but is rather a term which evolved out of reader response criticism. The term *textual community* may be used broadly, as Juliana Spahr does in *Everybody's Autonomy: Connective Reading and Collective Identity*, to discuss the sense of connection readers of an individual work feel toward each other about their collective, dynamic participation in the text through their shared experience as readers of it. Spahr builds on the earlier usage by Thomas Kuhn, further developed by David Olson, who writes in *The World on Paper: The Conceptual and Cognitive Implications of Writing and Reading* that "to be literate it is not enough to know the words; one must also participate in the discourse of some textual community," meaning that within that community, one knows whether an individual text is important and, again within that community, how to read and understand it. While these definitions of textual community have significance for Chicana writings, including the anthologies *This Bridge Called My Back* and *Chicana Voices*, especially in discussions of their importance as consciousness-raising texts, I am using the term to convey a different sort of community. A *textual community*, within this work and my larger project on Chicana editorship, refers specifically to a group of writers and editors who identify with each other as part of, or as representing, a larger community or movement, and/or are identified by readers as belonging to this common collective publication.

My definition of textual community begins with and draws heavily on the historical and sociological studies of physical communal settlements in the United States described as "developmental communalism." Donald Pitzer, in *America's Communal Utopias*, writes that the three central assumptions of developmental communalism are that

1. "communal living is a generic social construction"

2. "communal structuring usually is adopted in an early stage of development"

3. "communal arrangements that are not adjusted over time to changing realities or long-range objectives may contribute to the decline or demise of the original movements"

Using Pitzer's three assumptions, but opening them further in order to discuss text-centered communities, the textual communities formed by collectively run and relatively short-lived 1970s Chicana-edited journals and newspapers (such as the publications *Hijas de Cuauhtemoc*, *Encuentro Femenil*, *Regeneration* and *El Grito del Norte*) can be discussed as textual communities as well as physical collectives. These early publications played a significant part in the development of Chicana feminist writings, and had influence which lasted far longer than the short-lived publication history of each journal or newspaper, partly because they evolved out of these physical collectives and communities into textual communities — what Chicana scholar Maylei Blackwell calls "print communities." Via re-printing, early Chicana writings were distributed far wider than each newspaper's relatively small printing, moving between Chicana/o publications and communities. Enriqueta Vasquez's text, "The Women of La Raza," for example, with its multiple re-printings and re-publications, is an example of a text gaining cultural capital by its distribution in multiple venues. Rather than seeing these publications as having "failed" due to their small print runs and often short lives, these collectives can be judged to have succeeded to the degree they both furthered the goals that prompted their founding and influenced the development of their participants, who continued to engage in activist writing.

Not all anthologies fit this definition of textual community, but collections that represent their communities, speaking both for and to them, such as *Chicana Voices* and *This Bridge Called My Back*, do. As Barbara Christian wrote in her discussion of anthologies for *New Black Feminist Criticism*, one of the first functions of a women's representative community anthology is to "confront … the issue as to whether a community of women writers actually represent their community." The textual community created via the Chicana anthology is created by these imaginings — that is, the authors become a community as they imagine their own connection to (whether or not they have face-to-face connection) and representation of Chicanas, and that connection between authors is reified by their readers, who see the writers as connected to themselves and each other.

CHAPTER 34.

LOVE IN THE TIME OF PEER REVIEW

MARISOL BRITO, ALEXANDER FINK, CHRIS FRIEND, ADAM HEIDEBRINK-BRUNO, ROLIN MOE, KRIS SHAFFER, VALERIE ROBIN, AND ROBIN WHARTON

Over the weekend of November 21-23, 2014, the Hybrid Pedagogy *editorial board gathered in Washington D.C. for an intensive working retreat. During that time, we collaborated on the following article — 8 authors with Sean Michael Morris and Jesse Stommel as reviewers working together in a single document over three hours to brainstorm, draft, and revise the piece. What we offer here is both an experiment in peer review and also a treatise on peer review.*

Love as Pedagogy

Love is patient and kind; love does not envy or boast; it is not arrogant or rude. It does not insist on its own way; it is not irritable or resentful; it does not rejoice at wrongdoing, but rejoices with the truth. Love bears all things, believes all things, hopes all things, endures all things.

~ I Corinthians 13:4-7, ESV

Love, patience, kindness, humility, truth — we don't often talk about these things in the academy. Even those of us who eschew discussion of "efficiency" and "effectiveness" in favor of "empowerment" often stop short of genuine affection. But education, at its core, is an act of love — it seeks to empower as its very nature. And this care fuels our desire to help each other become full agents in our own right.

When we truly love, we humanize rather than normalize. Much of what the academy does — both in teaching and in scholarship — is about norms. Even our new wine ends up in old skins, as the norms of academic discourse dominate the dissemination of our work in journals, monographs, textbooks. But love does not "insist on its own way." In *Teaching to Transgress*, bell hooks advocates for "an openness of mind and heart that allows us to face reality even as we collectively imagine ways to move beyond boundaries, to transgress. This is education as the practice of freedom" (207). Empowering another human to be a mindful agent in their own learning requires a great deal of patience, kindness, and determination. These things only coexist with conscientious effort. This is the work that we all do as we exist simultaneously as authors, editors, and students.

As editors of *Hybrid Pedagogy*, ourselves also educators, we strive for love-as-peer-review. We seek, as Sean Michael Morris says, to "give any author a voice" ("Collaborative Peer Review: Gathering the Academy's Orphans"), bringing our voices to them in a meaningful and accessible way through a specific style of peer review. In this, we spread a little love around so that we leave the world in better shape than we found it.

A common myth in our culture is that knowledge comes from distance — from fact and not from feeling. Thus, in search of knowledge, as if in search of the atomic properties of iron, editors are so often scripted to discover truth by objectively dismantling and critiquing a piece of work. But that is not the full story. The search for knowledge must include feeling.

The guiding principle of our editorial process is not a relationship between an editor and a document, but a relationship between editor and author. This type of relationship is only possible in a space of love, from which we strive to understand others, what they are trying to say, and support them in their search.

A space of love is a space of learning.

In part, this is because when we have love as a foundation we are able to be vulnerable with one another, revealing our selves, our stories — our vulnerabilities make us both idiosyncratic and collectively human. Thus, when we share our vulnerabilities, we offer a new story to the world, one that has the potential to resonate with many.

bell hooks describes teaching-and-learning as a process that produces some degree of pain. This is true about writing-and-editing, too. These processes are much the same: editing is teaching, and writing is learning. And, while it is the vulnerability that makes us susceptible to that pain, it is also the force that inspires our humanity. Writing should be painful, and editors must respond to that pain with love.

We understand that a submission to *Hybrid Pedagogy* is an invitation into a private space — where ideas form words and inhabit that place with the author. This practice allows people — both authors and reviewers — to surprise themselves, again and again. While we often do not know exactly where an idea may go, there is a way in which our process designs for epiphany. The author may end up somewhere new, and the article may arrive somewhere unexpected. Ideas are emergent.

Editing from a place of love is grounded in relationships. Somewhere along the way in education, we forgot that peer review is a conversation. Opening the peer-review process reminds us of those human connections.

Charting the Traditional

In her presentation about open peer review at the 2014 OpenEd conference, Eva Amsen challenged her audience by asking: "Why are people so mean?" She argues that allowing the public to see the review process, and allowing readers to know their reviewers, demands that the reviewers be nicer and more human, a stark contrast from traditional academic peer review. Amsen noted that graduate students are introduced to the process of peer review by observing the way academics treat one another. It is an informal process defined at least partly by fear, where students "learn to be vicious" from receiving vicious blind reviews. Because the author and reviewers don't know each other, they don't respond to one another's needs; instead, they work based on individual conceptions of what they believe the reader needs. The silence of the traditional review process reduces a "review" to a set of orders to be followed, an indifference to the author as a person and a resistance to the relationship between author and editor. Amsen's presentation called for an intervention.

Traditional review processes (such as those used by Taylor & Francis or Elsevier) generally involve comments from reviewers, a single revision from the author, followed by publication. The exchange is brief, limited in duration, and transactional. These reviews involve a sender and a receiver rather than a conversation, eliminating the ability of writing to be responsive. As Björk and Solomon explain, the time an article spends in traditional peer review has grown substantially over the past generation, often taking more than two years between the time of submission and the time of publication. We believe a lack of communication is what leads to the long waits for publication. At *Hybrid Pedagogy*, enabling conversations keeps the article in the present and on the forefront for all parties. It also allows for exploration of topics, opportunities to follow potential arguments and theories in the hope of furthering arguments. It's a great benefit to scholarship, more so than a desire to be, as Kenneth Burke says, "rotten with perfection." The turnaround on articles is dependent on the relationship between author and editors: we have seen turnaround in months, weeks, days, and even in as short as seven hours. Traditionally, articles go from submission to publication in under a month, and articles that extend beyond that do so responsive to the authors' needs and not the editors'.

We adhere to the warning from Wilhelm Stekel, and popularized by Elie Wiesel, that "the opposite of love is not hate, but indifference." In this, we equate "indifference" with "objectivity," so highly valued in the traditional peer review process. Objectivity casts a glaze of inauthenticity on the work, rendering it a static text of content rather than an active text of conversation. This is not objectivity; it is the de-humanizing, the killing, of writing. We must ensure that the author not only remains in a text but is nurtured. The conversations between author and editors at *Hybrid Pedagogy* do not exchange "rigor" for community; they augment the practices of academia with advocates. Such personal connections can be created within the traditional peer-review structures by pulling back the curtain, by removing peer review's blinders. Erin McKiernan, who presented along with Eva Amsen, encourages academics to sign their names to their reviews and to explicitly give editors permission to share their identities with the authors. "The voice in your head becomes nicer."

Traditional peer review is often more about the review than the peer. But an empowering, loving peer review is more about the peer than the review. That's what we advocate for in *Hybrid Pedagogy*: a collaborative peer review process in which authors and editors work together to create a supportive structure that fosters a relationship between the author and the journal. It's a rejection of the flow charts and -isms of much publication and a celebration of relationships and situated environments. It is not a process that can be diagrammed, and it is neither Humean nor Humanist; it is a belief in people. The one-way communication of sending an author a self-proclaimed objective review is replaced with a two-way communication focused on working together in an organic process.

Love, Learning, and Transformation

A loving approach to peer review transforms the work, the authors, the reviewers, the process — and this transformation bleeds into every aspect of our personal and professional lives. Putting love into practice is our way of approaching everything we do, a way of integrating rather than compartmentalizing our academic selves.

> "Thich Nhat Hanh says that love and understanding are the same thing. ... If this is true, then how do we as teachers read and respond lovingly to all of our students' writing, even those we are confused by or do not understand? Is it our job to understand our students' writing, or is it simply to assess its worth or quality? Obviously, I think the first. The question is how do we do it?"
>
> ~ Asao B. Inoue

If academic writing is a cathedral, then peer review is the flying buttress. The shape of the process determines the shape of what we build. When we are inside the cathedral, we cannot perceive the whole buttress. Part of it is outside, but it is nonetheless still there. The peer review — and the reviewers — is both apparent and hidden. Whether we notice it, and how much, depends on our orientation (temporal, physical, psychical, intellectual, political...) to the finished structure and how carefully we're observing. As Pete Roarbaugh, Sean Michael Morris, and Jesse Stommel write elsewhere in this collection, rigor is important to *Hybrid Pedagogy*'s peer review process. The infrastructure that provides that rigor is, however, one structured by understanding, a desire to build relationships and amplify messages, rather than a relentless and futile pursuit of best practices, objective assessment, or perfection.

> "[F]or me all writing is a gift. The person who shares their writing ... is giving you a gift. Now, just like with any gift, it isn't always thoughtful, or to your taste, or beautiful, or — let's admit it — liked. BUT, just like with any gift, you should be appreciative, tactful, and compassionate. You may have to return it, you may have to tell the giver why you didn't like it — but you never have to hurt them needlessly or make them think you didn't recognize and appreciate their effort."
>
> ~ Dometa Brothers

Publishing is a pedagogical activity: for the author, the reviewer, the reader, the (re)user. Like all pedagogy, it sits in the present

286

tense. And yet, it also holds to an emergent vision for the future. At *Hybrid Pedagogy*, we believe all forms of peer review are synonymous, and thus, "peer review" is a symbolic thread that can join a unified whole from the bits and pieces of our professional identities. Students review each other. Sometimes they review the work we've reviewed for them, and the texts we work with in our classrooms have been through many peer reviews. When love, understanding, and relationships enter the equation, the concept of peer is transformed. It becomes about who's peering, how they're peering, when they peer, and what they're peering at, more than about a reified concept of "peer" that excludes those traditionally left out of the conversations. We should expand the signifying power of "peer review" in the academic publishing context to include how we use these words as teachers, mentors, students, children, friends, parents, and lovers.

Just as in pedagogical spaces, where we learn through peering review and peer reviewing — peer review is an opportunity to learn and teach simultaneously. In this way we transform scholarship into pedagogy and pedagogy into a form of love.

AUTHOR BIOGRAPHIES

Nora Almeida is an instruction and outreach librarian at the New York City College of Technology (CUNY) and a volunteer at Interference Archive, an archive of social movement ephemera in Brooklyn. She researches and writes about critical pedagogy, social justice, neoliberalism, performance, and place. You can find her on twitter: @nora_almeida.

Maha Bali / مها بالي is Associate Professor of Practice, Center for Learning and Teaching, American University in Cairo, Egypt. Co-founder of Virtually Connecting and co-facilitator of Equity Unbound, and its Continuity with Care Spin-off, which started during the COVID-19 pandemic. Open, connected educator. Learnaholic and writeaholic. Blogs at blog.mahabali.me and tweets at @bali_maha.

Ruha Benjamin is an Associate Professor of African American Studies at Princeton University, where she studies the social dimensions of science, technology, and medicine. She is also the founder of the JUST DATA Lab and the author of two books, *People's Science* (Stanford) and *Race After Technology* (Polity), and editor of *Captivating Technology* (Duke). She writes, teaches, and speaks widely about the relationship between knowledge and power, race and citizenship, health and justice.

Lee Skallerup Bessette is a Learning Design Specialist in the Center for New Designs in Learning and Scholarship (CNDLS) at Georgetown University. Her current research focuses on affective labor, autoethnography as a form of critical pedagogy, and narrative as a means of communicating our work in digital pedagogy and learning. You can find her on Twitter as @readywriting and all of her writing at readywriting.org.

Margaret Betz is an Assistant Teaching Professor of Philosophy at Rutgers University in Camden, NJ. She is the author of *The Hidden Philosophy of Hannah Arendt*, as well as various articles on feminist theory, political philosophy, and applied ethics.

Kate Bowles is Associate Dean International in the Faculty of Law Humanities & Arts, University of Wollongong, Australia, and co-lead of NiCHE: Narrative informed Codesign in Health and Education.

Marisol Brito is a living-wage earning philosopher at Metropolitan State University in Minnesota. Marisol's teaching and research focus on race, gender, education, and generally rethinking the world — especially the academic one.

Karen Cangialosi is Professor of Biology and Open Education Faculty Fellow at Keene State College. She integrates the principles and practices of Open Pedagogy and Open Science into all of her courses and spearheaded a movement to replace traditional textbooks with OER and other free resources for nearly all KSC biology courses. She also runs a youth education and coral reef monitoring program in the Turks and Caicos Islands contributing to an open international reef survey database.

Cathy N. Davidson is Founding Director of The Futures Initiative and Distinguished Professor of English and the MA in Digital Humanities and MS in Data Analysis and Visualization at the Graduate Center CUNY. She is CoFounder and CoDirector of the world's first and oldest academic social network, HASTAC.org ("haystack"), the Humanities, Arts, Science, and Technology Alliance and Collaboratory and has published more than twenty books, most recently, *Now You See It: How the Brain Science of Attention Will Transform the Way We Live, Work, and Learn* (Viking Penguin 2011) and *The New Education: How to Revolutionize the University to Prepare Students for a World in Flux* (Basic Books, 2017).

Janine DeBaise is author of the book *Body Language* and the chapbook *Of a Feather*. Her essays have been published in numerous journals including *Orion Magazine*, the *Southwest Review*, and the *Hopper*. She teaches writing and literature at the SUNY College of Environmental Science and Forestry in Syracuse, New York. The best part of her job is that she gets to teach students who are passionate about environmental issues.

Catherine Denial is the Bright Distinguished Professor of American History, chair of the History department, and Director of the Bright Institute at Knox College in Galesburg, Illinois. She was the 2019 recipient of the Eugene Asher Distinguished Teaching Award from the American Historical Association, is a former member of the Digital Public Library of America's Educational Advisory Board, and is a Distinguished Lecturer for the Organization of American Historians.

Jonan Phillip Donaldson is a learning scientist with a position as a postdoctoral research associate in the Center for Teaching Excellence at Texas A&M University. He has a Ph.D. in Educational Leadership and Learning Technology from Drexel University. He has taught online courses in education, technology, learning experience design, and critical pedagogy at Drexel University, Oregon State University, Western Oregon University, and other higher education institutions. His specialties include constructionist learning, critical pedagogy, epistemic learning, design thinking, and creativity. His current research involves using theory and methods from the learning sciences, complex systems theory, and linguistics to investigate the relationship between conceptualizations of learning and practices in teaching and learning.

Joshua Eyler is the Director of Faculty Development and the Director of the ThinkForward QEP at the University of Mississippi where he is also on the faculty in the Department of Writing and Rhetoric. He is the author of *How Humans Learn: The Science and Stories behind Effective College Teaching* (WVU Press, 2018).

Julie Fellmayer is an international elementary school teacher of English and Drama. She encourages students to be caring and courageous in their work. She holds degrees in Peace and Conflict studies and Social Justice Education from the University of Toronto and an MA in English Language Education from the University of Nottingham. She likes kids, dogs, aquariums, knitting, reading and writing.

Alexander Fink is a Researcher in Youth Studies at the University of Minnesota, where he works to support young people to lead social change. Through his collaborations with young people, he studies strategies for supporting strong youth leadership in non-profit organizations and government, developing youth leadership skills, and working with adults to do better at including youth at the table. In the last few years, his work has focused on building capacity within organizations to support youth leadership, while simultaneously dismantling systems that exclude or oppress young people — with a special eye toward the data systems that track, surveil, and punish youth.

Chris Friend welcomes people to new ways of thinking. He teaches first-year writing courses, helping students see writing as rhetoricians. He also teaches pedagogy courses, introducing educators to empowering and liberatory praxis. He feels most at home building courses that trick students into achieving more than they thought they could. Being an obsessive fan of Apple software, Tesla hardware, Asimov fiction, Star Trek utopias, Pixar storytelling, and NASA spaceflight makes him a special kind of nerd, but his cat doesn't seem to mind.

Richard H. Godden is an Assistant Professor at Louisiana State University. His research interests include representations of monstrosity and disability in Premodern cultures, with a current focus on the materiality of prosthesis in medieval literature.

Adam Heidebrink-Bruno is a Ph.D. student in Lehigh University's Literature and Social Justice program. He studies twentieth-century American literature with a focus on class, labor, and economics.

Dorothy Kim is a medievalist, digital humanist, and intersectional feminist. She teaches at Brandeis University.

Tiffany Kraft is an Educator, Organizer, & Activist with a PhD in English from the University of Nottingham (2008). As a Training Organizer at SEIU Local 503 in Portland, Tiffany supports a statewide caregiver training initiative funded by the Department of Human Services (OR DHS).

Amanda Licastro is an Assistant Professor of Digital Rhetoric at Stevenson University in Maryland. Amanda's fields of research include digital humanities, composition and rhetoric, and textual studies. Recent publications include "The Past, Present, and Future of Social Annotation," published in Digital Reading and Writing in Composition Studies, and "The Problem of Multimodality: What Data-Driven Research Can Tell Us About Online Writing Practices" in Communication Design Quarterly. Amanda won the prestigious Paul Fortier award at the 2017 Digital Humanities Conference for her work on teaching empathy through Virtual Reality as well as the Innovative Teaching with Technology Award at Stevenson University. Amanda serves on the Executive Council of the Modern Language Association and the Editorial Collective of the *Journal of Interactive Technology and Pedagogy*.

Aisha Damali Lockridge is currently an Associate Professor of English at Saint Joseph's University. Her research focuses on African American Literature, Black popular culture, and pedagogy. Committed to an engaged pedagogy, Aisha's teaching style encourages students to engage meaningfully with Black texts and to interrupt spaces of privilege and power.

Rolin Moe is dean of Academic Support & Learning Technologies at Skyline College. For over a decade, he has worked as an education administrator across multiple institutions: K-12, higher education, and informal spaces. Rolin is a prolific author in both popular and scholarly press; his work has appeared across the publishing landscape, including at magazines such as *Real Life*, and journals like *Learning, Media and Technology, Cur-*

rent Issues in Emerging eLearning, and *Hybrid Pedagogy*. Rolin holds a doctorate in learning technologies from Pepperdine University. His teaching background mixes his unique background as a social scientist with experience in the creative arts.

Sean Michael Morris is the Director of Digital Pedagogy Lab and Senior Instructor in Learning, Design, and Technology at the University of Colorado Denver. He tweets @slamteacher and blogs at www.seanmichaelmorris.com.

Danielle Paradis is a writer, editor and podcaster who lives in Edmonton, Alberta. You can read or hear her work at *Canadaland, Star Metro Edmonton, Gig City, BUSTLE, Canadian True Crime Podcast*, and *The Sprawl* to name a few.

Annemarie Pérez is an assistant professor in the interdisciplinary studies department at California State University Dominguez Hills. Her interests include digital humanities and digital pedagogy work and its intersections with ethnic and cultural studies. Her specialty is Latinx literature, with a focus on Chicana feminist writer-editors from 1965-to the present She is currently writing a book on Chicana feminist editorship.

Katie Rose Guest Pryal, J.D., Ph.D., is a bestselling author, columnist, speaker, and occasional law professor in Chapel Hill, North Carolina. The author of more than ten books, she writes regularly for magazines on topics such as mental health, writing, and parenting. When not writing, she raises two incredible children alongside a house full of shelter pets and a very supportive spouse.

Sue Renes is Professor Emeritus at the University of Alaska Fairbanks. Her research focuses on factors related to Indigenous and rural student recruitment and retention in higher education. In 2013, she received the Elders Award given by Alaska Native Elders to acknowledge those whose deeds and practices promote cultural understanding and balance in all things for a better world community. Dr. Renes has chaired and has served on panels addressing Reclaiming Indigenous Spaces In Higher Education: Examining Recruitment, Retention, and Mentoring Of

Alaska Native Students in Saskatoon, Saskatchewan; Anchorage, Alaska; and in Akureyri, Iceland.

Howard Rheingold is the author of a dozen books, including *The Virtual Community, Smart Mobs,* and *Net Smart,* was editor of *Whole Earth Review* and *Millennium Whole Earth Catalog,* and taught courses on digital journalism, social media issues, and social media literacies at UC Berkeley and Stanford.

Valerie Robin studied Rhetoric and Composition at Georgia State University, and now works for an aeronautics IT company focusing on communication and collaboration. Dr. Robin still loves teaching and makes sure to pick up a class here and there in the evenings. She loves to read, write, and make things, and can often be seen jogging trails not looking where she's going.

Pete Rorabaugh is an assistant professor in the English Department at Kennesaw State University just outside of Atlanta. He studies digital culture, online community building, and grass-roots activism; Pete teaches digital rhetoric, content creation, composition, and literature.

Kris Shaffer is a data scientist and Technical Director, Web Intelligence for Yonder. He co-authored "The Tactics and Tropes of the Internet Research Agency", a report prepared for the United States Senate Select Committee on Intelligence about Russian interference in the 2016 U.S. presidential election on social media. Kris has consulted for multiple U.S. government agencies, non-profits, and universities on matters related to digital disinformation, data ethics, and digital pedagogy. Kris is the author of *Data versus Democracy: How Big Data Algorithms Shape Opinions and Alter the Course of History,* published July 2019 by Apress. In a former (professional) life, Kris was an academic and digital humanist. He has taught courses in music theory and cognition, computer science, and digital studies at Yale University, the University of Colorado–Boulder, the University of Mary Washington, and Charleston Southern University. He holds a PhD from Yale University.

Bonnie Stewart is an educator and social media researcher interested in the implications of digital networks for institutions and society. Assistant Professor of Online Pedagogy and Workplace Learning at the University of Windsor in Canada, Bonnie is interested in what it means to know, to learn, and to be a citizen in our current information ecosystem.

Jesse Stommel is co-founder of Digital Pedagogy Lab and *Hybrid Pedagogy*: the journal of critical digital pedagogy. He has a PhD from University of Colorado Boulder. He is co-author of *An Urgency of Teachers: the Work of Critical Digital Pedagogy*. Jesse is a documentary filmmaker and teaches courses about pedagogy, film, and new media. Jesse experiments relentlessly with learning interfaces, both digital and analog, and his research focuses on higher education pedagogy, critical digital pedagogy, and assessment. He's got a rascal pup, Emily, two clever cats, Loki and Odin, and a badass daughter, Hazel. He's online at jessestommel.com and on Twitter @Jessifer.

Joseph Stommel (@JoeStommel) has been a mental health professional and instructor since 1974 and was Colorado Department of Corrections Administrator of Alcohol and Drug Services from 1990-2008. He has done extensive training and authored numerous publications. He retired in 2008 and is now a consultant and online college instructor.

Shea Swauger is a librarian and Senior Instructor at the Auraria Library which serves the Community College of Denver, Metropolitan State University of Denver, and the University of Colorado Denver.

Audrey Watters is a writer and independent scholar who focuses on education technology – its politics and its pedagogical implications. She is the author of several books, including *The Monsters of Education* series and the forthcoming book *Teaching Machines*. Her work can be found online at Hack Education.

Robin Wharton is a writer who lives and works in Atlanta, Georgia. She holds a law degree and a PhD in English, both from the University of Georgia. You can follow her as @rswharton on Twitter and Instagram.

Anne-Marie Womack is a Professor of Practice in English at Tulane University. Her work focuses on disability studies and writing pedagogy and has appeared in *College Composition and Communication, Pedagogy,* and *The Chronicle of Higher Education.* She runs AccessibleSyllabus.com, a universal design guide for instructors.

ORIGINAL PUBLICATION DATES

All chapters originally published on *Hybrid Pedagogy: the journal of critical digital pedagogy*, unless otherwise noted.

1. Occupy the Digital: Critical Pedagogy and New Media by Pete Rorabaugh [2012]

2. Technology 101: What Do We Need To Know About The Future We're Creating? by Howard Rheingold [1998, republished on *Hybrid Pedagogy* in 2014]

3. Maggie's Digital Content Farm by Audrey Watters [2014]

4. A Guide for Resisting Edtech: the Case against Turnitin by Sean Michael Morris and Jesse Stommel [2017]

5. Disruptive Pedagogy and the Practice of Freedom by Julie Fellmayer [2018]

6. Our Bodies Encoded: Algorithmic Test Proctoring in Higher Education by Shea Swauger [2020]

7. Critical Pedagogy: Intentions and Realities by Maha Bali [2014]

8. Why Start With Pedagogy? 4 Good Reasons, 4 Good Solutions by Cathy N. Davidson [2015, republished from HASTAC]

9. Best Practices: Thoughts on a Flash Mob Mentality by Janine DeBaise [2014]

10. But You Can't Do That in a STEM Course! by Karen

Cangialosi [2018]

11. Travelling in Troy With an Instructional Designer by Jonan Phillip Donaldson [2019]

12. Building in the Humanities Isn't New by Robin Wharton [2013]

13. Three Lines of Resistance: Ethics, Critical Pedagogy, and Teaching Underground by Kris Shaffer [2014]

14. Listening for Student Voices by Sean Michael Morris and Chris Friend [2013]

15. On, On, On by Kate Bowles [2014, republished from Kate Bowles's blog]

16. A Lecturer's Almanac by Katie Rose Guest Pryal [2013]

17. Adjunctifcation: Living in the Margins of Academe by Tiffany Kraft [2013]

18. Librarian as Outsider by Nora Almeida [2015]

19. Contingent Mother: The Role Gender Plays in the Lives of Adjunct Faculty by Margaret Betz [2014]

20. Making Disability Part of the Conversation: Combatting Inaccessible Spaces and Logics by Richard H. Godden and Anne-Marie Womack [2016]

21. Amplifying Indigenous Voices by Sue Renes [2014]

22. Finding My Voice as a Minority Teacher by Chris Friend [2014]

23. Correctional Pedagogy: Prison Reform and Life-or-Death Learning by Joseph Stommel [2014]

24. The Pleasures, the Perils, and the Pursuit of Pedagogical Intimacy by Danielle Paradis [2014]

25. Practice and Performance: Teaching Urban Literature at the Less than Liberal Arts by Aisha Damali Lockridge [2014]

26. A Pedagogy of Kindness by Catherine Denial [2019]

27. Beyond Rigor by Pete Rorabaugh, Sean Michael Morris, and Jesse Stommel [2013]

28. Conversations: Instructional Design, Trust, and Discovery by Sean Michael Morris and Joshua Eyler [2016]

29. Learning at the Intersections by Amanda Licastro [2017]

30. In Public: The Shifting Consequences of Twitter Scholarship by Bonnie Stewart [2015]

31. The Rules of Twitter by Dorothy Kim [2014]

32. Social Media, Service, and the Perils of Scholarly Affect by Lee Skallerup Bessette [2015]

33. Textual Communities: Writing, Editing, and Generation in Chicana Feminism by Annemarie Pérez [2015]

34. Love in the Time of Peer Review by Marisol Brito, Alexander Fink, Adam Heidebrink-Bruno, Rolin Moe, Kris Shaffer, Valerie Robin, Robin Wharton, and Chris Friend [2014]

BIBLIOGRAPHY

Ackerman, D. (2000). *Deep play*. Random House.

Adichie, C. N. (2013). *Americanah*. Fourth Estate.

Alexander, B. (2016, Apr 15). Future trends forum #9 with Gardner Campbell: Full recording, notes, and Storify [Blog post]. Bryan Alexander. https://bryanalexander.org/future-trends-forum/future-trends-forum-9-with-gardner-campbell-full-recording-notes-and-storify

Amer, K. & Noujaim, J. (2019). *The great hack* [Film]. The Othrs.

American Folklore Society. (2011, Oct 25). *AFS position statement on research with human subjects*. https://www.afsnet.org/page/Human-Subjects

American Historical Association (2019, Jun). *Statement on standards of professional conduct*. https://www.historians.org/jobs-and-profes-sional-development/statements-standards-and-guidelines-of-the-discipline/statement-on-standards-of-professional-conduct

Amidon, T. (2016, Sep 8). (Dis)owning tech: Ensuring value and agency at the moment of interface. *Hybrid Pedagogy*. https://hybridped-agogy.org/disowning-tech-ensuring-value-agency-moment-inter-face/

Amsen, E., Berrios-Otero, C., & McKiernan, E. (2014, Nov 20). *Open peer review as educational resource* [Conference session]. OpenEd 2014, Washington, D.C. http://openedconference.org/2014

Austen, J. (1864). *Sense and Sensibility*. Harvard University Press.

Badke, W. (2011). Why information literacy is invisible. *Communications in information literacy, 4*(2), 129-141. https://doi.org/10.15760/comminfolit.2011.4.2.92

Bakis, M. (n.d.) A comics dissertation. *Diamond Bookshelf.* https://www.diamondbookshelf.com/Home/1/1/20/835?articleID=117751

Baldwin, J. (1998). A Talk to Teachers. In T. Morrison (Ed.). *Collected essays.* University of Michigan.

Bali, M. [م، بالي] (2016, Jun 30). Critical digital citizenship: Promoting empathy and social justice online. *Connected Learning Alliance.* https://clalliance.org/blog/critical-digital-citizenship-empathy-social-justice-online/

Bali, M. [م، بالي] (2016, Jul 18). On whose terms are we (digital) citizens? #MyDigCiz #DigCiz. EdConteXts. Retrieved from the Internet Archive. https://web.archive.org/web/20160806020104/http://edcontexts.org/contexts-matter/on-whose-terms-are-we-digital-citizens-mydigciz-digciz/

Benjamin, R. (2019). *Race after technology: Abolitionist tools for the new Jim Code.* Wiley.

Benjamin, W. (1968). Unpacking my library: A talk about book collecting. in H. Zohn (Tr.). *Illuminations.* Harcourt Brace Jovanovich.

Bassow, S., Campbell, D. & Stockwell, L. (2008). Nontraditional academics: At home with children and a PhD. In E. Evans & C. Grant (Eds). *Mama, PhD: Women write about motherhood and academic life.* Rutgers University Press.

Baumbach, N. (2005). *The squid and the whale* [Film]. Samuel Goldwyn Films.

Beatty, J. F. (2015, Jun 2). Reading Freire for first world librarians [Conference presentation]. Canadian Association of Professional Academic Librarians, Ottawa. http://hdl.handle.net/1951/70036

Beilin, I. (2015, Feb 25). Beyond the threshold: Conformity, resistance, and the ACRL information literacy framework for higher education. *In the Library with the Lead Pipe.* http://www.inthelibrarywiththeleadpipe.org/2015/beyond-the-threshold-conformity-resistance-and-the-aclr-information-literacy-framework-for-higher-education/

Bessette, L. S. (2010, Jul 22). How higher ed makes most things meaningless. *University of Venus, Inside Higher Ed.* Retrieved from Internet Archive. https://web.archive.org/web/20121207085353/ https://www.insidehighered.com/blogs/university_of_venus/ how_higher_ed_makes_most_things_meaningless

Bessette, L. (2010, Jul 29). How higher ed makes most things meaningless (Long Version). *College Ready Writing.* https://collegereadywriting.blogspot.com

Bessette, L. (2011, Dec 4). Taking action for contingent faculty. *College Ready Writing, Inside Higher Ed.* https://www.insidehighered.com/ blogs/college-ready-writing/taking-action-contingent-faculty

Bessette, L. (2011, Dec 6). Killing two birds with one giant stone: Tenure. *College Ready Writing, Inside Higher Ed.* https://www.insidehighered.com/blogs/college-ready-writing/killing-two-birds-one-giant-stone-tenure

Berube, C. T., Berube, M. R. (2010). *The moral university.* Rowman & Littlefield.

Bérubé, M. & Ruth, J. (2015). *The humanities, higher education, and academic freedom: Three necessary arguments.* United Kingdom: Palgrave Macmillan.

Bezerra, C. (2014, Aug 12). An education(al) anecdote from Brazil. *EdConteXts.* Retrieved from the Internet Archive. https://web.archive.org/web/20160229152828/http://edcontexts.org/teacher-education/an-educational-anecdote-from-brazil/

Björk, B. and Solomon, D. (2013, Oct). The publishing delay in scholarly peer-reviewed journals. *Journal of Informetrics* 7(4), 914–23. https://doi.org/10.1016/j.joi.2013.09.001

Blackwell, M. (2011). *¡Chicana power!: Contested histories of feminism in the Chicano movement.* United States: University of Texas Press.

Blikstein, P. (2008). Travels in Troy with Freire: Technology as an agent of emancipation. In C. A. Torres & P. Noguera (Eds.) *Social justice education for teachers: Paulo Freire and the possible dream.* Brill | Sense. https://doi.org/10.1163/9789460911446_015

boyd, d. (2007, May). Social network sites: Public, private, or what?

Knowledge   Tree (13).   http://kt.flexiblelearning.net.au/
tkt2007/?page_id=28

Bradbury, R. (2018, Aug 13). Preserving snapshots of Cambridge's anti-women protests. *Varsity*. https://www.varsity.co.uk/features/15985

Braungart, M. & McDonough, W. (2010). *Cradle to cradle: Remaking the way we make things*. Farrar, Straus and Giroux.

Brothers, D. (2014, Mar 27). *I think of it in the fact that for me all writing is a gift. The person who shares their...* [Post comment]. Facebook. https://www.facebook.com/asao.inoue/posts/10203558637030450?comment_id=10203559314767393

Bruff, D. (2015, Sep 15). In defense of continuous exposition by the teacher. *Agile Learning*. https://derekbruff.org/?p=3126

Bruner, J. S. (1986). *Actual minds, possible worlds*. Harvard University Press.

Burke, K. (1966). *Language as symbolic action: Essays on life, literature, and method*. Berkley: University of California Press, p. 16.

Butler, O. E. (2000, May). Brave new worlds: A few rules for predicting the future. *Essence, 31*(1). Essence Communications.

Carby, H. V. (1987). *Reconstructing womanhood: The emergence of the Afro-American woman novelist*. Oxford University Press.

Cassuto, L., Ryan, V., & Shumway, D. R. (2015, Jan 9). *Teaching, research, service: A close reading* [Conference session]. MLA, Vancouver. http://mla15.org/270

CCCC-Intellectual Property Caucus. (2012). *CCCC-IP Caucus recommendations regarding academic integrity and the use of plagiarism detection services* [Draft position statement]. http://culturecat.net/files/CCCC-IPpositionstatementDraft.pdf

Center for Open Science. (n.d.). *Our mission*. https://www.cos.io/about/mission

Chao, L. (1995, Winter). Anthologizing the collective: The epic struggles to establish Chinese Canadian literature in English. *Essays on Canadian Writing* (57), 145–170. https://search.proquest.com/docview/197239113/39DF2D8304B8483CPQ/1

Chatelain, M. (2014, Aug 25). How to teach kids about what's happening in Ferguson: A crowdsourced syllabus about race, African American history, civil rights, and policing. *Education, The Atlantic.* https://www.theatlantic.com/education/archive/2014/08/how-to-teach-kids-about-whats-happening-in-ferguson/379049/

Chavez, C. (1969). *Letter from Delano.* https://libraries.ucsd.edu/farmworkermovement/essays/essays/Letter%20From%20Delano.pdf

Chelsea Green Publishing. (2010, Mar 4). Anya Kamenetz on alternative education [Video]. *YouTube.* https://www.youtube.com/watch?v=nvr_L_jMC14

Chernik, A. F. (2014, May 13). The phenomenology of participation: Derrida and the future of pedagogy. *Hybrid Pedagogy.* https://hybridpedagogy.org/phenomenology-participation-derrida-future-pedagogy

Christian, B. (2007). *New Black feminist criticism, 1985-2000.* Bowles, G., Fabi, M. G., & Keizer, A. R. (Eds.) University of Illinois.

Coalition on the Academic Workforce. (2012, Jun). *A portrait of part-time faculty members* [Report]. http://www.academicworkforce.org/CAW_portrait_2012.pdf

Coburn, C. (1988). The case against coeducation: An historical perspective. *Feminist Teacher, 3*(3), 19-22. https://www.jstor.org/stable/25680560

Córdova, T., Cantú, N., Cardenas, G., García, J., & Sierra, C. M. (Eds.) (1993). *Chicana voices: Intersections of class, race, and gender.* University of New Mexico.

Cormier, D. (2008, Jun 3). Rhizomatic education: Community as curriculum. *Dave's Educational Blog.* http://davecormier.com/edblog/2008/06/03/rhizomatic-education-community-as-curriculum/

Cormier, D. & Siemens, G. (2010, Aug 5). Through the open door: Open courses as research, learning, and engagement. *EDUCAUSE Review 45*(4), 30–39. https://er.educause.edu/articles/2010/8/through-the-open-door-open-courses-as-research-learning-and-engagement

Cornbleth, C. (1990). *Curriculum in context.* Taylor & Francis.

Cottom, T. M. (2014, Dec 2). Racists getting fired: The sins of whiteness on social media [Blog post]. https://tressiemc.com/uncategorized/racists-getting-fired-the-sins-of-whiteness-on-social-media

Cottom, T. M. (2015) "Who do you think you are?": When marginality meets academic microcelebrity. *Ada: A Journal of Gender, New Media, and Technology, 7.* http://dx.doi.org/10.7264/N3319T5T

Crenshaw, K. (1989). Demarginalizing the intersection of race and sex: A black feminist critique of antidiscrimination doctrine, feminist theory and antiracist politics. *University of Chicago Legal Forum, 1989*(1), 139–167. Available at: http://chicagounbound.uchicago.edu/uclf/vol1989/iss1/8

Curry, M. (2005). *Street fight* [Film]. Marshall Curry Productions.

Curzan, A. (2014, Aug 25). Why I'm asking you not to use laptops. *Lingua Franca, The Chronicle of Higher Education.* Retrieved from the Internet Archive. https://web.archive.org/web/20181024224524/http://chronicle.com/blogs/linguafranca/2014/08/25/why-im-asking-you-not-to-use-laptops

Davidson, C. (2012, Apr 8). Single best way to transform classrooms of any size! [Blog post]. *HASTAC.* https://www.hastac.org/blogs/cathy-davidson/2012/04/08/single-best-way-transform-class-rooms-any-size

Davidson, C. (2015, Feb 2). The single best method for class (or any kind of) participation (Thx scifi genius Samuel Delany). *HASTAC.* https://www.hastac.org/blogs/cathy-davidson/2015/02/02/single-best-method-class-or-any-kind-participation-thx-scifi-genius

Davis, A. Y. (2012). *The meaning of freedom: And other difficult dialogues.* City Lights.

Davis, L. J. (1995). *Enforcing normalcy: Disability, deafness, and the body.* Verso.

Davis, M. (2006). *City of quartz: Excavating the future in Los Angeles.* Verso.

Dayton, J. & Faris, V. (2006). *Little Miss Sunshine* [Film]. Fox Searchlight Pictures.

Dean, M. (2017, Apr 26). What an open pedagogy class taught me about myself [Blog post]. *The Current Human Condition.* https://thechc-explored.wordpress.com/2017/04/26/what-an-open-pedagogy-class-taught-me-about-myself

Denzin, N. K. (2018). *The qualitative manifesto: A call to arms*. Taylor & Francis.

Deresiewicz, W. (2007, Jun 1). Love on campus. *The American Scholar*. Phi Beta Kappa. https://theamericanscholar.org/love-on-campus/

DeRosa, R. (2017, Nov 26). Open pedagogy at the program level: The #PlymouthIDS case study. *Actualham*. http://robinderosa.net/uncategorized/open-pedagogy-at-the-program-level-the-plymouthids-case-study

DeRosa, R. & Jhangiani, R. (2019, Mar 30). Open pedagogy. *Open Pedagogy Notebook*. http://openpedagogy.org/open-pedagogy

Dolmage, J. (2008). Mapping composition: Inviting disability in the front door. In B. J. Brueggemann & C. Lewiecki-Wilson (Eds). *Disability and the teaching of writing: A critical sourcebook*. Bedford/St. Martin's.

Doubek, J. (2016, Apr 17). Attention, students: Put your laptops away. *Weekend Edition Sunday*. NPR. https://www.npr.org/2016/04/17/474525392/attention-students-put-your-laptops-away

Downes, S. (2012, Apr 23). The rise of MOOCs [Blog post]. *Half an Hour*. https://halfanhour.blogspot.com/2012/04/rise-of-moocs.html

Drago, R. and Williams, J. (2000, Nov). A half-time tenure track proposal. *Change*. The Center for WorkLife Law, UC Hastings. https://worklifelaw.org/publication/a-half-time-tenure-track-proposal

Dziech, B. W. & Weiner, L. (1990). *The lecherous professor: Sexual harassment on campus*. University of Illinois Press.

Eisenhower, C. & Smith, D. (2010). The library as a "stuck place": Critical pedagogy in the corporate university. In M. T. Accardi, E. Drabinski, & A. Kumbier (Eds.) *Critical library instruction: Theories and methods*. Library Juice Press.

Ekins, S. & Perlstein, E. O. (2014, Aug 21). Ten simple rules of live tweeting at scientific conferences. *PLOS Computational Biology*. https://doi.org/10.1371/journal.pcbi.1003789

Ellsworth, E. (1989, Sep). Why doesn't this feel empowering? Working through the repressive myths of critical pedagogy. *Harvard Educational Review* 59(3), 297-325. https://doi.org/10.17763/haer.59.3.058342114k266250

Elmborg, J. (2006, Mar). Critical information literacy: Implications for instructional practice. *The Journal of Academic Librarianship 32*(2), 192–199. https://doi.org/10.1016/j.acalib.2005.12.004

Everhart, J. (2014, Aug 5). Exploring the dungeon: The importance of "play" to learning. *Hybrid Pedagogy.* https://hybridpedagogy.org/exploring-dungeon-importance-play-learning/

Fish, S. (2012). *Save the world on your own time.* Oxford University Press.

Foster, F. (2005). A narrative of the interesting origins and (somewhat) surprising developments of African-American print culture. *American Literary History, 17*(4), 714-740. http://www.jstor.org/stable/3567947

Fotheringham, W. (2012). *Put me back on my bike: In search of Tom Simpson.* Random House.

Freeman, S., Eddy, S. L., McDonough, M., Smith, M. K., Okoroafor, N., Jordt, H., & Wenderoth, M. P. (2014, Jun). Active learning boosts performance in STEM courses. *Proceedings of the National Academy of Sciences 111*(23), 8410-8415. doi:10.1073/pnas.1319030111

Freire, P. (1973). *Education for critical consciousness.* Seabury.

Freire, P. (1987). Letter to North-American teachers. In I. Shor (Ed.). *Freire for the classroom: A sourcebook for liberatory teaching.* Boynton/Cook.

Freire, P. (1998). *Pedagogy of freedom: Ethics, democracy, and civic courage.* Rowman & Littlefield.

Freire, P. (2014). *Pedagogy of the oppressed: 30th anniversary edition.* Bloomsbury.

Friend, C. (2013, Jan 17). Built beyond the walls [Blog post]. *Thinking Aloud.* https://chrisfriend.us/built-beyond-the-walls/

Friend, C. (2013, Feb 16). Built beyond the walls: Bringing MOOC strategies into the composition classroom [Conference presentation]. North Carolina Symposium on Teaching Writing, Raleigh. https://www.slideshare.net/chrisfriend/built-beyond-the-walls-bringing-mooc-strategies-into-the-composition-classroom

Friend, C. (2012, Aug 24). Learning as performance: MOOC pedagogy and on-ground classes. *Hybrid Pedagogy.* https://hybridpedagogy.org/learning-as-performance-mooc-pedagogy-and-on-ground-classes

Friend, C. (2017, Feb 6). CFP: Politicizing critical digital pedagogy. *Hybrid Pedagogy.* https://hybridpedagogy.org/politicizing-critical-digital-pedagogy/

Friend, C. & Morris, S. M. (2013, Oct 15). Listening for student voices. *Hybrid Pedagogy.* https://hybridpedagogy.org/listening-for-student-voices

Friend, C., Morris, S. M., and Stommel, J. (2015, Feb 11). CFP: The scholarly & the digital. *Hybrid Pedagogy.* https://hybridpedagogy.org/cfp-scholarly-digital

Fruscione, J. (2013, Oct 23). Not a scarlet letter: Talking with students about being an adjunct. *Hybrid Pedagogy.* https://hybridpedagogy.org/not-a-scarlet-letter-talking-with-students-about-being-an-adjunct

Gallop, J. (1997). *Feminist accused of sexual harassment.* Duke University Press.

Giroux, H. A. (2011). *On critical pedagogy.* Bloomsbury Academic.

Hall, R. (2014, Jul 10). Notes on the university as anxiety machine [Blog post]. *Richard Hall's Space.* http://www.richard-hall.org/2014/07/10/notes-on-the-university-as-anxiety-machine/

Hamilton, S. (2016, Apr 26). Risk taking is a form of playing it safe. *Hybrid Pedagogy.* https://hybridpedagogy.org/risk-taking-is-playing-it-safe/

Hanson, C. (2000). *Wonder boys* [Film]. British Broadcasting Corporation.

Harry, S. (2014, Apr 16). Attacking the stream. *Dissent.* https://www.dissentmagazine.org/online_articles/attacking-the-stream

Hattie, J. (2008). *Visible learning: A synthesis of over 800 meta-analyses relating to achievement.* Taylor & Francis.

Hirt-Manheimer, A. (2017, Aug 23). Channeling Elie Wiesel: Words from the past bring comfort in the present. *Reform Judaism.* https://reformjudaism.org/blog/2017/08/23/channeling-elie-wiesel-words-past-bring-comfort-present

Hoffman, A. L. (2018, Apr 30). Data violence and how bad engineering choices can damage society. *Medium*. https://medium.com/s/story/data-violence-and-how-bad-engineering-choices-can-damage-society-39e44150e1d4

Holstead, C. E. (2015, Mar 4). The benefits of no-tech note taking. *The Chronicle of Higher Education*. https://www.chronicle.com/article/The-Benefits-of-No-Tech-Note/228089/

hooks, b. (1994). *Teaching to transgress: Education as the practice of freedom*. Routledge.

hooks, b. (1997). *Back to reality? Social experience and cultural studies*. Manchester University Press.

hooks, b. (2004). *The will to change: men, masculinity, and love*. Atria Books.

hooks, b. (2013). *Teaching community: A pedagogy of hope*. Taylor & Francis.

hooks, b. (2014). *Yearning: Race, gender, and cultural politics*. Taylor & Francis.

Howard, R. M. (2013, May 4). Arguing against Turnitin [Blog post]. *Chenango Metonymy*. https://rmoorehoward.wordpress.com/2013/05/04/arguing-against-turnitin/

Inoue, A. B. (2014, Mar 27). *Thich Nhat Hanh says that love and understanding are the same thing. I think our experience with those whom we...* [Status update]. Facebook. https://www.facebook.com/asao.inoue/posts/10203558637030450

Jacobs, A. (2014, Aug 31). The end of big Twitter. *TextPatterns, The New Atlantis*. http://text-patterns.thenewatlantis.com/2014/08/the-end-of-big-twitter.html

Jones, R. P. (2014, Aug 21). Self-segregation: Why it's so hard for whites to understand Ferguson. *The Atlantic*. https://www.theatlantic.com/national/archive/2014/08/self-segregation-why-its-hard-for-whites-to-understand-ferguson/378928

Ḵaayastaan Olson, M. (2014, Mar 16). Opening remarks [Conference presentation]. Alaska Native Studies Conference, Juneau. http://hdl.handle.net/11122/5829

Kamenetz, A. (2010). *DIY U: Edupunks, edupreneurs, and the coming transformation of higher education*. Chelsea Green.

Kern, M. (2012, Sep 21). Part-time faculty pay reaching poverty level. *People's World*. https://www.peoplesworld.org/article/part-time-faculty-pay-reaching-poverty-level/

Kerschbaum, S. L. (2015, Fall). Anecdotal relations: On orienting to disability in the composition classroom. *Composition Forum* (32). http://compositionforum.com/issue/32/anecdotal-relations.php

Keyes, O. (2018, Nov). The misgendering machines: Trans/HCI implications of automatic gender recognition. *Proceedings of the ACM on Human-Computer Interaction*. https://doi.org/10.1145/3274357

Keyes, O. (2019, Sep 4). Our face recognition nightmare began decades ago. Now it's expanding. *Motherboard, Vice*. https://www.vice.com/en_us/article/d3a7ym/trump-didnt-create-our-face-recognition-nightmare-hes-just-expanding-it

Kim, D. (2014, Jan 7). #MedievalTwitter. *In the Middle*. http://www.inthemedievalmiddle.com/2014/01/medievaltwitter.html

Kim, D. & Kim, E. (2014, Apr 7). The #TwitterEthics manifesto. *Funding, Model View Culture*. https://modelviewculture.com/pieces/the-twitterethics-manifesto

Kim, S. (2012, May 9). The number of Ph.D.s on public aid triples in U.S. *ABC News*. https://abcnews.go.com/Business/growing-number-americans-phds-receiving-food-stamps-aid/story

Kincheloe, J. L. (1991). *Teachers as researchers: Qualitative inquiry as a path to empowerment*. Falmer Press.

Kincheloe, J. L. (2007). Critical pedagogy in the twenty-first century: Evolution for survival. In J. L. Kincheloe & P. McLaren (Eds). *Critical Pedagogy: Where are We Now?* Peter Lang.

Kincheloe, J. L. (2008). *Knowledge and critical pedagogy: An introduction*. Springer.

Kingeistí Katzeek, D. (2014, Mar 16). Elder response [Conference presentation]. Alaska Native Studies Conference, Juneau. http://hdl.handle.net/11122/5829

Kolowich, S. (2012, Oct 2). The academic twitterazzi. *Inside Higher Ed*.

https://www.insidehighered.com/news/2012/10/02/scholars-debate-etiquette-live-tweeting-academic-conferences

Kovalik, D. (2013, Sep 18). Death of an adjunct. *Pittsburgh Post-Gazette.* https://www.post-gazette.com/opinion/Op-Ed/2013/09/18/Death-of-an-adjunct/stories/201309180224

Ladson-Billings, G. (1995). Toward a theory of culturally relevant pedagogy. *American Educational Research Journal, 32*(3), 465–491. https://doi.org/10.3102/00028312032003465

Latif, H. A. (2012). *Never going back: 7 steps to staying out of prison.* Alden-Swain.

Lee, S. (1988). *School daze* [Film]. Columbia Pictures.

Mandell, H. (2015, Jul 6). No phones, please. This is a communications class. *The Chronicle of Higher Education.* https://www.chronicle.com/article/No-Phones-Please-This-Is-a/231235/

Marvit, M. Z. (2013, Oct 9). Interview with an adjunct organizer: "People are tired of the hypocrisy." *Dissent.* https://www.dissent-magazine.org/online_articles/people-are-tired-of-the-hypocrisy-an-interview-with-dan-kovalik

Mason, A. S. (2013, Oct/Nov). Buona sera, social clubs? *Boston Review.* http://bostonreview.net/archives/BR28.5/mason.html

Mason, M. A., & Goulden, M. (2002). Do babies matter? *Academe, 88*(6), 21-27. https://search.proquest.com/docview/232303988

Merculieff, L. & Roderick, L. (2013). *Stop talking: Indigenous ways of teaching and learning and difficult dialogues in higher education.* University of Alaska Anchorage.

Meulemans, Y. N, & Carr, A. (2013). Not at your service: Building genuine faculty-librarian partnerships. *Reference Services Review, 41*(1), 80-90. https://doi.org/10.1108/00907321311300893

Moraga, C. & Anzaldúa, G. E. (Eds.) (1983). *This bridge called my back: Writings by radical women of color.* Kitchen Table, Women of Color Press.

Morris, S. M. (2013, Dec 10). Collaborative peer review: Gathering the academy's orphans. *Hybrid Pedagogy.* https://hybridpedagogy.org/collaborative-peer-review-gathering-the-academys-orphans/

Morris, S. M. (2015, Apr 8). Call for editors. *Hybrid Pedagogy.* https://hybridpedagogy.org/call-for-editors/

Morris, S. M. (2016, Jan 11). MOOC MOOC: Instructional design. *Digital Pedagogy Lab.* https://www.digitalpedagogylab.com/mooc-mooc-instructional-design

Morris, S. M. (2016, Aug 16). Not enough voices. *Hybrid Pedagogy.* https://hybridpedagogy.org/not-enough-voices

Morris, S. M. (2017, Oct 27). A call for critical instructional design [Blog post]. *Sean Michael Morris.* https://www.seanmichaelmorris.com/a-call-for-critical-instructional-design

Morris, S. M. & Stommel, J. (2017, Jun 15). A guide for resisting edtech: The case against Turnitin. *Hybrid Pedagogy.* https://hybridpedagogy.org/resisting-edtech/

Morris, S. M., Wharton, R., & Stommel, J. (2013, Oct 8). CFP: The problem of contingency in higher education. *Hybrid Pedagogy.* https://hybridpedagogy.org/cfp-the-problem-of-contingency-in-higher-education/

Morrison, A. (2015, Apr 8). Teaching and all the feels. *Hook and Eye.* Retrieved from the Internet Archive. https://web.archive.org/web/20161201000440/https://hookandeye.ca/2015/04/teaching-and-all-feels.html

Mothers Movement Online. (2005, Apr). Playground revolution [Interview]. http://www.mothersmovement.org/features/05/playground_rev/print.html

Nall, J. (2012, Nov 27). Working for change in higher education: The abysmal state of adjunct teacher pay. *Toward Freedom, AlterNet.* https://www.alternet.org/2012/11/working-change-higher-education-abysmal-state-adjunct-teacher-pay/

Oxford. (2019). Intimacy. In the *New Oxford American Dictionary.* Oxford University Press.

Noble, S. U. (2018). *Algorithms of oppression: How search engines reinforce racism.* NYU Press.

Olson, D. R. (1996). *The world on paper: The conceptual and cognitive implications of writing and reading.* Cambridge University Press.

O'Neil, C. (2016). *Weapons of math destruction: How big data increases inequality and threatens democracy.* Crown.

Pacifico, L. N. (2013, Feb 1). *@HybridPed Students literally own their education. They must be allowed to co-create and steer it in order to reach their own goals. #digped* [Tweet]. Twitter. https://twitter.com/LansSolo/statuses/297409359888125952

Packer, Z. (2004). *Drinking coffee elsewhere.* Riverhead Books.

Paetzold, R. L., García, M. F., Colella, A., Ren, L. R., del Carmen Triana, M. & Ziebro, M. (2008, Jun 2). Perceptions of people with disabilities: When is accommodation fair? *Basic and Applied Social Psychology 30*(1), 27–35. https://doi.org/10.1080/01973530701665280

Pagowsky, N. & DeFrain, E. (2014, Jun 3). Ice ice baby: Are librarian stereotypes freezing us out of instruction? *In the Library with the Lead Pipe.* http://www.inthelibrarywiththeleadpipe.org/2014/ice-ice-baby-2/

Palmer, P. J. (2009). *The courage to teach: Exploring the inner landscape of a teacher's life.* Wiley.

Papert, S. (1993). *The children's machine: Rethinking school in the age of the computer.* Basic Books.

Papert, S. (2002, Jun 24). How to make writing 'hard fun'. *Bangor Daily News.* https://archive.bangordailynews.com/2002/06/24/how-to-make-writing-hard-fun

Park, S. & Kim, E. (2014, Mar 17). Hashtags as decolonial projects with radical origins. *Mythology, Model View Culture.* https://modelview-culture.com/pieces/hashtags-as-decolonial-projects-with-radical-origins

Park, S. & Leonard, D. J. (2014, Feb 3). In defense of Twitter feminism. *Form, Model View Culture.* https://modelviewculture.com/pieces/in-defense-of-twitter-feminism

Parker, A. (2003). *The life of David Gale* [Film]. Universal Pictures.

Parks, S. (2000). *In the blood.* Dramatists Play Service.

Peskowitz, M. (2005). *The truth behind the mommy wars: Who decides what makes a good mother?* Basic Books.

Peskowitz, M. (2008). Foreward. In E. Evans & C. Grant (Eds). *Mama,*

PhD: Women write about motherhood and academic life. Rutgers University Press.

Pew Research Center. (2019, Jun 12). *Social media fact sheet* [Fact sheet]. https://www.pewresearch.org/internet/fact-sheet/social-media/

Piaget, J. (1971). *The construction of reality in the child*. Ballantine Books.

Pitzer, D. E. (Ed.) (1997). *America's communal utopias*. University of North Carolina.

Priego, E. (2012, Oct 3). Live-tweeting at academic conferences: 10 rules of thumb. *Universities, The Guardian*. https://www.the-guardian.com/higher-education-network/blog/2012/oct/03/ethics-live-tweeting-academic-conferences

Proctorio. (2017, Feb 10). Proctorio student intro video [Video]. *YouTube*. https://www.youtube.com/watch?v=oEH55Iv73Is

Pryal, K. R. G. (2010, Autumn). Intimate Pedagogy: The practice of embodiment in university classrooms. *Assuming Gender 1*(2), 62–77. https://ssrn.com/abstract=1754015

Q'um Q'um Xiiem [Archibald, J.] (2008). *Indigenous storywork: Educating the heart, mind, body, and spirit*. UBC Press.

Ramsay, S. (2014). The hermeneutics of screwing around; or what you do with a million books. In K. Kee (Ed.) *Pastplay: Teaching and learning history with technology*. University of Michigan.

Resnick, M. & Rosenbaum, E. (2013). Designing for tinkerability. In D. E. Kanter & M. Honey (Eds.). *Design, make, play: Growing the next generation of STEM innovators*. Routledge.

Reticulatrix. (2013, Sept 6). Outsider learning. *Reticulatrix*. Retrieved from the Internet Archive. https://web.archive.org/web/20160912170658/https://reticulatrix.wordpress.com/2013/09/06/outsider-learning/

Rheingold, H. (2012). *Net smart: How to thrive online*. MIT Press.

Rich, A. (1979). *On lies, secrets, and silence*. Norton.

Robin, V. (2013, Feb 1). *@caty_posch @HybridPed Internet and general play are important to learning. We often teach ourselves out of pure interest. #digped* [Tweet]. Twitter. https://twitter.com/vrobin1000/status/297412540214939648

Rockmore, D. (2014, Jun 6). The case for banning laptops in the classroom. *The New Yorker.* https://www.newyorker.com/tech/elements/the-case-for-banning-laptops-in-the-classroom

Rorabaugh, P. & Stommel, J. (2013, Jul 21). Twitter vs. Zombies: New media literacy & the virtual flash mob. *Jesse Stommel.* Retrieved from the Internet Archive. https://web.archive.org/web/20150219112247/http://www.jessestommel.com/blog/files/twitter_vs_zombies.html

Romano, A. (2020, Mar 2). Twitter CEO faces backlash over site's abuse policies during live Q&A. *Tech, Daily Dot.* https://www.dailydot.com/debug/askcostolo-hashtag-backfires-over-twitter-abuse-policies/

Ronson, J. (2015, Feb 12). How one stupid tweet blew up Justine Sacco's life. *The New York Times.* https://www.nytimes.com/2015/02/15/magazine/how-one-stupid-tweet-ruined-justine-saccos-life.html

Roy, A. (2020, Apr 3). The pandemic is a portal. *Financial Times.* https://www.ft.com/content/10d8f5e8-74eb-11ea-95fe-fcd274e920ca

Sample, M. (2009, Mar 12). What's wrong with writing essays [Blog post]. *Sample Reality.* https://www.samplereality.com/2009/03/12/whats-wrong-with-writing-essays

Sample, M. (2013, May 22). The poetics of non-consumptive reading [Blog post]. *Sample Reality.* https://www.samplereality.com/2013/05/22/the-poetics-of-non-consumptive-reading

Sanders, J. (2018). "In dreams begin possibilities — Or, anybody have time for a change?" In E. Evans & C. Grant (Eds). *Mama, PhD: Women write about motherhood and academic life.* Rutgers University Press.

Schön, D. A. (2017). *The reflective practitioner: How professionals think in action.* Taylor & Francis.

Schuman, R. (2014, Jul 15). Revise and resubmit! *Human Interest, Slate.* https://slate.com/human-interest/2014/07/the-easy-way-to-fix-peer-review-require-submitters-to-review-first.html

Schuman, R. (2014, Jul 28). The peer-review jerk survival guide. *Community, The Chronicle of Higher Education.* https://community.chronicle.com/news/628-the-peer-review-jerk-survival-guide

Seawell, S. (2014, Mar 12). #NotYourAsianSidekick: Rethinking protest spaces and tactics. *Click Here to Continue, HASTAC.* https://www.hastac.org/blogs/sseawell/2014/03/12/noty-ourasiansidekick-rethinking-protest-spaces-and-tactics

Seeber, Kevin P. (2016). The failed pedagogy of punishment: Moving discussions of plagiarism beyond detection and discipline. In N. Pagowksy & K. McElroy (Eds.) *Critical library pedagogy handbook.* ACRL Press. http://digital.auraria.edu/IR00000048/00001

Shaffer, K. (2014, Jan 6). An open letter to my students. *Hybrid Pedagogy.* https://hybridpedagogy.org/open-letter-students/

Shor, I., Freire, P. (1987). *A pedagogy for liberation: Dialogues on transforming education.* Bergin & Garvey.

Simmons, M.H. (2005). Librarians as disciplinary discourse mediators: Using genre theory to move toward critical information literacy. *Portal: Libraries and the Academy* 5(3), 297-311. doi:10.1353/pla.2005.0041

Smith, A. & Kaba, M. (2014, Feb 1). Interlopers on social media: Feminism, women of color and oppression. *Truthout.* https://truthout.org/articles/interlopers-on-social-media-feminism-women-of-color-and-oppression/

Sommers, N., & Laura Saltz. (2004). The novice as expert: Writing the freshman year. *College Composition and Communication, 56*(1), 124-149. doi:10.2307/4140684

Souljah, S. (1996). *No disrespect.* Vintage.

Spahr, J. (2001). *Everybody's autonomy: Connective reading and collective identity.* University of Alabama Press.

Spivak, G. C. (2005). Commonwealth literature and comparative literature. In S. Duangsamosorn (Ed.). *Re-imagining language and literature for the 21st century.* Rodopi.

Stager, G. & Martinez, S. L. (2013). *Invent to learn: Making, tinkering, and engineering in the classroom.* Constructing Modern Knowledge Press.

Steiner, S. & Valdez, L. (1972). *Aztlan: An anthology of Mexican American literature.* Vintage Books.

Stekel, W. (1921). *The beloved ego: foundations of the new study of the psyche.* London: Kegan Paul, Trench, Trubner, p. 16.

Stewart, B. E. (2014, Sep 2). Something is rotten in the state of... Twitter.

The Theoryblog. http://theory.cribchronicles.com/2014/09/02/ something-is-rotten-in-the-state-of-twitter

Stewart, B. E. (2015). In abundance: Networked participatory practices as scholarship. *The International Review of Research in Open and Distributed Learning, 16*(3). https://doi.org/10.19173/irrodl.v16i3.2158

Stewart, B. E. (2015, Mar 9). Open to influence: what counts as academic influence in scholarly networked *Twitter* participation. *Learning, Media and Technology 40*(3). https://doi.org/10.1080/ 17439884.2015.1015547

Stewart, M. (2014, Aug 20). Designing for emergence: The role of the instructor in student-centered learning. *Hybrid Pedagogy.* https://hybridpedagogy.org/designing-emergence-role-instructor-student-centered-learning

Stommel, J. (2012, Dec 2). Online learning: A manifesto. *Hybrid Pedagogy.* https://hybridpedagogy.org/online-learning-a-manifesto

Stommel, J. (2013, Oct 1). How to build an ethical online course. *Hybrid Pedagogy.* https://hybridpedagogy.org/how-to-build-an-ethical-online-course

Stommel, J. (2014, Feb 10). MMDU: "I would prefer not to." *Hybrid Pedagogy.* Retrieved from the Internet Archive. https://web.archive.org/ web/20190807003000/https://hybridpedagogy.org/mmdu-prefer/

Stommel, J. (2014, May 11). CFP: Critical digital pedagogy. *Hybrid Pedagogy.* https://hybridpedagogy.org/cfp-critical-digital-pedagogy/

Stommel, J. (2014, Dec 17). Critical digital pedagogy: A definition. *Hybrid Pedagogy.* https://hybridpedagogy.org/critical-digital-pedagogy-definition/

Stommel, J. (2015, Jan 7). Who controls your dissertation? *Community, The Chronicle of Higher Education.* https://community.chronicle.com/news/852-who-controls-your-dissertation

Stommel, J. (2017, Jul 30). Queering open pedagogy [Keynote address]. *Digital Pedagogy Lab Vancouver,* Vancouver. https://youtu.be/tM-jJNXYNF8?t=1011

Stommel, J. (2020, Feb 2). The human work of higher education pedagogy. *Academe.* AAUP. https://www.aaup.org/article/human-work-higher-education-pedagogy

Stommel, J. & Morris, S. M. (2013, Jul 22). MOOCagagy: Assessment, networked learning, and the meta-MOOC. *Hybrid Pedagogy.* https://hybridpedagogy.org/moocagogy-assessment-networked-learning-and-the-meta-mooc/

Stommel, J. & Morris, S. M. (2014, Jan 7). CFP: Pedagogical alterity: Stories of race, gender, disability, sexuality. *Hybrid Pedagogy.* https://hybridpedagogy.org/cfp-pedagogical-alterity-stories-race-gender-disability-sexuality/

Straumsheim, C. (2015, Jul 14). What is detected? *Inside Higher Ed.* https://www.insidehighered.com/news/2015/07/14/turnitin-faces-new-questions-about-efficacy-plagiarism-detection-software

Sun, P. (2014, Jul 8). Thoughts on work-life imbalance from those left behind. *PrawfsBlawg.* https://prawfsblawg.blogs.com/prawfsblawg/2014/07/thoughts-on-work-life-imbalance-from-those-left-behind.html?

Thomas, W. G., III. (2015, Feb 28). What is digital scholarship? A typology. [Blog post]. http://railroads.unl.edu/blog/?p=1159

Tufekci, Z. (2013). "Not This One": Social movements, the attention economy, and microcelebrity networked activism. *American Behavioral Scientist, 57*(7), 848–870. https://doi.org/10.1177/0002764213479369

Tufekci, Z. (2014, Jan 13). Social media is a conversation, not a press release. *Technology and Society, Medium.* https://medium.com/technology-and-society/social-media-is-a-conversation-not-a-press-release-4d811b45840d

Tufekci, Z. (2014). Big questions for social media big data: Representativeness, validity and other methodological pitfalls. In *International AAAI Conference on Web and Social Media.* https://www.aaai.org/ocs/index.php/ICWSM/ICWSM14/paper/view/8062/8151

Tufekci, Z. & Wilson, C. (2012, Apr). Social media and the decision to participate in political protest: Observations from Tahrir Square.

Journal of Communication, 62(2), 363–379. https://doi.org/10.1111/
j.1460-2466.2012.01629.x

Tufekci, Z. (2014, Aug 14). What happens to #Ferguson affects Ferguson:
Net neutrality, algorithmic filtering, and Ferguson. *The Message,
Medium.* https://medium.com/message/ferguson-is-also-a-net-
neutrality-issue-6d2f3db51eb0

Tufekci, Z. (2014, Sep 4). Why Twitter should not algorithmically curate
the timeline. *The Message, Medium.* https://medium.com/message/
the-algorithm-giveth-but-it-also-taketh-b7efad92bc1f

Turner, N., Chunichi, & Glenn, R. (2004). *Girls from da hood.* Urban
Books.

Twitchell, L. A. [X_'unei / Du Aaní Kawdinook / Ḵ'eijáakw]. (2015). *Haa
wsineix_ haa yoo x_'atángi: Our language saved us.* Troubled Raven.

U.S. Department of Health and Human Services (2014, Jan 28). *Correctional therapeutic community for substance abusers.* Retrieved from the
Internet Archive. https://web.archive.org/web/20150905191853/
http://www.nrepp.samhsa.gov/ViewIntervention.aspx?id=338

U.S. Department of Health and Human Services (2014, Jan 28). *Modified
therapeutic community for persons with co-occurring disorders.* Retrieved
from the Internet Archive. https://web.archive.org/web/
20140316064840/http://www.nrepp.samhsa.gov/ViewInterven-
tion.aspx?id=144

Vaidhyanathan, S. (2018). *Antisocial media: How Facebook disconnects us
and undermines democracy.* Oxford University Press.

Verhoeven, D. (2014). Doing the sheep good: Facilitating engagement
in digital humanities and creative arts research. *Advancing Digital
Humanities: Research, Methods, Theory.* Springer, New York.

Vygotsky, L. (1978). *Mind in society: Development of higher psychological
processes.* Harvard University Press.

Wallis, L. (2015, Mar 23). Smashing the gates of academic discourse: Part
1 [Blog post]. *Do-It-Yourself Library Instruction.* https://laurenwal-
lis.wordpress.com/2015/03/23/smashing-the-gates-of-academic-
discourse-part-1/

Wallis, L. (2015, May 12). Smash all the gates, part 2: Professional silenc*
[Blog post]. *Do-It-Yourself Library Instruction.* https://laurenwal-

lis.wordpress.com/2015/05/12/smash-all-the-gates-part-2-pro-fessional-silenc/

Walker, R. (2005). *Black White & Jewish*. Penguin Publishing Group.

Wan, A. J. (2011, Sep). In the name of citizenship: The writing classroom and the promise of citizenship. *College English 74*(1). https://library.ncte.org/journals/ce/issues/v74-1

Watters, A. (2013, Mar 3). Hacking at education: TED, technology entre-preneurship, uncollege, and the hole in the wall [Blog post]. *Hack Education*. http://hackeducation.com/2013/03/03/hacking-your-education-stephens-hole-in-the-wall-mitra

Watters, A. (2017, Apr 7). Education technology's completely over. *Hack Education*. http://hackeducation.com/2017/04/07/prince

Wecker, M. (2014, Jan 2). Conference season is here. Don't stink at Twitter. *Community, The Chronicle of Higher Education*. https://com-munity.chronicle.com/news/242-conference-season-is-here-don-t-stink-at-twitter

Weller, M. (2011). Reward and Tenure. In *The digital scholar: How technol-ogy is transforming scholarly practice*. London: Bloomsbury Academic. http://dx.doi.org/10.5040/9781849666275

Wetherbe, J. C. (2013, Mar 13). It's time for tenure to lose tenure. *Har-vard Business Review*. https://hbr.org/2013/03/its-time-for-tenure-to-lose-te

Wharton, R. (2006, Mar 24). Re-thinking plagiarism as unfair compe-tition: Presented at CCCC, Chicago, IL [Blog post]. *Robin Wharton, PhD*. http://www.robinwharton.com/2013/01/re-thinking-plagia-rism-as-unfair-competition-presented-at-cccc-chicago-il-24-march-2006/

Willis, J. (2006). *Research-based strategies to ignite student learning: Insights from a neurologist and classroom teacher*. ASCD.

Winner, L. (1978). *Autonomous technology: Technics-out-of-control as a theme in political thought*. MIT Press.

Wright, E. O. (2019). *How to be an anticapitalist in the twenty-first century*. Verso.

Wright, R. (1945). *Black boy: A record of childhood and youth*. Harper.

Wylie, I. (2012, Apr 8). Schools have the final word on plagiarism. *Finan-*

cial Times. https://www.ft.com/content/
97a2c816-57ca-11e1-ae89-00144feabdc0

Yancey, K. B. (2009, Feb). Writing in the 21st century. *National Council of Teachers of English.* https://secure.ncte.org/library/NCTEFiles/Press/Yancey_final.pdf

Yergeau, M., Brewer, E., Kerschbaum, S., Oswal, S. K., Price, M., Selfe, C. L., Salvo, M. J., & Howes, F. (2013). Multimodality in motion: Disability and kairotic spaces. *Kairos: A Journal of Rhetoric, Technology, and Pedagogy, 18*(1). http://kairos.technorhetoric.net/18.1/coverweb/yergeau-et-al

Young, R. (2017, Oct 3). Why James Baldwin's "A talk to teachers" remains relevant 54 years later. *Here & Now.* WBUR. https://www.wbur.org/hereandnow/2017/10/03/james-baldwin-talk-to-teachers

Printed in Great Britain
by Amazon